"If, concerning the person and work of the Holy Spirit, you feel caught between fear, cynicism, and scandal on the one hand, and thoughtless, overzealous craziness on the other, and are worried that no sane thinking or practice can be found today, then read *Gift and Giver*. Keener assures us that we can love and embrace God the Holy Spirit and his gifts with intellectual integrity and a genuine humility that breaks the back of divisiveness."

—**Todd Hunter**, Anglican bishop; former director of Vineyard USA and of Alpha USA

"Keener has already demonstrated his ability to guide readers through difficult biblical and theological issues with splendid pastoral sensitivity and sharp exegetical acumen. Here he tackles key debates between charismatics and cessationists with similar aplomb."

—**Craig L. Blomberg**, Denver Seminary

"Both scholarly and warmly personal, this book should be helpful to Pentecostals, charismatics, evangelicals, and any others needing a fresh perspective on the Holy Spirit's work today."

—**Vinson Synan**, Regent University, Virginia

"Those wishing to walk successfully through the minefield of questions that both the Bible and contemporary experience raise will find this a welcome guide. I heartily commend it."

—**Ben Witherington III**, Asbury Seminary

"Keener's conclusion is to seek not a single experience but a continuing relationship. This represents a sound contribution against the present-day polarization that plagues much of the literature in this field."

—*Calvin Theological Journal*

Gift & Giver

The Holy Spirit for Today

Craig S. Keener

WITH A NEW AFTERWORD

B
Baker Academic
a division of Baker Publishing Group
Grand Rapids, Michigan

© 2001 by Craig Keener

Published by Baker Academic
a division of Baker Publishing Group
PO Box 6287, Grand Rapids, MI 49516–6287
www.bakeracademic.com

Repackaged edition published 2020
ISBN 978-1-5409-6361-1

Printed in the United States of America

The Library of Congress has cataloged the original edition as follows:
Keener, Craig S., 1960–
    Gift and giver : the Holy Spirit for today / Craig S. Keener.
        p.   cm.
    Includes bibliographical references.
    ISBN 0-8010-2266-5 (pbk.)
    1. Gifts, Spiritual. I. Title
BT767.3.K44 2001
234′.13—dc21   00-050768

Unless otherwise indicated, Scripture quotations are the author's translation.

Scripture quotations identified NIV are from the HOLY BIBLE, NEW INTERNATIONAL VERSION ®. NIV®. Copyright © 1973, 1978, 1984 by International Bible Society. Used by permission of Zondervan Publishing House. All rights reserved.

Scripture quotations identified KJV are from the King James Version of the Bible.

To the memory of church planters
Everett and Esther Cook,
two of my earliest mentors in ministry

Contents

Contents

Preface

Gift and Giver is a nontechnical survey of New Testament teaching about the gift of the Spirit and is thus about our relationship with the Lord and our empowerment for our Lord. For a summary of what I would say exegetically about the Spirit in the New Testament, this book is the best place to start. The main text of the book thus remains unchanged from the 2001 edition.

Individual gifts of the Spirit consumed only a minority of the pages of *Gift and Giver*. Because these gifts have remained quite controversial in the intervening years since original publication, I have taken this opportunity to add some comments about gifts of the Spirit in the afterword.

Nomenclature has also shifted since the first (2001) edition of *Gift and Giver*. Most importantly, I should emphasize that by "charismatic" I mean simply a practicing continuationist—that is, someone who believes that the gifts are for today and puts this belief into practice.

Unfortunately, extreme voices have polarized the discussion, at least on the unregulated internet. Some more extreme charismatics highlight and pursue unique "revelations" more than biblical teaching; some extreme cessationists (who believe that most spiritual gifts have ceased) have acted as if only the gift of teaching remains—and it had better be *their* teaching or it might be dangerous. Some charismatics have propounded claims that contradict Scripture, at least the way they have worded them; some cessationists have denounced virtually all charismatics as heretics, often by cherry-picking video clips out of context or painting all charismatics by the most extreme examples. Being *biblical* helps avoid these polarizations.

Genuine life in the Spirit is more radical than I perceived in 2001, but it is also more balanced. We need Word and Spirit together. I hope the discussion that follows and the new afterword make that point abundantly clear.

Special thanks to my editors at Baker, Jim Kinney, Jennifer Hale, Bob Hosack, and Melinda VanEngen; also to Amanda Beckenstein and Jonathan and Melissa Fettig, my students at Eastern Seminary, who retyped much of the manuscript after a disk error destroyed the computerized form of some chapters. I should also thank my colleague Kristin Frederich-Smoot, dean of spiritual formation at Palmer Seminary of Eastern University (where I was teaching in 2001) and a person of prayer, for her helpful comments, as well as my friend Alyn Waller, pastor of Enon Tabernacle Baptist Church in Philadelphia.

Because much of the material from *3 Crucial Questions about the Holy Spirit* remains in this work, I must also thank some dear friends who hold various perspectives on the more controversial questions and read through this manuscript. They include Melesse and Tadesse Woldetsadik, two charismatic brothers from Ethiopia who led hundreds of people to Christ while living in refugee camps in Kenya; Sharon Saunders, a former Baptist missionary with Africa Inland Mission; and Jackie Reeves, a charismatic African Methodist Episcopal (AME) minister in New Jersey. I am also grateful to my editors on that first project: Richard Jones, Grant Osborne, Jim Weaver, and Wells Turner.

Everett and Esther Cook, to whom this book is dedicated, spent much of the twentieth century pioneering Pentecostal churches in the western United States. Afterward, they opened a street mission with their retirement income and mentored the college students who worked with them at the mission, treating us like their own children. Although they had never been able to attend college and I was initially more impressed with my growing academic knowledge, I ultimately learned from their lives of humble faithfulness what no book could have taught me.

Introduction

Perspectives and Labels

Christians agree on much of what the Bible teaches about the Holy Spirit, such as the fruit of the Spirit and the Spirit's work in salvation. Most of us also agree that the Spirit empowers us for evangelism, and we also agree on at least some spiritual gifts and some ways of hearing God's voice. But Christians often differ on details such as the importance of particular gifts (especially tongues) and whether a person is baptized in the Spirit at conversion, after conversion, or (in some sense) at both times.

My goal in writing this book is to help Christians better understand how the Spirit empowers us to live. Most of the book, therefore, addresses practical areas in which the Spirit helps us live the Christian life. That being said, however, I also seek to help Christians with some of the controversial questions concerning the Holy Spirit, because answers to these questions also affect the church's life and ministry. In those sections of the book, I attempt to present various sides fairly, though in the end I make a case for what I believe are biblical positions. Only if Christians listen to one another's reasons for holding different views will we be able to work for consensus, or at least for unity in God's work despite our differences.

Defining Terms: *Charismatic* and *Evangelical*

In an earlier book, I freely described myself as "charismatic." In much of North America, this term commonly means Christians who affirm and practice spiritual gifts but are not members of a Pentecostal church. Sometimes it also refers somewhat more specifically to those who pray in tongues; naturally this group also affirms and practices spiritual gifts. I have tried to allow for both of these traditional definitions, encompassing anyone who feels comfortable describing themselves in this way. For the sake of one overarching, convenient designation, I also include in this designation Third Wave and other groups that might not use the label "charismatic"; the contours of today's church differ from when charismatic essentially meant noncessationist, but so far no one term has come along to replace it.

Since I wrote 3 *Crucial Questions about the Holy Spirit*, however, I have learned that people apply the term in different ways in different circles. Some Nigerian friends from the Evangelical Church of West Africa (ECWA) and an evangelical friend from Mexico warned me that in their circles charismatic means advocates of health and wealth teachings, people who "claim" material blessings for themselves. I would rather abandon the title than risk anyone thinking that I advocate such teachings! (In fact, I am coauthoring a book for Nigeria with a Nigerian professor and pastor, challenging those very beliefs and practices.) In his book, *I Was Wrong*, former health and wealth teacher Jim Bakker confesses his discovery that for years he taught exactly the opposite of Jesus' teachings. Studying the Bible in context changed his thinking and led him to renounce his former beliefs on this matter. Millions of Bible-reading Christians who today call themselves charismatics do not believe in health and wealth teachings.

I do not wish to risk confusion by using a label that means different things to different readers. Although I have used the term *charismatic* less frequently in this book, however, I have had to retain the term a number of times, for the simple reason that no other term available in English encompasses all who affirm and practice spiritual gifts. *Pentecostal* usually applies specifically to those who belong to Pentecostal denominations, and as much as I like Pentecostal denominations (and personally share the "Pentecostal experience"), most people would not use that title to describe me: I was ordained in a Baptist church, not a Pentecostal one. I should also emphasize that not all charismatics and Pentecostals agree with everything that has been practiced in the name of "charismatic." People have wrongly justified all sorts of things in the name of the Spirit (just as they have wrongly justified all sorts of things in the name of the Bible, or in the name of Christ).

Not everyone uses the term *evangelical* in the same way either. I use the term to describe those who embrace and seek to obey the Bible as God's Word and are committed to evangelizing the world because they recognize

Christ as the only way of salvation. It has been applied more narrowly in a denominational or subcultural sense, but I mean it in the broader historic sense. The circles in which I move and the largest part of this book's audience have determined to some extent the issues I address and in how much detail. (For example, I do not deal at length with sacramental views of the Spirit at confirmation, though many committed Christians in many parts of the world do hold these. This is not to devalue the importance of such a discussion, but many parts of that debate hinge on the needs of the early church after the completion of the New Testament; my own area of expertise and study is the New Testament itself.) I trust that the book will nevertheless contain enough useful information that all readers will profit from it, whether they are Pentecostal, Baptist, Anglican, or from other circles.

I have done my best to write a book that is fair to various views, but I have especially tried to be faithful to what I believe I find in the Bible. Nevertheless, because one's background and spiritual experiences (or lack of particular experiences) often help shape a Christian's approach to the subject of the Holy Spirit, it is only fair to my readers that I recount briefly my own background.

My Background on the Subject

I have been miraculously healed, experienced supernatural gifts such as prophecy, followed the Spirit's leading in witnessing, and had deep experiences in the Spirit during prayer (including, regularly, prayer in tongues). I consider such experiences (and others mentioned later in the book) an advantage in writing a book on the Holy Spirit that includes controversial questions.

Some may object that such experiences bias my treatment of whether or not such experiences can happen today. From their standpoint, this is a legitimate objection (although many Pentecostals would respond that non-experience can also produce a sort of bias in the other direction). I could not deny that such works happen today any more than I could deny the existence of someone I know personally, because I have witnessed their reality firsthand. I do not, however, expect others to embrace the reality of these experiences on the basis of my testimony if they do not believe that such experiences are biblical. I can merely invite them to listen to my biblical arguments, and, if they wish, to a few of the stories I tell.

But I am an evangelical New Testament scholar who has published commentaries on various New Testament books. God called me to understand and teach the Bible, and if I had found my experiences to be unbiblical, I would have needed to find some other explanation for what they really were. It would not be the first time the Bible made me change my mind on something!

I am also part of the larger evangelical movement that is committed to evangelizing the world across denominational lines. Fundamental Baptists led me to Christ, I was ordained in a black Baptist church, and I teach in an interracial, evangelical Baptist seminary that serves evangelical students from a broad range of denominations (Presbyterian, Methodist, Mennonite, Assemblies of God, and others). My Methodist cousins prayed me into the kingdom, and I taught for four years in an AME Zion seminary. (I therefore sometimes jest that I am a Methobapticostal.) When I teach in Africa, I teach workers from a much wider range of denominational circles: Anglican, Church of Christ in Northern Nigeria (COCIN), ECWA, Salvation Army, Deeper Life, and so on. I therefore move in a variety of circles. Many (perhaps most) of my closest friends have not experienced the same spiritual gifts I have experienced, and I have good friends who teach at seminaries such as Dallas and Westminster, which hold that some spiritual gifts have ceased.

My own church background has varied. Early in my education I studied especially under Pentecostals; later I studied under Presbyterian, Baptist, Methodist, Church of Christ, and other professors (and was discipled by an even wider range of writings). I pastored a charismatic congregation. During seminary, I belonged to a nondenominational, noncharismatic congregation. When I relocated to begin my Ph.D., I joined a Pentecostal church for two years until going on staff with a Baptist church. When I relocated again to teach, I went on staff with a campus AME Zion church and later a Baptist church. At present, I belong to and minister in a black Baptist church and sometimes attend a charismatic Messianic Jewish congregation and travel to speak in a variety of circles. My background probably suggests to readers that I am eclectic—or hopelessly confused! But the biblical body of Christ is not circumscribed by denominational boundaries; our circles of fellowship should be as wide as Christ's body.

I thus write this book with the larger body of Christ in mind, from Pentecostals to moderates to cessationists (those who believe supernatural gifts have ceased)—though my cessationist friends may wish to skip a few of the later chapters! Most of the church probably falls in the range between Pentecostal and cessationist; most Christians today seem to accept that experiences described in the Bible are valid today, even though not every Christian will have all of them. But this book will address enough practical issues that even cessationists will profit from at least some of it.

Many other charismatic or Pentecostal scholars also write for wide Christian audiences, scholars such as Michael Brown, Peter Davids, Gordon Fee, Michael Green, Rebecca Merrill Groothuis, Wayne Grudem, Richard Hays, Michael Holmes, and Ben Witherington, as well, I am told, as some widely read writers such as Martin Lloyd-Jones.

A Different Book

Although it was an honor to have a book in the 3 Crucial Questions series alongside authors such as Grant Osborne, Clint Arnold, and Tremper Longman, I am grateful to Baker for the opportunity to revisit the subject in a fresh way. While this book is based on the same material I used for *3 Crucial Questions about the Holy Spirit,* it represents a significant reorganization of that material. I have written five other books between that work's release and the present time, so hopefully I have more experience in knowing how to write a readable book. I have tried to package the material in more interesting ways. I have also had time to grow in my own relationship with the Lord and my relationships with brothers and sisters who hold a wide range of views on matters of spiritual gifts. In terms of its direct value for the church, this book may be the most important book I have written, with the possible exception of *The IVP Bible Background Commentary: New Testament.*

I have included a few more personal stories to spice up the book; indeed, a couple stories I originally told in the third person to avoid talking about myself too much I am now retelling in the first person. The stories are to illustrate, not to argue a case; the case (when I am making one) depends on biblical arguments. I include the stories, however, for several reasons.

First, I want to underline the importance of applying biblical principles to daily life, and concrete examples are a good way to invite application. My ministry students and colleagues desire practical examples of how the principles we learn about in the Bible should influence our lives. I have found that my students respond to my personal illustrations because they demonstrate that I grapple with the task of applying the text to my own life; I don't just teach theory.

Further, when the stories are my own, verification becomes simpler. I am an eyewitness to the events and experiences I describe. If I am credible, my stories should be credible as well. Finally, by observing Jesus' teaching techniques and by noticing what contemporary books hold readers' attention, I have learned the value of stories for communicating points I endeavor to convey. Stories capture the attention of people in most cultures in a way that a more traditional textbook format does not.

The Need

Christians differ on their views about some aspects of the Holy Spirit's work, but we can all agree on most of the central questions. The early Christians were dependent on God's Spirit from start to finish, and we must be too.

Each revival in history has been the result of a fresh outpouring of God's Spirit, usually accompanied by experiences or commitments that threatened the comfortable status quo of religious institutions of the day. Yet the strength of the flesh, or proud human intellect that seeks to control God's power by reducing it to terms we can explain, can pretend to be sufficient for God's work only when the kingdom of Satan appears to be dormant. Now is not such a time.

Those of us involved in various forms of frontline evangelism recognize that our world has little time to spare; we stand in desperate need of revival. Will we dare to submit our lives to the giver of the Spirit, regardless of what price the Spirit may call us to pay to reach our contemporaries for Christ? On the answer to that question hangs the fate of our generation.

1

Recognizing the Spirit's Voice

Recently converted in high school, I began sharing Christ with other students on the way home from school. Sometimes I was afraid to witness, but I would feel the Spirit prompting me to talk with the person behind me, or to walk to the next block and find someone there to share Christ with, or to follow up with someone I had led to Christ the preceding week. Often the leading came from the Holy Spirit, but sometimes my feelings were simply the product of indigestion, and I was not very skilled at discerning the difference.

I wanted to know God's leading better, but to know God's leading better I had to know something more important than his specific leading: I had to know his heart, what God was like. Too often we hold misconceptions about God's character. We have our own mental idols and we conceive of God in an image that does not correspond with the true God of the Bible. Paul says that we know in part and prophesy in part (1 Cor. 13:9). We may not always hear God perfectly, either in prayer or in our study of Scripture, but if we know what he is like enough to love him the way he is, he has ways to work out our imperfections in hearing him. When we perceive and reflect his heart, especially the love that nailed Jesus to the cross, we can best say we "know God" (1 John 4:7–12).

This chapter lays the groundwork for knowing and recognizing the Spirit; the next chapter provides further comments on learning to hear the voice of the Spirit. Often we experience God's leading in evangelism (chapter 3). Chapter 4 also remains central to this issue: The fruit of the Spirit tells us about the Spirit's character, hence, enabling us to recognize him when he speaks to us.

Why Hear God's Voice?

In Western Christianity today, people are often far more eager to attend to controversial issues such as Spirit baptism and spiritual gifts than discussions about the Spirit's character. By these priorities, however, we may miss the most important matter we could learn about the Spirit—learning God's heart. (Someday, when we know God fully, the gifts will not even be necessary, useful as they may be now [1 Cor. 13:8–12].)

Several years ago, when the pressures of trying to find time for teaching, writing, and speaking were overwhelming me, I walked into a worship service and suddenly felt God's Spirit prompt me to consider something in my heart. "My son," I felt him say, "you will not always have this ministry or that ministry. These gifts will pass away when you stand before me. But you will *always* be my son." I wept as I felt his comfort (and perhaps a tinge of gentle reproof). I had gotten so wrapped up in all the work I was doing for God—like Martha—that I had forgotten what mattered most: sitting at Jesus' feet like Mary. God graciously uses us to serve others, but first he graciously saves us from sin, from our selfish rebellion against him and his ways. Anything we do for God is simply the fruit of his new life within us. I felt that God was pleased with my work, but even more than my work he desired my fellowship with him, my continual acknowledgment of him in all my ways. I won't always be a teacher or a writer, but I will always be his child, and that means more to me than anything else.

The Holy Spirit, like the Father and the Son, is not just a doctrine, an idea, or an experience to be tagged on to the other doctrines and experiences of our Christian life. He is the God who has invaded our lives with his transforming presence.

Many of us need guidance to recognize more accurately when and how the Spirit speaks. Some circles in the church tend to exclude the Spirit's work almost altogether, content to depend on human programs and abilities. As one preacher remarked, "Were the Spirit to be withdrawn suddenly

from the earth today, most of the church's work would continue unabated."
In other circles, nearly everything that happens is attributed to the Holy
Spirit, though much of what happens there has nothing to do with him.

In this chapter, therefore, we begin with one of the less controversial but,
nevertheless, crucially practical questions: How can we recognize the Spirit?
The answer to this question must affect our discussion of the gifts of the
Spirit later in the book, our discussion of the Spirit's leading in evangelism,
and why discussions about the meaning of baptism in the Holy Spirit even
matter. After briefly commenting on the Spirit and his character as God, we
will consider some ways to improve our sensitivity to the Spirit's voice.

Some Introductory Principles

If we desire to hear God, the best place to start is by asking him to open
our ears. God often grants such gifts (compare 1 Cor. 14:13) and encourages us to seek them (1 Cor. 12:31). His voice may come through such means
as gentle nudges, calm assurances, specifically Spirit-guided dreams, a powerful urge, clear wisdom, or an unyielding sense of calling or direction.

If we ask to hear, however, we must also be willing to obey what we hear.
James invites us to ask for wisdom (James 1:5) but insists that we ask in faith
(1:6)—a faith that elsewhere in his letter must be confirmed as genuine by
obedience (2:14–26). The more we obey the Spirit's leading, the more adept
we become at hearing it. We must take it seriously and pay attention; God
will not continue to give us leadings if we use them merely to gauge our spirituality or keep ourselves emotionally excited (compare John 14:23).[1]

Yet this raises the question, How do we discern what is God's leading,
apart from trial and error? In situations in which it would do no harm to
step out in faith, trial and error may work. In more critical matters, we may
need to ask for God's confirmation or assurance (for example, Judg. 6:36–40;
1 Sam. 14:9–10). But knowing God's character in Scripture is the most
important way to begin recognizing God's voice. Although our voices
change over time, the character of God's voice has not changed in the past
two thousand years.

Who Is the Spirit?

Christians today agree on many details about the Spirit. We recognize
that the Spirit is God, just as the Father and the Son are God. Although

the Father, Son, and Spirit each focus on some different aspects of our salvation, we can learn about the Spirit's ways by looking at Jesus the Son, because the Bible reveals God's character most clearly in Jesus.

Perhaps because their Jewish contemporaries were less inclined to debate the personhood of the Spirit than, say, Christ's deity, the New Testament writers usually assume, rather than defend, the distinct personhood of the Spirit. Nevertheless, they do teach that the Spirit is personal and divine (Matt. 28:19; John 14:16–17; 16:13–15; Acts 5:3–5; Rom. 8:26–27; 2 Cor. 13:14). But while Jewish people before Jesus did not think of the Spirit as a distinct person, as Jesus' followers did, they all took for granted that the Spirit was divine, belonging to God's being (see, for example, Isa. 40:13; 48:16; 63:10–11). That the Spirit was divine was never in question.

I should pause momentarily to explain why I call the Spirit "he" rather than "it." As early church fathers also recognized, the word for "spirit" is feminine in Hebrew, neuter in Greek, and masculine in Latin. Because the New Testament is written in Greek, it is therefore not surprising that pronouns for the Spirit are normally neuter in the Greek New Testament. (The exceptions are passages in John that refer to the Spirit as the Paraclete, or counselor, a masculine term in Greek.) Because God is Spirit, Christians do not believe that God has biological gender, but neither would we describe him as neuter. I thus use Christian tradition's masculine pronoun for the Spirit here to remind readers that he is a divine person, an individual, not an impersonal force.

Knowing the Spirit Personally

Greek philosophy might seek to define what God is; the Bible, by contrast, shows God to us in how he related to people throughout history. The Old Testament does not clearly provide the arithmetical components for the Trinity (although it allows for it); God is "one," but so is a married couple (Gen. 2:24). The Old Testament does, however, reveal God's character, the same character we meet in the flesh in Jesus in the Gospels. This is also the same divine character we experience in our interactions with God through the Holy Spirit.

Some people suppose that learning theology means learning about God only in an abstract, rational sense, and feel this has little influence on their personal relationship with him. But when the Bible talks about knowing God, it speaks of a relationship characterized by intimacy and obedience, not by merely intellectual knowledge. Knowledge about God is clearly essential for knowing him, because a relationship with someone demands that we get to know about that person and the people and things important to that person. But knowledge about God is inadequate unless we apply it in practical ways to our relationship with him. In fact, merely knowing about him without applying that knowledge leads to more severe judgment than if we did not know about him (Luke 12:47–48; Rom. 2:12–16; James 3:1).

One of the first steps we should take in knowing God's voice is knowing God's heart. If we know the God of the Bible—the God of the cross—we will recognize the true Spirit of God when he speaks to us. Of course, God sometimes reveals himself to us by his Spirit within us first before we understand Scripture fully. But the heart of God we come to know through prayer is the same heart of God we find in Scripture when we search it with hearts humbled before him.

Knowing someone's background and significant relationships and what matters to that person are important if we want to really know and care for someone. Each day as we study the Bible and watch God in his relationships with others throughout history—confronting the arrogant, comforting the broken, calling and using the humble—we should hear God speaking to us. We learn God's character and get to know him in Scripture and must recognize the same God in our experience. As Dallas Willard points out, we need to see the people in the Bible as being just as human as we are. We can *believe* the Bible and enter into its experience only if we study it "on the assumption that the experiences recorded there were basically of the same type as ours would be if we were there."[2]

Knowing God through the Spirit

Although we will look at many passages in the Bible, we will return often to the Gospel of John in this chapter and the next. John especially emphasizes the theme of knowing God personally through the Holy Spirit. The Holy Spirit undoubtedly led John to emphasize this theme because it was so important to his readers, mainly Jewish Christians, in their difficult situation. Leaders of some synagogues had expelled them from the synagogues and in some cases may have handed them over to hostile Roman authorities because of their faith in Christ. These local Jewish leaders appealed to their superior knowledge of religious traditions to justify their actions, but John encouraged the Christians to appeal to a more essential kind of knowledge: We know God himself, because the Spirit of his Son lives in us (compare 1 John 4:13).

As I will mention several times in this book, many Jewish people felt that the Spirit of prophecy had departed from Israel. From the time of Malachi on, prophecies were rare, and most people believed that Israel lacked prophets in the authoritative, Old Testament sense. But Jewish people recognized that someday God would pour out his Spirit on his people in a fuller way, as the biblical prophets had promised (Joel 2:28–29). By appealing to their continual experience with the Spirit, the Christians not only appealed to a supernatural empowerment their opponents did not even claim. They also declared that the time of promise had arrived in Jesus of Nazareth! The presence and manifestation of the Spirit constituted the clearest proof that Jesus was the promised deliverer.

John encourages his readers by telling them that their experience marks them as God's true servants, but he also calls them to a deeper relationship with God by presenting the ideal meaning of that relationship. By listening to John's words of encouragement to his first readers, we can deepen our own sensitivity to the Spirit.

Jesus' Sheep Know His Voice

How do we recognize the Spirit when he speaks to us? Paul tells us plainly that we do not yet know as we are known (1 Cor. 13:12); yet if we are to grow in our relationship with God, we need to begin somewhere. John's Gospel teaches that all who are born again have a relationship with Jesus. We have already begun to know God; we simply need to develop the relationship that God has already established with us.

The Bible describes many people who were intimate with God, while at the same time imperfect just as we are. God became so intimate with his friend Abraham that he asked, "Shall I hide from Abraham what I am about to do?" (Gen. 18:17 NIV), and Elisha seemed disturbed to discover that God had not revealed something to him (2 Kings 4:27). Yet this same Abraham acted in unbelief in having relations with Hagar (Gen. 16:1–3, reported immediately after God's confirmations of Genesis 15). Noah and Enoch walked with God (Gen. 5:22, 24; 6:9), but this same Noah got drunk (9:21). Likewise, Jesus came in the flesh to imperfect disciples (who could sleep through a prayer meeting or even deny him) and made them examples of the transformation he can bring about in us through intimacy with him.

The Bible says that Jesus' sheep know him and know his voice (John 10:4–5, 14). They recognize him when he speaks because they are already acquainted with his character. The Gospel of John, which includes this saying of Jesus, illustrates this point with various examples. Nathanael, undoubtedly a student of Scripture (1:45–46), recognized the Lord he already served when the Lord confronted him (1:49). Similarly, Mary did not recognize the risen Jesus by his physical appearance (20:14–15), but when he called her by name—as the Good Shepherd promised to do with his sheep (10:3)—she immediately knew who he was (20:16). In the context of Jesus' promise that his sheep would know his voice, a broken man whose need Jesus touched embraced him readily, whereas the arrogant who rejected Jesus showed that they were not his sheep (9:35–10:10).

God's Nature

Because the Father, Son, and Spirit are one in nature (though distinct in person and role), what we learn about the character of one member of the Trinity applies to all three. Just as we cannot have a relationship with the Father except through the Son (1 John 2:23), we cannot have a relationship with the Son except through the Spirit (John 16:14; Rom. 8:9), or vice versa (John 14:17). Thus, whatever we learn about our relationship with the Father or the Son also applies to our relationship with the Spirit, through whom we experience the presence of the Son and the Father.

How, then, can we learn about God's character so that we can recognize his voice? Countless Bible passages teach us about him—about a God so merciful and patient that human analogies portray him as almost foolishly indulgent (Matt. 18:24–27; Mark 12:6; Luke 15:12). At the same time, Scripture reveals that God's patience does have its limits with those who continue to take his mercy for granted (Exod. 4:24–26; 32:35; Ps. 78:17–31; Hosea 2:8–10; 11:1–7; Rom. 2:4–5; 9:22).

God disciplined his people for their continual disobedience to him, but when they repented, Judges tells us that God "could endure their pain no longer" (Judg. 10:16), so he raised up a deliverer for them. In Jeremiah he weeps that his people have forsaken him, the true source of water, in exchange for broken containers (Jer. 2:13); in Hosea he laments that they oppose him, their help (Hosea 13:9).

God often chose to illustrate his character by comparing his relationship with his people to human relationships. Thus, through Hosea we learn of God's wounded heart, broken by the betrayal of his unfaithful people. Just as we are ready to condemn Hosea's unfaithful wife, Gomer, Hosea reminds us that Gomer did nothing to him that all of us have not done to the God who loves us (Hosea 1:2–2:23). Hosea speaks further of how God redeemed Israel from slavery, then adopted the people as his own children. God says he taught Israel how to walk, carried them in his arms, bent down and fed them like a loving father (Hosea 11:1–4). But they rejected his message, so he warned in grieving anger that he would send them back to captivity (11:5–7)!

In the midst of pronouncing judgment in this passage, however, God's voice breaks. "How can I punish you like this, my people?" he cries out. "How can I treat you like Admah and Zeboiim?" (11:8), referring to two cities God overturned and burned when he overthrew Sodom (Deut. 29:23). Rather, he says, "My own heart is overturned within me, and all my compassion burns" (Hosea 11:8). God is saying, "My people, if I could bear the judgment in your place, I would." And then he forgave his people (11:9–11). This is the God of the cross.

God's Supreme Revelation of Himself

Some issues are more central in the Bible than others (e.g., Matt. 23:23–24, where the Pharisees neglected the "weightier matters" of Scripture). The same principle is true in how God reveals his character; all of his revelation is important, but some of his revelation is clearer to us than other parts.

John teaches us about God's character in a special way: He tells us to look at Jesus. When one of Jesus' disciples fails to recognize that Jesus perfectly reveals the Father's character, Jesus responds, "Anyone who has seen me has seen the Father" (John 14:9 NIV). Indeed, even John's prologue introduces this point: Jesus is God's "Word" made flesh.

All that God revealed of himself in the written Word, God revealed even more fully in his Word made flesh. Jewish people recognized that God had revealed himself in the Scriptures, and the synagogue leaders who had expelled John's readers from their assemblies apparently believed they knew the Scriptures better than the Christians did (compare John 5:39; 9:28–29). But John claims that the same Word of God we confront in the Scriptures has stepped into human history in the person of Jesus of Nazareth. John thus counters the claims of the Christians' enemies, who emphasized their own zeal for God's law: Those who claim to know God's law but reject Jesus reject the true message of the Word itself (5:45–47).

By alluding to the Old Testament story of Moses on Mount Sinai, John shows how Jesus revealed God's character. As the Word, Jesus had always existed alongside the Father (1:1–13), until finally God spoke his Word as flesh (1:14). Then Jesus became one of us, embracing our humanity and our mortality. In so doing, Jesus revealed the Father's glory, "full of grace and truth" (1:14), a fullness of grace and truth that we all receive when we receive Christ (1:16; compare 1:12–13).

God Showed His Heart to Moses

By telling us that Jesus' glory was "full of grace and truth," John tells us about God's heart. He alludes to Moses' climbing up Mount Sinai the second time to receive God's law. God told Moses that he was angry with his people and did not wish to dwell among them any longer, but he also said that Moses was his friend (Exod. 33:3, 17). "If I am your friend, then I ask only this," Moses requested. "Show me your glory" (Exod. 33:18). God then explained that his full glory would be too much for Moses—no one can see God and live—but that he would reveal part of his glory to Moses (Exod. 33:19–23). The Lord then passed before Moses, showing him part of his glory (Exod. 34:5–7). Yet what God showed his servant was not just some cosmic spectacle of fireworks (although there were enough "fireworks" to make Moses' face glow); God revealed his character, his heart, to Moses. He made his "goodness" pass before him (Exod. 33:19).

As the Lord passed before Moses, he declared, "The LORD, the LORD, abounding in covenantal love and covenantal faithfulness. His anger against sin is so great that he punishes it for three or four generations—but his love is so great that it stretches to the thousandth generation—so much greater is his mercy than his wrath" (Exod. 34:6–7; see also Exod. 20:5–6; Deut. 7:9–10). In other words, God's glory was summarized as "full of covenant love and covenant faithfulness," which could be translated from Hebrew to Greek and Greek to English as, "full of grace and truth." "Grace" means God accepts us because that's the way he is, not because of how we are. The Hebrew word for "truth" in this context means God's integrity, his unfailing faithfulness to his character and to the promises he made in his covenant. When God finished his revelation, Moses acted on his deeper understanding of God's character, pleading again for God to forgive Israel and dwell among them (Exod. 34:8–9). And God, being gracious and merciful, agreed (Exod. 34:10).

God Showed Us His Heart in Jesus' Sufferings

Some thirteen centuries later, God revealed his Word again, "full of grace and truth." But this time, more than part of God's glory was revealed. This time the Word became flesh, and the grace and truth revealed in him was complete, unlike the partial revelation in the law of Moses (John 1:17). Although no one had seen God at any time, the only begotten God, who is in the most intimate relationship with the Father, expounded his character and nature for all the world to see (1:18). What Moses saw in part, the eyewitnesses of Jesus, who could say "we beheld his glory" (1:14), saw in full. The same principle applies not only to those who walked with Jesus on earth but also to those who have subsequently come to know his glory, understanding his character in the gospel (2 Cor. 3:2–18).

But though we may expect some fireworks when Jesus comes back, there were no fireworks at his first coming. God's Word came in a hidden way, recognized only by those who had developed some acquaintance with God's character beforehand (for example, John 1:47–51). Jesus revealed his glory through various signs, often to only a handful of people (2:11). But the supreme revelation of his gracious and truth-filled glory was the ultimate expression of his full identification with our humanity: his death! God "glorified" Jesus when his enemies "lifted him up" on the cross (12:23–24, 32–33). We crowned our Lord Jesus with thorns and enthroned him "King of the Jews" on a cross, but in Jesus' sacrifice, God accounted him Lord of creation and reserved for him the seat at God's own right hand. In the ultimate act of our rebellion, when we shook our fist in God's face and declared our hatred of our Creator, when we pounded the nails into his wrists, God's emissary offered the ultimate demonstration of God's love for us. "For this is how God loved the world: He gave his uniquely special Son, so whoever depends on him will not perish, but share in the life of the world to come" (John 3:16).

God revealed his glory throughout history, but the ultimate expression of his glory—the supreme revelation of his grace and truth—occurred on the cross. Do we want to know God's heart? John declares that we must look at the cross to find it. Paul informs us of this same reality: While we were yet sinners, enemies of God, he proved his love for us by sending Jesus to die for us (Rom. 5:6–8). Now "God has poured out his love toward us by the Spirit he has freely given us" (Rom. 5:5; see also Eph. 3:16–19)—an experience that in this context means the Spirit has come into our hearts and now points to the cross, assuring us over and over again, "See! I love you! I love you! I love you!"

To the abused child, to the abandoned spouse, to the unappreciated, workaholic pastor, to all the other broken people of our world, Jesus declares the heart of God. When we hear the voice of the one who sent his Son not to condemn the world but rather to save the world from its sin, we truly hear the voice of God's Spirit. Sometimes we can get so caught up in doing God's work that we forget to pause to listen to God's reassurance of love for us, his Spirit reminding us that we are truly his children (Rom. 8:16; 1 John 3:24; 4:13; 5:6–8). But once we have experienced the soothing touch of God's love in prayer, we are content only when walking in loving intimacy with him.

To recognize God's voice, we should begin by knowing, as best as possible, God's character as he has revealed it already. That is, before we listen for what God might say, we should heed what he has already said. Listening to the Spirit means listening to the God of the Bible, the God of the cross.

The Spirit and Jesus' Presence

An important step in getting to know God is to realize how available he is to us. In learning to hear God, it helps us to take on faith the fact that we are already in his presence. If we must make ourselves worthy of his presence first, we will never get there. As a young Christian, I felt I had to "pray through" for an hour before I could earn my way into God's presence. Having grown more conscious of the need to use my time responsibly, I realize I wasted many hours that could have been spent instead in intimate communion with the God I was growing to love.

If we must "feel" God's presence before we believe he is with us, we again reduce God to our ability to grasp him, making him an idol instead of acknowledging him as God. I find that I often do feel an overwhelming sense of God's majesty and love and character now, but usually (in my better moments) I neither seek it nor use it to gauge my relationship with him.

Back when I waited for a feeling before believing God was present, I often felt merely frustrated. Feelings should follow faith; God himself, rather than feelings, should be the object of our seeking.

Approaching God's Throne

The writer of Hebrews summons us to approach God's throne of grace confidently (Heb. 4:16), and Paul reminds us that Christ has provided us perfect access to God, which we could not have achieved on our own (Rom. 5:2; Eph. 2:18). The Gospel of John again provides a helpful approach to this step in learning to hear God's voice.

John informs us that we can approach God intimately at any time because we are already in his presence (John 14:16–23; 15:1–11). Our relationship with God comes by grace (Phil. 3:9–10), so we act on it by faith. It is true that disobedience can obstruct our relationship with God (John 14:23–24); certainly God does not waste his words on those living lives of deliberate disobedience. But Jesus' triumph on the cross freed us from both the consequences and the power of sin. We overcome temptation by appropriating God's gracious power, not by waiting until our lives are holy enough to earn his power (Ezek. 36:27). We learn to appreciate God's abiding presence with us in the same way.

Many Dwellings

Jesus promises his disciples his continuing presence after his departure. After Jesus uses his coming death for us as the new standard of love that believers should follow (John 13:31–38), he addresses the next inevitable issue: He must go away. But he assures his anxious disciples that though he is going away to the Father, he will return to them again (14:3, 18, 23).

We often read the first few lines of John 14 as a promise of Jesus' second coming, but although Jesus promises the second coming in other passages in John, that is probably not what the promise of John 14:2–3 means. In this passage, Jesus assures his disciples that he is going to the Father's house to prepare a place for them among the many dwellings there (14:2; KJV's "mansions" mistranslates, based on the Latin Vulgate). He promises that he will return to them and that they will be with him forever in his Father's house. It is not surprising if we are unsure what Jesus was talking about, for even Jesus' original disciples were confused (14:5)! The context, however, goes on to clarify Jesus' point.

First, Jesus explains what he means by his coming again. In this context, he means he will come to his disciples after the resurrection (14:16–20; 16:16, 20–22). At that time he will give them his Spirit, through whom they will experience his presence and resurrection life (14:16–17, 19; 20:22). Second, Jesus explains what he means by the "dwellings" in the Father's house: our current dwelling in God's presence. The noun I translate here as "dwellings" appears only one other time in the entire New Testament— later in this passage, where Jesus expands on the information he has already given his disciples about dwellings. Through the Spirit, Jesus and the Father will come and make their dwelling within each disciple (14:23), thus making them temples of the Lord (the Father's house). The term *dwell*, or *abide*, which is the verb form of *dwelling*, appears several times in John 15, where Jesus talks about dwelling with us and we with him (15:4–7, 9–10).

Further, Jesus' disciples did not understand what he said, so his explanation to them instructs us as well. When Jesus noted that they already knew where he was going and how he would get there, one confused disciple protested, "Lord, we do not even know *where* you are going; how can we know the way to get there?" Jesus replied that he was going where the Father was, and Jesus was the way the disciples would get there (14:6; see also 16:28). But *when* do the disciples get to the Father through Jesus?

John 14:6 is talking about salvation; we come to the Father through Jesus when we become believers in Jesus. This being the case, Jesus' earlier words in 14:2–3 must also speak of a relationship beginning at conversion. When we come to the Father through Jesus, we become his dwelling by the Spirit he has given us. If John 14:6 refers to salvation (and it does), then the question it answers (how do we get where you are going?) cannot merely refer to the second coming of Jesus that we look for in the future.

God Lives in Us

But even if one rejects my argument concerning John 14:2–3, the rest of the context (14:16–17, 23, 26) makes the point that God comes to live inside us. The same Jesus who washed his disciples' feet, who died on the cross for our sins, is the same Jesus who is with you now as you read this book. You are in his presence at all times, and he is pleased when you trust his presence.

God's continuous presence and life-giving empowerment is important in the New Testament, but it would have shocked some people in John's day. Jewish people during this period spoke of God purifying his people through his Spirit or empowering some to speak for him through his Spirit. But the first Christians who experienced the Spirit recognized that the Spirit living inside them meant something more; it meant that God himself lived inside them, that they were God's holy temple (1 Cor. 3:16; Eph. 2:22; 1 Peter 2:5; compare the "Father's house" in John 14:2 with John 2:16). Although not to the same degree, this experience already had biblical precedent before Jesus came (Gen. 41:38; Num. 27:18; 1 Peter 1:11; compare Dan. 4:8–9, 18; 5:11, 14; 1 Peter 4:14).

God not only wanted to save us from hell, he wanted to cleanse us from sin. And God not only wanted to deliver us from sin, but once he has purified our house, he wants to live in it with us. Although some Jewish people, such as the writers of the Dead Sea Scrolls, already saw their community as a new temple for God, early Christians went beyond this. Viewing not only the church but each individual believer as a temple (1 Cor. 6:19), they recognized that the Spirit dwelt continually in each believer's heart and provided each believer with continual, intimate communion with God (Eph. 3:17–19). It was expedient for us that Jesus go away so that he could return to be present with each of us in a deeper and more intimate way than before (John 16:7, 12–15). How marvelous is God's great love for us!

Once the Spirit has made us God's temple, the Spirit equips us for worship. More than any other activity, with the possible exception of evangelism, worship helps us focus on God's glory. By doing so, worship invites us to pay attention to the very one whose heart we wish to know. It allows us to translate what we know *about* God into a dynamic conversation *with* God.

Spirit-Empowered Worship

I had been hearing wonderful news about worship services at a particular church. I knew, of course, that God's presence there would not differ from the presence of God I already knew; there is only one true God. Still, I also recognized that sometimes people in different places have a better picture of some aspect of God's infinite character, and sometimes their intensity or the intensity of God's gracious response to their worship can affect others who come (compare 1 Sam. 19:20–24 for a dramatic example). God is consistent with his nature and declared purposes in Scripture, but he is not limited to our finite understanding of him or the ways we think he should work.

When I was visiting that city, I worshiped in that particular church, but during the first hour or so of worship, I experienced nothing out of the ordinary. A couple thousand young people enthusiastically danced and shouted praises to Jesus, but because of where I was seated, I could not hear the words, and hence, could not sing with them. I had come to worship, not to watch others worship, and was beginning to think sadly that, in my thirties, I was already becoming old and out of touch with youthful exuberance. I spent much of that time searching my heart before the Lord. I seemed to worship so differently from everyone else. Was there something wrong with me? But then as a moment of silence swept over the international congregation, in the midst of the silence I felt God's deep compassion and love. I began quietly singing in tongues, as did a few other people. Soon most of the worshipers were singing in tongues or spontaneously in their own languages.

It was then that I felt God's Spirit speak to my heart. He said that he had created each of us unique and different. Of course, I already knew that; our DNA signatures are far more diverse than snowflakes! But knowing something in the back of one's mind and applying it to one's circumstances are two different things. I felt God say that because he had created each of us unique, the worship of each of us was special to him. Even if ten thousand people were present, my own worship mattered to God. Only Craig Keener could offer God the worship that God had created Craig Keener to offer him. I might see myself as a stodgy scholar, but God saw me as his child who would worship him through all eternity! I fell to my knees weeping, completely overwhelmed by God's grace and mercy.

The Book of Acts reveals the character of Spirit-empowered *evangelism*. Paul's letters often focus on the importance of Spirit-empowered *behavior*. But the Bible also teaches us about Spirit-empowered *worship*. God wants us to bring our needs to him, to express our dependence on him. But it is in an even more intimate form of worship that we pause before God to focus not on what we need from him but on God's glory. Without worship we may remember what God is like on paper, but we will not experience it as fully as we can in relationship with him. God yearns for our worship both because we reveal our love for him in this way and because he knows we need to worship him. It is most fully in worship that our hearts can embrace who God is, adoring him and finding the ways of his heart.

Biblical Examples of Worship

How involved is the Spirit in worship? The Spirit inspired the Old Testament psalms so God's people could praise him fully. In fact, the Bible often records an interplay between worship and prophetic inspiration (for example, Exod. 15:20–21; 1 Sam. 10:5; 2 Kings 3:15; Hab. 3:19). David himself appointed orderly but prophetically inspired worship leaders in the tabernacle (1 Chron. 25:1–7). Many of the psalms originated in this Spirit-inspired worship (2 Chron. 29:30) and were perpetuated there (Neh. 12:45–46). Worshipful celebration of God's goodness was essential for all his people in the Old Testament (see 1 Chron. 6:31–32; 15:16, 28–29; 16:4–6; 23:27, 30; 2 Chron. 31:2; Neh. 12:24, 27, 36, 43), and the major revivals in Israel's history included revivals of worship (2 Chron. 8:14; 20:20–22; 29:25; Ezra 3:10–11).

If God's Spirit empowered his people in worship in the Old Testament, he certainly deserves worship today that is no less Spirit-led. Scripture, in fact, marks the believer as one who will worship God not merely in traditional temples (such as those in Samaria or Jerusalem) or with traditional ritual (such as circumcision) but "in the Spirit" (John 4:24; Phil. 3:3 in context).

Much of the worship in the Bible involves singing, and singing involves emotions (and our body) as well as intellect. We should know and celebrate God with our whole person. While too many Christians neglect to serve God with the mind, others cultivate only their minds and neglect the emotional aspects of worship. To know the Holy Spirit involves more than knowing facts about him. One need only to survey the psalms to realize that God touches the affective (emotional) dimension of our personality as well as the intellectual. The psalms emphasize joy (over one hundred times), shouting (over twenty times), and even dancing.[3] Of course, different cultures and personalities lead us to express emotion in different ways, and different kinds of circumstances may invite different kinds of responses from our hearts (James 5:13). But knowing the Holy Spirit means pursuing a personal and intimate relationship with him, and relationships involve intellect, emotions, and commitment.

The Biblical Meaning of Worship

Worship does not involve merely enjoying the rhythm of a song, experiencing an emotional feeling, or comprehending a liturgy, helpful as any of these may sometimes be for inviting our attention to God. Nor does it involve repeating glib phrases without recognizing the one who deserves the phrase. When the psalmist declares, "Hallelujah!" (in English, "Praise the Lord!") this is a strong Hebrew imperative—that is, it is an urgent, strong command uttered by the worship leaders in the temple to the people who had come to worship. It is not so much worship itself as a call to worship! But even in summoning ourselves or others to worship, we may begin to turn our hearts toward God.

Worship involves giving the appropriate honor to God; it is an ultimate act of faith, in which we acknowledge God's greatness directly to him. God often responded to such genuine worship and faith by acting on behalf of his people (for example, 2 Chron. 20:20–24). We need to glorify God and allow him to express his power among us today as well. As a royal priesthood (1 Peter 2:5, 9; Rev. 1:6), we must offer a more meaningful sacrifice than that of bulls and goats, offering both our lips and our hearts in magnifying God.

Our mission in this world involves bringing people from all cultures to exalt the name of Christ (Rev. 5:9–10), even though we do not always see the responses we work for. Yet whatever the visible results on this side of eternity, our very labors fulfill part of our mission by glorifying God. God created us to bring him honor with both our lips and our lives, yet God is so great that only his Spirit working within us can create genuine, sincere praise appropriate to his majesty.

Early Christians recognized that the Spirit needed to empower them to offer praise worthy of a God greater than all his creation. As we have noted, they spoke of worship in the Spirit (John 4:24; Phil. 3:3; see also Eph. 6:18; Jude 20). Some passages provide glimpses into the early Christians' Spirit-led worship, which apparently included singing, sometimes in tongues not even known to the worshipers (1 Cor. 14:13–15; compare Eph. 5:18–20). God is no less great today than he was in the Old Testament and in the early church, and no less deserving of Spirit-empowered praise. We should seek the Spirit's presence and empowerment for our worship of God today, for he dwells near the sincere and humble heart that desires his honor above all. We do not all need to express our worship in the same way, but God wants us to worship him in sincere desire for his honor. We should ask him and trust him to turn our hearts toward him.

Worship as a Foretaste of the Future

No earthly temple can contain God's glory (1 Kings 8:27; 2 Chron. 2:6; 6:18); no sacrifices we finite creatures offer could prove worthy of the eternal, infinite Creator of the universe. But when Solomon and Israel determinedly offered God their very best—and it was a considerable offering

(1 Kings 8:5, 63)—God met them there. He filled his earthly house with glory, as he had previously done with the tabernacle (Exod. 40:34–35). By so doing, God confirmed his love for his worshipers. Today, as then, God remains eager to meet us and make up for our finiteness if we will just come to him with the greatest zeal we have to offer.

Lest we underestimate the intensity of God's confirmation, we should note that the priests were not even able to minister in the temple because of God's glory (1 Kings 8:10–11; compare Exod. 40:35; Ezek. 44:4; Hag. 2:7). Yet, though God's glory filled his earthly house of worship in the Old Testament, someday, God promises a greater glory. He declares that his glory will fill the whole *earth*, just as the waters cover the sea (Hab. 2:14). We may need "bodies of glory" (1 Cor. 15:43; Phil. 3:21) to be able to withstand the fullness of God's glory in that time (compare Rev. 22:4–5). Our present experiences in worship are merely a foretaste of eternal worship— but if we earnestly yearn for eternity with Christ, we should relish the foretaste we have now.

The Book of Revelation abounds with scenes of worship. The Lord gave John this revelation for churches in Asia Minor, churches very much like churches in various parts of the world today. Some of these churches were suffering persecution, while others were compromising with the very world system that was persecuting their fellow Christians elsewhere! Most of John's scenes of earth are unpleasant (especially the slaughter of saints as the world worships the beast), but his scenes of heaven are glorious: the saints and all the creatures of heaven worshiping God.

In fact, heaven in Revelation looks like a temple: It includes a tabernacle, altar, incense censers, a sea (like Solomon's temple), trumpets, and so forth (Rev. 4:6; 5:8; 6:9; 8:2–6; 11:19; 15:2, 5). Heaven is a place designed for worship! Indeed, the New Jerusalem in 21:16 is shaped like the Old Testament holy of holies, but whereas access to God's presence was once severely limited, we will enjoy his presence in all its fullness forever! As the seven churches of Asia Minor heard this book read in their worship services, it summoned them to join all of heaven in worshiping the sovereign God. It is heaven's perspective that enables us to triumph over our present sufferings and temptations. And we are never as close to our heavenly future in this life as when we worship God.

The Spirit enables us to participate in this future kingdom in the present. In the midst of severe hardships, the Spirit guarantees our future inheritance, the greater glory resulting from our present testings (Rom. 8:16–18). The Old Testament linked the Spirit's coming with the age to come, so early Christians, who knew the Old Testament well, understood that the Spirit connected them with the future. They recognized that those who have the Spirit taste the powers of the coming age in advance (Heb. 6:4–5). The Spirit makes us people of the future and enables us to view our identity in terms of our destiny in Christ, rather than by how the world's pressures define us (1 Cor. 2:12–16).

Thus, Paul speaks of the Spirit as the "firstfruits" (Rom. 8:23). The offering of firstfruits marked the actual beginning of a coming harvest (Lev. 23:10). We who long anxiously for our Lord's return have the foretaste of the coming harvest. We do not simply await a theoretical hope for the distant future; we await something we know beyond any shadow of a doubt, because we have already begun to experience the life of the coming world.

Elsewhere Paul speaks of the Spirit as the "down payment" or "earnest" of our future inheritance (2 Cor. 1:22; 5:5; Eph. 1:13–14). Businesspeople in Paul's day used this very term to speak of the first installment, the initial payment, on what was to come. God has advanced us part of our inheritance now, so we can experience the life of the Spirit, "eternal life," in this present age (John 3:16, 36). Some promises await Jesus' return, but God's presence and power in our lives right now should enable us to live as heaven's people on earth. Can you imagine how it would revolutionize the lives of believers and churches if we actually recognized and believed this reality? We should mean it when we pray, "Your will be done on earth as it is in heaven"!

Conclusion

If we desire to recognize the voice of the Spirit, we should begin by cultivating the means he has already given us. That is, we should get to know God's character by means of what he has already said in the Bible. Such knowledge will sensitize us to the true voice of the Spirit when he speaks. We should also recognize by faith that God has already given us his presence; we can begin to relate to him even before we feel him. Finally, we should worship him, bringing what we know about God into the intimacy of our relationship with God.

These basic principles help prepare us to hear the voice of the Spirit more accurately. In the next chapter, we investigate some other principles and practices that can prove helpful in learning to hear God's voice.

2

Learning to Hear God's Heart by the Spirit

As a young Christian, I was praying fervently one day for guidance on a particular issue when I felt the Spirit gently interrupt. I was shocked to think I heard him suggest that I was too busy seeking his will. How could that be? Then I heard the rest of his suggestion. "Don't seek my will in this matter. Seek me—and then you will know my will." Seeking God's will is important, but in this case my focus was wrong.

God often does provide specific guidance. After preaching at a church in Nigeria, I felt led to locate the Kenyan woman who had been at the service; she was working with an African ministry related to Campus Crusade. A friend who was with me at the time, who previously had worked with Crusade, suggested we try their headquarters. We located her and discovered she was to leave the country the next day. She was happy to receive one of the Bible Background commentaries I had brought. She was the only Kenyan I met while in Nigeria that summer.

Several months later I heard from her; it turned out her fiancé had been amazed when he saw the commentary. He was the one Ethiopian evangelist I knew in Kenya at that time, to whom I had sent a commentary a couple years before. God's hand in leading us all together was obvious. On many other occasions God has provided such leadings alongside providentially ordering my steps.

But as exciting as such guidance is in our service for him, we should not doubt God's leading when he does not arrange such evidently dramatic encounters. God often wishes to speak to us about his love for us, to give us insight, or to reprove us—all of which testify to our relationship with him. Whenever God speaks, whatever else we may learn from what he says, we are able to learn more about him.

Christians Sometimes Struggle to Discern God's Voice

Hearing God is sometimes easier at certain times than at other times. Even Elijah, who spoke for God and heard from God, at one point in his life apparently went forty days without hearing him (1 Kings 19:7–9). But Elijah was sensitive enough to who God was (see the last chapter) to recognize that God's voice was not in the wind or the earthquake caused by God's presence. He kept waiting until he heard God in a gentle whisper, when God came to him in a special way (1 Kings 19:8–13).

The Bible provides plenty of guidance in learning to hear the Spirit's voice in practical ways. When the Spirit bears witness with our spirits that we are God's children (Rom. 8:16; 1 John 3:24; 4:13) or through Scripture-guided wisdom we learn the mind of the Spirit (Rom. 8:5; 12:2–3; 1 Cor. 2:12–16), we know we hear his voice. Sometimes we also have an overwhelming sense that we need to act. When the Lord called me to Bible college, he made me so sure of his leading that I turned down a National Merit Scholarship offered for another school. A few years ago, I was sure that God wanted me to move, at least temporarily, to an urban area in a mid-Atlantic city. I was so certain of his leading that I prepared to leave my full-time teaching position in North Carolina without having a lead for another teaching position. It just so happened that Eastern Seminary in Philadelphia had an opening for a visiting professor that year. Not long after that, after a national search, Eastern offered me a long-term position on the day I needed to let another very good school know if I would accept their offer.

On the other hand, sometimes we may think God is leading us to a location for one reason and arrive only to find out that, while he was ordering our steps, it was for reasons other than those we expected. If we do our best to follow him, however, he proves trustworthy in accomplishing his purposes. And if we have an intimate relationship with him, we will ultimately have his guidance, whether by a specific sense of direction or by God simply ordering our steps.

Some sorts of situations prove especially ambiguous. Whereas some Christians discover God's leading in locating appropriate marriage partners in a fairly straightforward manner, others find it more difficult, especially when particular callings are involved. One friend studying at Dallas Seminary told me that she was toying with the idea of writing a thesis on why so many single Christians she knew thought God told them to marry someone but that person ended up marrying someone else. Whatever the other reasons, the involvement of our own emotions can make such areas difficult even for very committed Christians.

The foundation of knowing God, however, is not simply being able to determine specific guidance from him, important as specific guidance is. Knowing God is more than simply getting guidance for the details of our lives.

The Spirit Reveals Jesus to Us

There is much pressure today to preach what is directly relevant to behavior. Such sermons and Bible studies are important, but one of the most important things we learn when we study the Bible is the nature of God's relationship with his followers. Jesus is not just an idea or one doctrine among many; he is our only Savior and Master, through whom and for whom we were created.

The Spirit is the key in revealing Jesus to us, and the Jesus he reveals to us is the same Jesus we read about in the Bible. In fact, the Spirit often teaches us about Jesus by recalling to our hearts at appropriate times what he already inspired for us in Scripture. The Spirit does not waste his inspiration!

The Spirit Carries on Jesus' Work

Jesus had been telling his disciples that the Spirit would explain further the teachings he had given them (John 14:26; compare Neh. 9:20; Ps. 143:10; perhaps Prov. 1:23); he would not make up new things that had little to do with the Jesus they had known (1 John 4:2–6). In John 16, Jesus explains how the Spirit would carry on Jesus' mission. (John intends this promise for his readers, not just for Jesus' first hearers [see 1 John 2:20, 27].)

The Spirit not only reminds us of Jesus' words in the Bible, but he actively stands up for us in our conflict with the world. John 16:1–11 encourages persecuted Christians by telling them that the people who drag them into court are in fact the ones on trial, because God is the ultimate judge. In God's courtroom, the Spirit is believers' Paraclete (translated variously "comforter," "counselor," "advocate"; 14:16, 26; 15:26; 16:7), a term that often meant "defense attorney" (as in 1 John 2:1). In the same way, the Spirit testifies along with us as a "witness" for Christ (John 15:26–27) and "prosecutes" the world concerning sin, righteousness, and judgment (16:8–11).

Although Jesus has gone, John tells us, he remains present, because the Spirit stands in for him, providing his presence and continuing his work. Everything that Jesus says the Spirit will do in the world (16:8–11) Jesus himself had done (3:18–19; 8:46; 15:22). In other words, the Spirit carries on Jesus' mission of revealing the Father, so that by the Spirit, Jesus continues to confront the world as he did personally two thousand years ago. The Spirit does not, however, reveal Jesus in a vacuum; when Jesus sends the Spirit to convict the world, he sends the Spirit, not directly to the world itself but to us (16:7, the Spirit is sent "to you," that is, to those who follow Jesus). The Spirit continues to confront the world with the person of Jesus through our proclamation of him (15:26–27).

Intimate Friends with Jesus

We discuss the Spirit's power for our witness for Christ in chapter 3. But the Spirit does not come merely to reveal Jesus to the world. Just as the Old Testament prophets knew God well before they proclaimed him, our proclamation should flow from a deep and intimate knowledge of God. The Spirit not only empowers us to proclaim Jesus to the world but testifies to us about Jesus for our own relationship with him (16:12–15; see also Eph. 2:18; 3:16). The Spirit will take the things of Jesus and reveal them to us, glorifying Jesus as Jesus himself glorified the Father (John 16:14–15; see also 7:18, 39; 17:4). As soon as he returned to them after the resurrection, Jesus gave his followers the Spirit so that they could continue to develop their relationship with him (16:16; 20:20–22).

Most important, Jesus promised that whatever the Spirit would hear, the Spirit would make known to the disciples (16:13). To someone reading the fourth Gospel from start to finish, this promise would sound strangely familiar. Jesus had just told his disciples, "I have not called you slaves, but friends, because a slave does not know what the master is doing, but whatever I have heard from the Father, I have made known to you" (15:15). What did

Jesus mean by calling us friends? Friendship meant many different things to people in the ancient Mediterranean world, but one aspect of friendship most often emphasized was intimacy: True friends could share confidential secrets with one another.[1] As God said to his friend Abraham, "Shall I hide from Abraham the thing which I am about to do?" (Gen. 18:17). Moses, too, as God's friend, could hear his voice in a special way (Exod. 33:11; Deut. 34:10). Some early church fathers noted that Jesus, who was in the Father's bosom (John 1:18), knew the Father's secrets.

Jesus shared God's heart openly with his disciples; he "bared" God's heart. Here Jesus explains that he shares the Father's secrets with his friends (15:15) and promises that the Spirit will be as open with the disciples after the resurrection as Jesus himself had been before the resurrection. Ancient philosophers emphasized that true friends shared all things in common; similarly, friends of a prince often received special favors from the king because of their relationship with the king's son. Jesus explained that all that belonged to the Father was his, and all that was his would therefore be the disciples' (16:14–15). In the context, Jesus especially meant God's truth (16:13). Members of God's household, friends of God's Son, would know the heart of God, Jesus' Father.

What does this promise mean for disciples today? It means that Jesus still calls us friends and shares his heart with us. It means that the Spirit passes on Jesus' words as clearly as Jesus passed on the Father's, that we should be able to hear Jesus' voice as clearly today as his disciples did two thousand years ago and—since we see things in light of the resurrection—understand his message better.

Some Safeguards in Listening for God's Voice

Of course, Christians have often abused the promise of hearing God's voice, hearing instead only what we wanted or expected to hear. What objective guidelines can help us learn sensitivity to the Spirit and enable us to hear God's direction accurately?

Safeguards in This Passage

First of all, the Spirit does not come to testify about himself; he comes to testify about Jesus (15:26; 16:14). He brings to our remembrance and explains what Jesus has already said (14:26). What the Spirit teaches us is therefore consistent with the character of the biblical Jesus, the Jesus who came in the flesh (1 John 4:2). The more we know about Jesus from the Bible, the more prepared we are to recognize the voice of his Spirit when he speaks to us. Knowing God well enough to recognize what he *would* say on a given topic can often inform us as to what God *is* saying, because God is always true to his character. But be warned: Those who take Scripture out of context (a common problem in today's church) render themselves susceptible to misinterpreting God's voice.

Second, the Spirit does not come merely to show us details such as where to find someone's lost property, although the Spirit is surely capable of doing such things and sometimes does (1 Sam. 9:6–20). Nor does the Spirit come just to teach us which sweater to put on (especially when it is obvious which one matches) or which dessert to take in the cafeteria line (especially if none of them is healthy), as a few young believers in their well-intentioned zeal for the details of God's will have supposed. The Spirit does, however, guide us in evangelism or in encouraging one another (for example, Acts 8:29; 10:19; 11:12). The Spirit also comes to reveal God's heart to us, and God's heart is defined in this context as love (John 13:34–35; 15:9–14, 17). To demonstrate unselfish love is to know God's heart (1 John 4:7–8; see also Jer. 22:16).

Another Safeguard

Third, the Spirit helps us when we are in fellowship with others who also are seeking to obey God's Spirit. In the Old Testament, older prophets mentored younger prophets (1 Sam. 19:20; 2 Kings 2:3–8). Likewise, Paul instructed first-generation prophets in the early church to evaluate each others' prophecies, to keep themselves and the church accurate in hearing God (1 Cor. 14:29).

Spiritual mentors or peers who are mature in their relationship with God and whose present walk with God we trust can seek God with us and provide us with a sort of "safety net." If we feel the Spirit is leading us to do something but recognize that much is at stake if we are wrong, we may do well to talk the matter over with other mature Christians. Proverbs advised rulers that wisdom rests in a multitude of counselors, and that advice remains valid for us as well. In the end, we may not always settle on the counsel others give us—like us, they too are fallible—but if they are diligent students of the Scriptures and persons of prayer, we should humbly consider their counsel. God sometimes shows us things that others may not yet see; at the same time, God may well show some of our brothers and sisters things we have not yet seen.

Other Ways to Hear

Many young Christians are understandably intrigued by the frequent experience of supernatural guidance from the Holy Spirit. While most of us who have learned to hear the Spirit in that way still experience such guidance regularly today, after a number of years, sensitivity to the Spirit's guidance in that form becomes almost second nature and thus becomes less of a focus than it once was.

Nor is this guidance, exciting as it may be to one discovering it for the first time, always the clearest form of guidance God's Spirit gives us. By this method of hearing the Spirit, we might help someone in need, because the Spirit specifically directs us to do so. But many of us have also learned to hear God's Spirit exegetically, as the Spirit has spoken in the Scriptures. By hearing the Spirit's voice in Scripture, we might help that same person in need simply because Scripture commands us to do so. But perhaps the deepest sensitivity to the Spirit comes when we learn to bear the Spirit's fruit in our lives—when our hearts become so full of God's heart that we help a person in need because God's love within us leaves us no alternative. All three forms of guidance derive from the Spirit and from Scripture. Yet where needs clearly exist, God's character, which we have discovered by means of Scripture and the Spirit, is sufficient to guide us even when we have no other specific leading of the Spirit or scriptural mandate, provided neither the Spirit nor the Bible argues against it. It is when the Spirit has written the Bible's teaching in our heart that we become most truly people of the Spirit.

The Spirit's Leading

Most of all the Spirit leads us into a deeper relationship with Jesus (John 16:13; compare 14:6). But this relationship occurs not only in prayer but in the context of our daily lives. In Romans 8:14, the context of being "led by the Spirit" evokes the language of the exodus, when God led his people in the wilderness (Isa. 63:10–14). Paul thus shows that the Spirit not only brings us into the Christian life, but he then guides us throughout, ensuring that we will safely enter our future "inheritance" as Israel entered theirs (Rom. 8:15–17).

Though we often do not realize it, the Spirit joins us and the rest of creation in "groaning" with birth pangs for the coming age (8:22–23, 26; the Greek term evokes the image of Israel sighing under Egyptian bondage).

Similarly, the Spirit often leads us without our realizing it. He takes the struggles of our daily lives and uses them to conform us to Christ's image (8:18, 28–30). In the context of Galatians 5:18, being "led by the Spirit" may also include ethical empowerment—God leading us in the ways of righteousness for his name's sake (Gal. 5:13–6:10; compare Pss. 23:3; 25:4–5, 8–10).

But while these texts present a general leading of the Spirit, various texts indicate that the Spirit clearly can speak and give direction on other matters too. The Spirit not only assures us of our relationship with God (Rom. 8:16; 1 John 3:24; 4:13), but he can guide us concerning specific matters of personal evangelism (Acts 8:29; 10:19; 11:12). To illustrate this point, I offer one example here (others may be found in my chapter on the Spirit and evangelism).

After my first or second year of Bible college, while I was home working for the summer, I was translating and studying Romans 8 in preparation for a midweek Bible study I was to lead two days hence. Suddenly I felt the Spirit impress on me that he wanted to demonstrate just how meticulously he can guide us when he wills to do so. Being a budding Bible student, I did not really want to interrupt my study, but I thought that I had better obey him if I wanted his help when I stood before the congregation on Wednesday night. The Spirit had sometimes led me like this before, so I knew how to be sensitive to his direction.

After I stepped outside, the Spirit led me up the street, down another street, up another street for some blocks, and finally onto a side street. After I had walked on that street for some distance, the impression left, so I stopped and turned around to get my bearings. As I turned around, I spotted an old friend I had not seen since high school, and beside him I saw a young woman I had first met on the other side of town three days before and for whose salvation I had since been praying. As I approached, my friend from high school (who was still not a Christian) began telling her how dramatically I had changed after my conversion. Although not yet a Christian himself, he witnessed to her for me!

After that, the woman trusted me enough to open her heart to me and my witness, but she had no permanent address. Sometimes she stayed with various friends and at other times lived on the street. On the occasions when I felt the Lord wanted me to speak to her, I would just start walking and trust the Holy Spirit to take me to her, as he invariably did.

This was not my everyday experience, but I believe that God cared so much about this young woman that he was prepared to use unusual means to show her his concern. (Jesus multiplied food for the five thousand because a miracle was needed; then he had his disciples collect the leftovers because they didn't need another miracle for their next meal. He does miracles when we *need* them—not for our entertainment or to make us feel "spiritual.") She had prayed as a child to accept Christ but grew up in a home where, among other things, her mother slept with various boyfriends in front of the children. The young woman was by this time an alcoholic, but Jesus had not forgotten her or stopped reaching out to her.

The Spirit can direct us in a number of ways. Although the Spirit testifies of our relationship with God to our spirit (Rom. 8:16), Paul also speaks of the "mind of the Spirit" (8:5–6) and the "renewing of our minds" (12:2; see also Eph. 4:23; Phil. 4:7–8; Col. 3:2). Proverbs encourages us to seek genuine wisdom based on the fear of God (1:7); such wisdom also provides us with God's guidance. Then too, if we are willing to obey him, we can trust God to order our steps and situations even when we have no specific guidance. At numerous critical points in my life, God has had me cross paths with individuals with whom the chance meeting was a one in a thousand "coincidence," yet that meeting significantly affected the subsequent course of either their life or mine.

Hearing God's Voice: A Personal Account

Although a convinced atheist by age nine, I was converted through the witness of some Baptist street evangelists at the age of fifteen, the first day I heard the gospel. I argued with them for forty-five minutes, but the Spirit worked me over for the next hour or so until, on the floor of my bedroom, I acquiesced and surrendered my life to him.

Over the next couple years I studied the Bible and led many people to Christ, but I felt frustrated; I wanted to ask God so many questions, but I did not know that he would still speak today. One day as I was walking down a deserted road praying, the Spirit sparked faith in my heart that he would grant the desire of my heart. God knew, of course, what I wanted most! So I asked him to open my ears to hear his voice. What I heard then was so wonderful that I almost could not believe it, yet it was so far beyond what I could have conceived by myself that I could not doubt it.

I had unconsciously expected God to be like some other authority figures I had known as a child—to say something like, "It's about time you showed up, Keener!" Instead, he said, "My son, I have been waiting so long to tell you how much I love you." And then he began to talk with me about his love for his people and how it broke his heart that we were so wrapped up in all our other pursuits (including many of our religious pursuits) that we did not really embrace his love. Some of us—like myself—were afraid to be intimate with him in prayer, because we doubted his love.

No one had ever loved me the way God did, and each day I would go out to walk along that same deserted road to listen to the voice of the one who had wooed me to himself. He told me that the measure of his love was the cross: "See the nails in Jesus' hands, the thorns in his brow, and see the blood. My child, that's how much I love you." I later discovered the same teaching in Scripture (Rom. 5:5–8; 8:16; Gal. 4:6; Eph. 3:16–19), and still later I realized that this teaching was what I had discovered as a seventeen-year-old seeking God's voice. God in his kindness showed it to me when I needed to hear it, before I had learned how to translate Greek and Hebrew and even before I had immersed myself in Scripture. Sometimes when we talked, God spoke about impending judgment and other less pleasant topics, but he always did so sorrowfully and always pointed me back to his heart of love.

I had prayed for the gift of prophecy, initially simply because 1 Corinthians 14:1–5 said it was the best gift to seek for building up the body of Christ. I wanted to please God and glorify him, so I sought the gift of prophecy. Yet when I began to exercise the gift, at first it seemed like a new toy to me. I began going to people and prophesying words that answered prayers for wisdom that only they and God knew about. In one case, someone had been praying for several months about whether God would allow them to date. They had told no one, yet I felt the Lord leading me to find them and tell them they were allowed to date. Since I was against dating myself and had not felt that the Lord had granted *me* permission to do so, I was quite annoyed with the message. I kept praying until I felt sure I would be disobeying God if I did not deliver it. When I reluctantly delivered the message (showing my annoyance even while doing it), the person began praising God and then explained the situation.

One day I felt led to pray for someone to be healed and felt directed to walk down a particular hallway on campus. I was sure the person I ran into must be the one and asked him if I could pray for his healing. He seemed surprised that I knew, but he allowed me to pray. Unfortunately, I had better guidance than faith; I realized as I began to pray that I really did not have confidence that God would heal him. Happily, God is gracious anyway; the young man suddenly straightened up and began thanking God for healing him. I was stunned and a little disappointed that God had acted without waiting for me to exercise some faith!

But as I matured, I realized that prophecy was not meant to be a toy; my heart needed to reflect God's heart. He also began to provide prophecies that were less pleasant than the sort described above (occasionally a reproof for someone's sin). God gave us the gift to show us his heart so we could do his work. Mistakes in finding guidance in my own life slowly persuaded me to take seriously the Bible's claim that all prophecy must be tested and that I remained a finite and fallible vessel. I was glad God corrected me in my own life before I caused harm in anyone else's. I continued to share what I felt God wanted me to share but learned to be more cautious and to try to distinguish better between what I was sure the Spirit was saying and what was merely an impression.

It was then that I discovered another method of hearing God's voice that could complement and anchor the prayerful, "charismatic" method. I had been reading the Bible steadily since my conversion, but now I learned to value much more highly sound Bible interpretation. When I was reading about forty chapters of the Bible a day, the Spirit enabled me to see the importance of understanding the Bible in context, and from context he led me to a passion for the Bible's cultural background. Whole new horizons of Bible study began to open to me. I worked hard to set aside my presuppositions and traditions and to go where the biblical evidence led. Those who have used any of my commentaries will know how seriously I take this commitment (even if we occasionally differ on a particular interpretation).

But in 1987, in the deepest crisis of my life, I learned still another way of hearing God's voice, related to the first two. Before that crisis I had been praying two hours a day; in the midst of the crisis, I could only weakly mutter Jesus' name over and over. Although I was so broken and overwhelmed that I could not hear him at all except on rare occasions, I still clung to what Scripture taught me about God's character.

During this deepest darkness time in my life, some African American Christians in the low-income neighborhood where I had moved unofficially adopted me into their family and took me to church with them. The family consisted of a grandmother and the five grandchildren she was raising by herself. Their own lives were difficult, yet they had learned how to draw on God's strength in ways that I had not. As I learned to let go of my ambitions and embrace brokenness, my personal pain began to bond me with others who were in pain. As I grew to feel their pain, I began to realize afresh God's pain—for he loved all people too much not to feel their pain.

John says, "Everyone who loves has been born of God and knows God. Whoever does not love does not know God, because God is love" (1 John 4:7–8 NIV). I will never doubt that God genuinely provided my prayerful and exegetical biblical experiences, but in my pain I also learned another way of hearing God to which both the Spirit and Scripture testify. As we begin to know God's character and become like him, we begin to share his heart as well as know about it. When we cannot only say what God is saying on some issue but actually feel what he feels about it, sharing in the fellowship of Christ's sufferings (compare Phil. 3:10), then we have begun to know him still more deeply.

Other Resources for Hearing God's Voice

We have discussed knowing God's character, trusting his presence, worshiping him, and believing that God is willing to reveal himself to us. But beyond that, we often learn by doing. As noted earlier, sometimes we must simply step out in faith on his leading, although it is usually best to start small if we are unsure. (I joke that walking on the Sea of Galilee may be troublesome if the ice cracks when I step on a frozen puddle.)

As when he was with his disciples two thousand years ago, Jesus is a patient teacher; he often will work with us. The first time I felt God impressing something on my heart to share with others, twenty-two years ago, I asked God to let someone else share it first so I could be sure. Someone suddenly offered a prayer, which used almost the same words I had been feeling. The next time I felt such an impression, I knew that I should speak out.

Most important in learning to hear God's voice is seeking God himself, asking him to reveal himself to us more deeply. Some of what I have recounted I intended merely to whet your appetite for more intimacy with God, but ultimately that intimacy comes only from his hand, not from reading about it. In some matters, how-to books have advantages, but when attempting to hear God, praying that he himself will open our ears is the best place to start. Before I began hearing God's voice, I prayed for that ability, based on what I had just learned from 1 Corinthians 14:1 (that one way to serve Christ's body is to pray for the gift of prophecy). We can trust that he who promises the Spirit to those who ask him (Luke 11:13) will not withhold the intimacy with himself for which he sent us the Spirit.

We should not straitjacket God's workings. God spoke differently to different prophets and others in the Bible, and we do not all need to hear him in the same way. At different times in my life, and sometimes from one day to another, I have heard him in different ways. What matters is our intimacy with God. If it is God himself more than his voice we seek, and if we seek his voice most of all so we can be and do what pleases him, we will hear his voice in every way we need to hear it.

We can often learn new things from the diversity of God's workings. Although I had previously written about hearing God's voice, Jack Deere's book on the same subject intrigued me with the question of hearing God in dreams, so I prayed that God would help me to hear him in this way too, if he wished. Some of my dreams are, of course, simply due to what I had for dinner or situations I am dealing with in life (compare Eccles. 2:23). Many of my dreams help me to experience other people's life situations (such as persecution, war, or slavery), which teaches me how to pray for them more sympathetically. As I immerse myself in Scripture, I sometimes dream Bible stories. Some dreams warn me about the future, bring to my mind someone for whom to pray, or deal with issues in my heart. But in a few dreams, God explicitly speaks to me, and when I awake I know I should pay attention.

We have already discussed worship; it is too easy for requests to consume all our prayer time, leaving no time for talking with God about his own greatness and works. At the same time, even bringing requests directs our hearts toward God. God is near us when we call on him, whether in the desperation of a broken heart in intercession, the jubilant cries of worship, or the discipline of a daily quiet time. Hearing God's voice in the Bible is also essential. There was a time right after Bible college when I thought I needed less devotional Bible study because I studied it academically much of each day. I quickly discovered, however, that I needed to read the Bible regularly to listen to God's voice in it. My academic work in cultural background makes the Bible come all the more alive to me when I study it devotionally, but it's my devotional life that makes my academic study alive and relevant.

Other spiritual disciplines can also turn our hearts toward God. Richard Foster, Dallas Willard, and others have written helpful books on these subjects. In my own life in the past decade, I have found that regular fasting helps me to direct my heart toward God and humble myself before him. When I started, I thought I could fast for a particular prayer request, but eventually I became overwhelmed when I realized I would have to fast every day to cover all the requests! I then changed my approach: I began fasting just as a spiritual discipline before God, to humble my heart so I could seek to please him more fully. God does not hear my prayers because I fast, but because I am his child who loves him. But I keep my love for him more attentive by spiritual disciplines. Jesus is my atonement and sin offering; fasting serves as more like a freewill offering or thank offering, a way I can voluntarily demonstrate further devotion to him.

If God has stirred in your heart a deeper desire for him, there are sacrifices you can make to demonstrate to him your total dependence on him. If you want God to stir your heart more, you can ask God, with whatever faith you start with, to do so. God meets even the smallest step on our part, and even the biggest step would go nowhere without his grace. God reckoned righteousness to Abraham—one chapter before Abraham acted unfaithfully regarding Hagar. Abraham's faith grew over the years (until he could even offer up Isaac), but at the beginning, God simply met him where he was. I pray every day for God to deepen my love for him, for my new heart and its continued renewing are his gift.

Conclusion

We may hear God's voice in Scripture, in worship, in the Spirit's leading, in God's voice in our hearts, and by knowing God's heart so fully that we know what he desires. All these ways of hearing God are important, but our goal is not just to receive guidance for our sake or so we can boast to others that we have heard from God. Our desire must be to know and obey him and reflect his character. If we desire to know him more intimately, we may start by asking him for this gift. One matter about which God often chooses to speak to us concerns our witness for him. To this subject we turn in the next chapter.

3

The Spirit Empowers Us for Evangelism

One day while I was doing Bible study with a new believer, one of his friends from high school dropped by. I felt led to begin sharing with her about the pain in her background, and for about half an hour I felt the Spirit strongly pouring into me the message of God's love for her and comfort about her past. Finally, she began to weep and surrendered her life to Christ, knowing that God had revealed the secrets of her heart. I had never met her before and knew nothing about her until that time—but God did.

Usually my witness proceeds by more "natural" means. But even then, I often feel the Spirit prompting me to say something or just to listen. Occasionally I have been talking with someone about having a personal relationship with God, and they have asked me whether someone can really be intimate enough with God to know him. Sometimes at that point I simply point out that Scripture claims that we can, but on occasion I have felt it appropriate to ask God out loud if he has anything he wants me to say to them. On those particular occasions, he did, and my hearers responded by respectfully pondering his message to them (which was often explaining why he had chosen this time in their life to bring the gospel to their attention). On the other hand, I can think of a few times when, led by my own knowledge about what was usually effective, I failed miserably to communicate the gospel.

We need the Spirit's guidance when we witness. Many of us do not realize how available that guidance already is! Consider the following illustration from a recent magazine article:

> Imagine visiting a town at night that appears to have no lights, no televisions—not even alarm clocks. And then imagine learning that the town's power supply is virtually infinite, but that no one in the town had thought to turn any of their electrical appliances on. Wouldn't that town seem like a silly place to you? Yet the Church is all too often like that town. God has given us the power of His Spirit to fulfill His mission in the world, yet few Christians have even begun to depend on His power.[1]

In this chapter we will focus on Pentecost and how the Spirit equipped believers for evangelism; how God sometimes confirms our witness with dramatic answers to prayer; the model of Elijah and Elisha for some frontline ministries of evangelism; and how empowerment to do God's work is inextricably bound with suffering in Mark's Gospel.[2]

The Power of Pentecost (Acts 1–2)

In modern terms, Jesus was (among other things) the disciples' "hero." They trusted him and could trust themselves only as he empowered them; they went out to minister (for example, Luke 10:1–2) only because he sent them. In Acts, after Jesus' ascension, they continued to do his work, knowing that he was still working through them. Today, it is still Jesus to whom we look. If we think the disciples ministered by their own power or holiness (contrary to Acts 3:12) and look only to the leaders of that first generation for guidance, naturally we will not witness miracles or Spirit-empowered evangelism today. If we still look to Jesus Christ, our hero and Lord, however, we should expect that God may continue to provide signs glorifying Christ.

Unlike some other biblical writers we will examine, Luke focuses almost exclusively on one special feature of the Spirit's power in our lives. Whereas John the Baptist, Paul, John the apostle, and others in the New Testament often spoke of the entire sphere of the Spirit's work, Luke focuses especially on the prophetic empowerment dimension of the Spirit. (By "prophetic" I do not mean only inspired speech—though that was most common in Acts—but also the kind of miracles associated with prophets in the Old Testament; see the comments on Elijah, below.) As many writers have shown, Luke emphasizes particularly the Spirit's role in various kinds of inspired speech (see Luke 1:15–17, 41–42, 67; 2:26; 12:12; Acts 1:2, 8; 2:4, 17; 4:8, 31; 5:32; 6:10; 7:51; 10:45–46; 11:28; 13:2, 4, 9; 20:23; 21:4, 11; compare 7:55; 8:29; 10:19, 38; 15:28; 16:6–9). There may be a few exceptions, for instance, the contrast between Spirit and fire in Luke 3:16, but the Spirit's prophetic activity is his activity most often emphasized in Luke and Acts.

Luke and Acts are two volumes of one long story, and in the second volume, the Book of Acts, Luke shows that the church continues much of what Jesus began. With some important limitations (for instance, Jesus alone is the Messiah), Jesus' ministry in the Gospel of Luke serves as the model for ministry in Acts. Writers have pointed out many parallels between the two volumes, but one parallel between Jesus and the church is especially clear in Acts 1–2. When Jesus announces his Spirit-anointing in Luke 4:18–19 on the basis of Isaiah 61, this sets the tone for the Gospel of Luke; in the same way, Luke uses Isaiah and Joel to announce the church's Spirit-anointing in Acts 1:8 and 2:16–21, setting the agenda for the rest of Acts.[3]

By emphasizing that the same Spirit who empowered Jesus empowers his followers, Luke reminds us that Christ's body has (in principle at least) the same kind of empowerment Jesus had in his earthly ministry. If that is not evident in our own ministry as God's church, it may be because we have failed to recognize the dramatic nature of his gift.

Why is Pentecost so central in discussions about the Holy Spirit? Why did God send the Spirit? Following the outline provided by Acts itself, we survey the promise of Pentecost (1:4–8); the preparation for Pentecost (1:12–2:1); the proofs of Pentecost (2:1–4); the peoples of Pentecost (2:5–13); the prophecy of Pentecost (2:14–21); the preaching of Pentecost (2:22–41); and finally, the purpose of Pentecost (2:41–47). The church can spread across cultural barriers because God's Spirit equips us to speak for him and to experience a foretaste of heaven.

First, Luke reports the promise of Pentecost (Acts 1:4–8). In the Old Testament, the Spirit empowered God's prophets to speak for him and promised that someday all God's people would prophesy (Joel 2:28). This special prophetic empowerment was so essential that Jesus commanded his disciples to wait in Jerusalem until it came (Luke 24:49; Acts 1:4–5).

But the promise of the Spirit was associated not only with power to speak for God; it was also associated with the end time. When the disciples heard Jesus' promise of the Spirit, they asked whether he was about to restore the kingdom to Israel. They asked the obvious question, given what they knew about the Spirit from the Old Testament: The Bible associated the Spirit with the time of the kingdom (see Isa. 44:3; Ezek. 36:24–28; 37:14; 39:29; Joel 2:27–3:1).

Had we been in their place, we probably would have assumed the same thing the disciples did; after all, the Messiah had come, the resurrection had begun (with Jesus), and the Spirit was about to be poured out. It would have seemed obvious to us that the end time was arriving (Acts 1:6–7). Jesus instead informed his followers that the Spirit was coming ahead of the future restoration—in other words, part of the future promise had invaded the present. As Paul puts it, the Spirit is the "down payment," the "first installment" of our future inheritance (Eph. 1:13–14); another writer says we have "tasted the powers of the coming age" (Heb. 6:5).

Jesus explained that the Spirit would empower his followers to carry their eyewitness testimony about him to all nations (Acts 1:8). Jesus is continuing the subject of end time prophetic empowerment. Isaiah had promised that in the end time, Israel's remnant would become God's witnesses to the nations (Isa. 43:10–12; 44:8–9). The end has not yet arrived, but we can do our part to prepare for the end by evangelizing the world as Jesus called the first disciples to do (Matt. 24:14; Rom. 11:25–26; 2 Peter 3:9, 12). The rest of the Book of Acts continues much of this focus. The promise that the Spirit equips disciples to evangelize the entire world provides a rough outline for the expansion of the church in Acts: Jerusalem, Judea, Samaria, and on to the ends of the earth. (Specific summary statements divide Acts even more neatly: 6:7; 9:31; 12:24; 16:5; 19:20; 28:31.)

Second, Luke reports the disciples' preparation for Pentecost (Acts 1:12–2:1). After Jesus told them to "wait" in Jerusalem (Luke 24:49; Acts 1:4–5), the disciples prayed together, which also contributed to their unity (Acts 1:12–14; 2:1). Luke probably wants us to notice this emphasis on prayer and unity, since he continues to stress these characteristics in succeeding chapters (prayer, for example, in 1:24; 2:42; 3:1; 4:31; 6:4; unity, for example, in 2:46; 4:24, 32; 5:12). Looking forward to what God had promised, the disciples also reorganized so that their leadership structure would be ready for what God had planned; this required both faith and foresight (1:15–26).

This is not to say that God is able to pour out his Spirit only under certain circumstances. But we do know that God sometimes filled his people with the Spirit in direct response to prayer (4:29–31), sometimes with effects similar to Pentecost (4:32–35); Jesus invited disciples to pray for the Spirit (Luke 11:13). Even in passages in which prayer is not recorded, we see that people were attentive to God before God filled them (Acts 8:17; 10:44; 19:6).

Third, Luke recalls the proofs of Pentecost (Acts 2:1–4). He reports three signs of Pentecost: wind, fire, and tongues-speaking. Because each of these promises was associated with the end time, God was assuring the disciples that, even if the final end had not yet arrived, they were experiencing a foretaste of the future (see 1:6–7). To the early Christians, the wind probably recalled Ezekiel 37: In the end time, God would send a mighty wind of his Spirit to resurrect Israel. The fire might have reminded them of John's prophecy as well as Old Testament prophecies of end time judgment (Luke 3:9, 16–17, for example, might be a reminder of Isa. 66:15–16 or Zeph. 1:18; 3:8). The fire did not mean God was sending judgment at this time; it did suggest, however, that he was offering signs of the future kingdom.

The empowerment to speak in languages they did not understand must have reminded the disciples of the Old Testament promise of end time prophetic enablement, as Peter goes on to make clear (Joel 2:28–29; Acts 2:16–18). These three signs constituted decisive proofs to the gathered Christians that many of the events of the end time were now taking place: The Messiah had been enthroned at God's right hand to rule until his enemies become his footstool (Ps. 110:1; Acts 2:34–35). (Because some Jewish people thought that Pentecost was the day Moses had ascended Mount Sinai to receive the law, some scholars also think that Jesus' ascension to give the Spirit parallels Moses' ascent to receive and give the law.)

Fourth, Luke surveys the peoples of Pentecost (Acts 2:5–13). Even though most of the visitors for the festival were Jewish, they took the gospel back with them to many locations and cultures. Their experience on Pentecost, therefore, provided a foretaste of the Christian mission in the rest of Acts (1:8; 11:17–18). What is the point of the list of nations here? The list may simply be an updated version of the list of nations in Genesis 10, nations scattered when their languages were separated at Babel in Genesis 11. If so, the different tongues here transcend the dividing of nations and call us together in Christ. In this passage, God shows that, even from the start, his plan was for "all flesh" (2:17, 39). This is true even though the Twelve themselves did not begin to understand what this meant until the seven bicultural ministers they appointed in chapter 6 began to pave their way (8:4,

25). As early as chapters 1 and 2, the Book of Acts emphasizes that multiculturalism is God's idea (compare Rev. 5:9–10; 7:9), though it should not surprise us that the world often perverts that ideal to their own ends (compare Luke 2:1; Rev. 13:7, 16).

Fifth, Luke reminds us of the prophecy of Pentecost (Acts 2:14–21). We learn both from Joel's prophecy and from how Peter paraphrases parts of it to bring out its meaning. Joel said that God would pour out his Spirit "afterward" (Joel 2:28). Knowing Joel's context, Peter emphasized that "afterward" means "in the last days" (Acts 2:17; see Joel 3:1). What did all the tongues-speaking mean? many of the bystanders asked (Acts 2:12–13, 15–16). Peter replied that this tongues-speaking meant that God was inspiring his servants to speak for him as the prophets did (Acts 2:17–18). If one can praise God in a language one does not know, one can surely be sensitive enough to the Spirit to prophesy or witness in a language one does know. Visions and dreams were typically prophetic activity (2:17), but just so no one misses the point that Peter refers to prophetic empowerment, he adds an explanatory line in his quotation of Joel: "and they shall prophesy" (2:18). This passage ties together two themes Luke has been hinting at all along: The Spirit gives us a foretaste of God's future power in us, and the Spirit equips us to speak for God.

Sixth, Luke reports Peter's preaching on Pentecost (Acts 2:22–41). If the Spirit was being poured out, then the rest of Joel's prophecy was also true: They were in the end time, the era of salvation (2:21). Following a typical Jewish method of preaching, Peter breaks off his quote from Joel here and picks up part of it at the end of his sermon ("as many as the Lord our God shall call," 2:39). This means that he will be preaching on the last line quoted: "Whoever calls on the name of the Lord will be saved." In Joel, the "Lord" is God himself; but Jewish people in Peter's day did not like to pronounce God's name. By citing various passages that identify the Lord with the risen and reigning king, Peter explains that the name of the Lord on whom they are to call is Jesus of Nazareth, God in the flesh.

When Peter calls for a public commitment, he does not ask them to bow their heads and close their eyes to call on Jesus. As a friend of mine puts it, he wanted them "altered"—changed—not just "altared" (as in our modern altar calls that presume people will find it too embarrassing to accept Christ publicly). Referring to the many pools on the temple mount, Peter summoned his hearers to turn from sin and be baptized as followers of Jesus Christ (2:38).[4]

As a Bible teacher listening to some of my former students preach, I have heard both sermons that delighted me and sermons that made me cringe with embarrassment. Yet in both cases I have seen people come to faith in Christ. God wants us to expound the Bible faithfully, but he does not need us to have all the details right to save people; he saves people through his gospel and by his Spirit.

Although some people are gifted for evangelism in particularly dramatic ways, the Spirit gifts all of us to witness for Christ—even if most of us do not recognize all the power that God has made available to us.

Finally, Luke depicts the true purpose of Pentecost (Acts 2:41–47). Prophetic empowerment was an initial expression of the Spirit's coming, but the long-range impact of Pentecost was the growth of the church and a community of believers who cared for one another in sacrificial ways. This passage provides the climax and focus of the Pentecost chapter: the Spirit's coming produces gifts, but especially fruit. The life of the Spirit in this passage contrasts starkly with the petty spiritual rivalries in many local churches today, even though some of them claim to be bearers of the Spirit. As both charismatic and noncharismatic Christians agree, the work of the Spirit must go deeper than Spirit-led utterances and initial experiences alone.

Signs in Evangelism Today

The message itself is more critical than the signs that attest to it, but in a book addressing the Holy Spirit's work, it seems appropriate to challenge the church in areas in which we need to grow. For some of Western Christianity, that means reappropriating the value of signs as resources for drawing people's attention to the gospel.

God's Spirit gives us boldness when we witness, and sometimes he may guide us dramatically when we witness. For example, one day during my doctoral work as I was walking home from the store, I felt urged by the Spirit to catch up to the young man in front of me and to call his name, "Matt." I had never met Matt before; in fact, it turned out that he had just moved to town a few days before. Unfortunately, I was afraid to call out his name, but when I caught up with him, I discovered his name was indeed Matt. Needless to say, the Spirit did lead the rest of our conversation.

Often I have felt the Spirit prompting to witness to a particular person, but he does not usually give me the person's name. I have other prayerful friends, however, who have often led people to Christ by confronting them with specifics about their life, the way Jesus did with Nathanael or the Samaritan woman. This has happened to me as well, though not very often.

In whatever ways he leads us, whether simply by emboldening us or by giving us wisdom how best to share with a particular person, God's Spirit leads our witness. This is a major emphasis of the Pentecost story: We witness for Christ, and we depend on God's power to make our witness effective.

Acts also mentions other aspects of prophetic empowerment for the church, such as visions and dreams (2:17). Although in Acts God often uses these to direct the progress of evangelism (9:10, 12; 10:3, 17, 19; 11:5; 16:9–10; 18:9; compare 27:23), Luke does not tell us that every believer must experience these. Acts also emphasizes the miracle-working ministries practiced by the original apostles (5:12), later apostles (14:3), and other Spirit-empowered witnesses (6:8). Signs and wonders remain the primary method of drawing people's attention to the gospel in Acts (for example, 2:5–41, 43; 3:11–4:4; 5:10–11, 12–16; 6:3, 5, 8–10; 8:6–7, 13, 39–40; 9:34–35, 40–42; 13:9–12; 14:9–10; 15:12; 16:25–34; 19:11–20; 28:5–6, 8–10; see especially 4:29–31; 14:3), although well-educated Christians also engaged in public lecture and debate forums (6:10; 17:2–3; 18:28; 19:8–10), and the gospel was also passed on through personal witness from individual Christians (8:4).

All believers can experience the leading of God's Spirit in our witness; dramatic healings as are often reported in Acts, however, may be a different matter. Although Acts does not limit these to the apostles as some have claimed (see 6:8; 8:13; 9:12), neither does it imply that all believers will experience these on the scale reported for particular believers in Acts. Nor does it imply that we have any means to guarantee that God will gift a particular servant in a particular way (Acts 8:18–23), though many of us have found God happy to share such gifts with those who seek him for them (compare 1 Cor. 12:31).

Nevertheless, although not all will experience dramatic miracles on the scale reported in the Bible for particular ministries, we need some people to exercise those ministries today. Further, we all can learn from biblical examples of faith related to such miracles, even if our prayers are not always on that scale.

On some occasions the person to whom I was witnessing was ill or facing a major crisis and permitted me to pray for them. God does not always heal people when we pray, but as Paul Little pointed out in one of his books on evangelism, people are rarely offended when we pray for them. God often does heal people, however, as I began learning as a young Christian. I had already been effective in evangelism. As a high school student newly converted from atheism, I prayed with perhaps fifty people to accept Christ before I left for college. But while doing maintenance work at apartments during one summer vacation, I began to discover in the Book of Acts that the most common (though not exclusive) method of attracting attention for the gospel in Acts was by signs and wonders. I began praying that I would be able to overcome the severe rationalism of my atheistic background and believe God to confirm his gospel in this way.

Nothing happened to the first person for whom I prayed, but I already recognized that God had not promised to do it every time. So when an older woman came by complaining that her doctors had not been able to do anything about her knee, I asked her for permission to pray over it. A few days later she returned, announcing that her knee had been better since I prayed and asking if I would pray for her lungs now. "I've been coughing up blood, and my doctor thinks I have lung cancer," she lamented. I wasn't expecting the stakes to rise so dramatically that afternoon, but on my lunch break I went to her apartment. I began by explaining that whether or not God answered my prayer to heal her, she would die someday and therefore needed to be ready to meet Christ. After she prayed with me to submit her life to Christ, I prayed for her healing. She immediately quit coughing up blood, and the doctor gave her a clean bill of health. She lived roughly fifteen more years.

Offering prayers of faith for people at work is not as dramatic as the stories in Acts, but I hoped that it was a start in the right direction. When people see that God cares about their desperate situations, they often become more ready to pay attention to the rest of what God wants to do in their lives.

Elijah as a Model for Jesus and the Church in Acts

The closest Old Testament parallels for most of Luke's accounts about the miracles of Jesus and his leading agents in Acts are the stories about Elijah and Elisha. Although Elijah and Elisha probably used Moses as a model for some of their miracles, they (and especially Elijah) lived during a period when Israel's rulers were basically hostile to their message. Thus, like Jesus in his earthly ministry, their ministry to Israel was more prophetic than administrative. While some aspects of Jesus' ministry resemble Moses, Luke also emphasizes those that resemble these prophets.

Connections with Elijah are easy to recognize, though they must not be pressed too far. People were expecting Elijah's return (Mal. 4:5). Clearly Jesus was not Elijah, though Elijah served as an important biblical model for Jesus and the church. John the Baptist functioned like the promised Elijah in one sense—as Jesus' forerunner (Luke 1:17); further, the literal Elijah, like Moses, is plainly subject to Jesus (Luke 9:30).

Nevertheless, most of Jesus' miracles were more like those of Elijah and Elisha than like those of other Old Testament prophets. Like Elijah, Jesus raised a widow's son (1 Kings 17:17–24; Luke 7:11–17; compare 2 Kings 4:32–37). Like Elijah and Elisha, Jesus multiplied food (1 Kings 17:13–16; 2 Kings 4:42–44; Luke 9:10–17). By speaking of a prospective disciple's "plow," Jesus even alluded to the account of Elijah's call of Elisha, emphasizing that his own demands for discipleship are greater than Elijah's were (1 Kings 19:19–21; Luke 9:61–62). Perhaps most significantly, Jesus' opening declaration compared his mission to the disenfranchised—ultimately to the Gentiles—with the ministries of Elijah and Elisha (Luke 4:24–27).

Many writers have pointed to the clear connections between Luke's Gospel and the Book of Acts, which constitute volumes one and two of Luke's history of the early Christian mission.[5] In volume two, Peter (the leading representative of Jewish Christianity) and Paul (the leading minister to early Gentile Christians) repeat many of Jesus' same miracles, showing how the church must carry on his mission in various cultures. Some commentators even think that Acts 1:1 summarizes Jesus' earthly mission as "all that Jesus *began* to do and to teach" because Luke recognizes that Jesus continues to perform his works through his church. Luke's Gospel closes and Acts opens with Jesus commissioning his church for a worldwide mission, empowered by the Spirit, until his return (Luke 24:47–49; Acts 1:8). As Elijah's mantle fell on Elisha and as other prophetic disciples sought to emulate their mentors, so the ascending Jesus empowered his church with the Spirit to carry on his mission to the ends of the earth (1:9–11).

Are Such Works Needed Today?

Because I am committed to the truth of Scripture, I must try to understand what Scripture says, even if it transcends my own experience. Although friends from other parts of the world have shared with me reports of similar events, I have rarely witnessed miracles on the scale of Elijah,

Elisha, the Gospels, or Acts. From the standpoint of my experience, it might therefore be easy for me to believe that such dramatic miracles do not occur today. But my desire is to learn what Scripture teaches and then to seek to bring my life and the church's life into line with that norm. Of course, we do not need miracles just to prove to ourselves that we are spiritual, but we may need them to accomplish the sort of mission that Elijah and similar prophets undertook.

In some parts of the world, God is sovereignly using miracles to bring people to himself. One of my students, a Baptist pastor from India, told me how he reached resistant Hindus by praying for those who were sick to be healed. God answered abundantly, and the church grew from a handful of members to over six hundred. He expressed his frustration that the same thing did not happen at times when he prayed for people in the United States while a student here. The church in Nepal rose from fifteen thousand Christians in 1970 to around four hundred thousand three decades later; a Western Christian observer reported that roughly half of these conversions stemmed directly from witnessing miracles.[6]

For power like Elijah's to be active in today's church does not mean that all believers must exercise miracles like Elijah's. John the Baptist, who like Elisha (2 Kings 2:9, 15) came "in the Spirit and power of Elijah" (Luke 1:17), preached God's message of repentance boldly and introduced the Messiah; but he performed no miracles (John 10:41). Different members of Christ's body have different gifts (1 Cor. 12:4–30). The church as a whole, through some of its members (usually especially evangelists and apostles evangelizing the unreached), must reappropriate these particular gifts. Further, God works in different ways in different times, according to the needs of that time. For example, God specially gifted Joseph and Daniel with dream interpretation, perhaps because they would serve in pagan courts where dream interpretation flourished. We should also remember that, though God rewarded the desperate faith of those seeking urgent miracles from him, the *maturest* faith appears in a deep relationship with God. Such a faith relationship develops over time as we persevere through trials (for example, Heb. 11:8–19, 23–29, 35–38).

Nevertheless, significant aspects of Elijah's ministry remain a model of Spirit-empowered ministry for the church as a whole and, in many respects, for individual believers as well. Thus, while exhorting believers that a righteous person's prayer for healing will be effective (James 5:14–16), James reminds us that Elijah was a person "of like passions" as we are (5:17–18).

If God heard Elijah when he requested drought or rain, the text declares, we who also serve God can trust him to hear our prayers.

Sometimes I have seen God answer prayers like Elijah's. One morning our campus ministry had scheduled a march in Livingstone College's homecoming parade, but we feared that the downpour outside was going to "dampen" our witness. So a student from the chapter of New Generation Campus Ministries at North Carolina A & T State University decided to lead us in prayer for the rain to stop. It couldn't hurt, I thought, though the college administration was at that moment in the process of calling off the parade. Yet no sooner had the student prayed than the rain became like the dripping of a faucet just turned off. Within a few minutes the rain had stopped entirely, and it did not rain again that day. I marveled at the faith of the students eager to witness, who did not pause to doubt whether God could control the rain. When I spoke at the campus church the next day, I spoke from James 5 and pointed out that God had fulfilled this passage in our midst the day before.

When James makes Elijah's faith a model for ours, why shouldn't we be able to trust God for miracles? The Holy Spirit gives us boldness to ask for things in accordance with God's will because we walk in his desires for his work in the world rather than our own agendas (1 John 3:21–24; 5:14–15).

One more text may support the use of Elijah as a model for the church's ministry. Although any suggestion on the Book of Revelation will be controversial, some scholars suggest that Revelation 11:3–6 may portray God's church (or some of its evangelists) as experiencing the kind of miraculous power exhibited in the ministries of Moses and Elijah. The angel describes two witnesses to John in language taken from Zechariah 4:2–3, where the words refer to a king and a priest leading God's work in Zechariah's day (Zech. 3:6–9; 4:6–14). In Revelation, however, all God's people are a kingdom and priests (1:6; 5:10; see Exod. 19:6). Further, by calling these witnesses "lampstands" (11:4), Revelation may suggest that they symbolize the church (1:20, though see also Zech. 4:2, 11).[7] If this suggestion is correct, the church performs miracles like Moses and Elijah in Revelation 11:6. Whether one concurs with this interpretation will depend largely on how one reads the Book of Revelation as a whole, but those who do agree would find here another case in which New Testament writers saw Elijah as a model for the church. At the least, we learn more about evangelists whose message God promotes through signs.

Practical Implications of Elijah's Model

The biblical portrayal of Elijah and Elisha challenges us in a variety of ways. Although Elijah and Elisha were miracle workers, they hardly look like many modern "prosperity" preachers who claim miraculous power. God provided for Elijah, but eating from ravens' mouths and drinking from a brook (1 Kings 17:4) is hardly luxury. In response to Gehazi's pursuit of moderate resources, Elisha explicitly repudiated the valuing of material possessions (2 Kings 5:26–27). Moreover, Elijah's ministry required him to confront hostile officials, to live outside the confines of his own society, and to risk death for the honor of the one who had called him (1 Kings 17–19). Unlike many, probably most, other prophets (Num. 12:1; 1 Kings 13:11; 2 Kings 4:1; Isa. 8:3; Ezek. 24:18)—but like Jeremiah (Jer. 16:2–4), John, Jesus, and Paul—the call of Elijah and Elisha apparently forced them to remain unmarried.

That Jesus calls us as disciples to even costlier commitment than Old Testament prophets (Luke 9:61–62; compare 1 Kings 19:19–21) indicates the seriousness of his call. A Spirit-filled life like Elijah's or Elisha's does not mean homelessness in all circumstances (according to 2 Kings 5:9 Elisha had a house), but it does mean that we must value nothing so much that we cannot readily surrender it for God's call. I suspect that too many of us, for all our claims to be people of the Spirit, are so in love with our worldly comforts, resources, and pursuits that if God is calling us to give them up for the gospel's sake, we cannot hear him.

Lest we think Elijah too holy to provide a model for us, we must also pause to remember that Elijah was human in the same way we are (James 5:17). This is not to deny that Elijah was exercising a faith nurtured by years of an intimate relationship with God, but this faith depended on God's power, not Elijah's (the apostles also recognized this for themselves; compare Acts 3:12–13). Elijah dared work his miracles only at God's command (1 Kings 18:36).

Presumptuously seeking to declare God's purposes or work miracles on one's own will lead only to public embarrassment for oneself and God's people (compare Lam. 3:37–38), and one who has not learned sensitivity to God's Spirit should not step out on presumption. Had Elijah himself been deciding what God should do, he undoubtedly would have gotten his food somewhere besides ravens, but Elijah's authority came only from God's commission. Unlike some of us, Elijah was forced to remember that he was God's servant, empowered only to do God's will.

But Elijah was so confident that God had spoken that he was extravagant in proving that the fire would have to be a miracle. Although water was a rare commodity in this time of drought, he had the people pour water around the altar (1 Kings 18:33–35). After the miracle, Elijah was able to take vengeance on the prophets of Baal for the blood of his fellow prophets (18:40), many of whom may have been Elijah's own disciples (compare 18:13).

Yet despite what appeared to be an initial turning of the people to God, Elijah's feeling of climactic success was short lived. Jezebel was neither persuaded nor weakened in her throne but forced Elijah to become a refugee again (1 Kings 19:1–2). Fire from heaven should have brought Israel to revival, but instead it simply seemed to increase the opposition. Many of us have labored in God's work and finally seen the fruit of our labors only to experience what seem insurmountable setbacks. Given the opposition against the gospel, we recognize that our own gifts and works for the kingdom can never accomplish all of God's purposes, unless he intervenes by his own power. Elijah, who was a person of flesh and blood just like us, became discouraged (19:3–5). The Spirit's power does not stop us from being human or facing discouragements.

Once we realize that the power and the orders come from God rather than from ourselves, we will be ready for God to send us and use us the way he sees fit. We should pray for God to grant signs to his church for its work of evangelism (Acts 4:29–30); we should also be ready for the life of faith God asks of each of us—with signs, suffering, and sufficiency in him alone. The ultimate objective goes beyond signs, and even beyond evangelism and church growth; the goal to which these other activities lead is presenting people who are mature in Christ (Col. 1:28). Although God will not empower most Christians individually with the same gifts to the same degree that he empowered Elijah, all of us may learn from Elijah's example of faith, perseverance, and faithfulness. We may also pray for God to raise up men and women of God with those kinds of spiritual gifts for our generation.

Satan does not mind trotting forth his power. If the world is to recognize that God's power is greater, God's representatives must believe it and act accordingly.[8] Sometimes we have no choice. During my first year in Bible college, I was preaching at a street mission when a demon-possessed man began shouting that he was "Antichrist" and "Lucifer." (Leave it to a demon to take Scripture out of context; neither title in the Bible referred to a demon. Lecturing the demon on elementary principles of biblical interpretation, however, would not have been a helpful approach to the situation.) I had always assumed that I was spiritually prepared to cast out a demon, but remembering the story of the seven sons of Sceva, I found myself too scared to attempt it. What if the man jumped on me and began ripping my clothes off, as in Acts 19? Other workers escorted the man out, and I finished my sermon as best I could. The man might have come to the mission for deliverance, but we cast out the man rather than the demon. Ashamed at my failure, I realized that most of the "demons" I'd tried to cast out in prayer previously weren't real demons at all and that I did not have enough faith for the real thing. I resolved to become a stronger man of faith, and some months later I was tested again.

This time I was visiting a recently converted widow whose daughter was experiencing some serious problems. As I was praying for them outside, the Spirit suddenly led me back into the house to a door that opened to a stairwell, and down the stairs toward another door in the basement. I found myself unable to approach that door, however. An evil presence radiated menacingly from that room, and it felt like it was the ghost of the widow's husband. Knowing that "ghosts" are merely demons impersonating deceased people, I prayed upstairs and then marched down the stairs again, my strength renewed. I threw open the door and in Jesus' name commanded the spirit to depart, never to return. Instantly it was gone. As I rejoined the widow, she informed me of three matters I hadn't known: (1) the basement room was directly beneath her daughter's bedroom; (2) her former husband had been involved with the occult, and his belongings were stored in that room; and (3) a man she had dated a year before, who claimed to have psychic powers, had tried to confront the "ghost" of her husband in that room, but it had chased him away instead.

Although it is most convenient for me to share my own, firsthand testimonies (because I know more of them), many others who are involved in frontline evangelism have far more dramatic accounts of the need for the Spirit's power. Given what we are up against in our cities and in many unevangelized regions of the world today, I am convinced that nothing short of radical faith, in many cases accompanied with signs, will allow us to evangelize the "hard" areas. Missionaries frequently testify of God granting signs. Among some people groups, most converts were first reached through dreams and visions.

Yet as we pray for God to raise up gifts for his church (Acts 4:30; 1 Cor. 12:31), we do not need only Elijahs. There are other models of ministry in the Bible; John the Baptist for example was in some respects more like Jeremiah (who performed no signs but called for repentance in the face of impending judgment) than like Elijah (John 10:41). The church as a whole may currently need more prophets like Jeremiah to shake us from our complacency about God's mission in the world. Let us pray that God's Spirit will give us the various voices we need most to reach our generation for Christ.

The Spirit Equips Us to Suffer in Doing God's Work (Mark 1:7–13)

As a young Christian, I witnessed in some situations in which suffering was likely. Two weeks in a row I had led someone to Christ on Sunday night in a particular part of town; the third week I decided to try it again. Unfortunately, the first person I spoke to was not in a pleasant mood; he descended on me immediately with anger, pummeling me with his fists and kicking me. I managed to get away, with him cursing that he would kill me if he saw me again. On some occasions when I was beaten, the physical pain remained for several days after the beating. Once, however, the Lord mercifully caused me to feel nothing, though my hair was being torn out and my head was being slammed repeatedly against the floor.

I have not found such occurrences to be commonplace in the United States, but my friends in other parts of the world have recounted more examples. One Nigerian professor told me that he had been on Campus Crusade staff during some extremist Islamic riots a decade ago. Although the riots appeared to be spontaneous, the radical Muslims had, in fact, mapped out where all the Christian ministers in that town lived. They went to one house after another, murdering the ministers and their families. My friend and his wife huddled beneath a table with their baby as rocks were thrown through their windows. They escaped death only because a moderate Muslim neighbor with whom my friend had shared Christ went out and in Arabic insisted that this was a "house of peace." More recently, close Nigerian friends of mine lost ministry colleagues and relatives as hundreds of people were massacred (on both sides of the ensuing conflict). Around the world, thousands of Christians are martyred every year, and events in Columbine High School and elsewhere indicate that such events may become increasingly common here.

Equipping us to suffer for Christ's name is part of the Spirit's mission to us. The Gospels tell us that John the Baptist announced that Jesus would baptize people in the Spirit. We will examine this promise in greater detail in Matthew later in this book, but here we turn to Mark's account. The Gospel of Mark offers us the most concise summary of this story, because

Mark includes this account in his introduction, and introductions were supposed to be short and to the point. Thus, Mark includes only the most relevant points and uses them to introduce the major themes of his Gospel.

Mark mentions the Spirit only six times in his Gospel, but three of these times are in his introduction. This suggests that the Spirit is considerably more important for Mark than one might guess from the few times he mentions the Spirit later—introductions typically prepare the reader for what will follow. Mark builds three successive, concise paragraphs around the topic of the Spirit: John announces the Spirit-baptizer (1:8); the Spirit descends on Jesus (1:10); and the Spirit drives Jesus into the wilderness for conflict with the devil (1:12).

The progression of these three paragraphs means that the promised Spirit-baptizer himself is the model for the Spirit-baptized life, and the Spirit-baptized life is a life of victorious conflict with the devil's kingdom. The rest of Mark traces the continuing conflict: Jesus defeats the devil by healing the sick and freeing those possessed by demons. The devil strikes at Jesus through the devil's religious and political agents. Jesus finally dies but conquers death itself in the resurrection. This is the model for Spirit-filled existence: A Christian must be ready to display God's power but also to pay the price of death for doing so. The Spirit who inspired the Scriptures (Mark 12:36) and empowered Jesus to do miraculous works that skeptics reviled (Mark 3:22–29) will also anoint Jesus' witnesses to speak his message in times of persecution (13:11).[9]

Mark was "charismatic" in the sense that he emphasized the power of the Spirit for doing God's work. But he was quite different from the kind of charismatics today who emphasize only the blessings of serving God. Mark recognized that the Spirit empowers us to do exploits for God but also to suffer for his honor. As in the Book of Acts, irrefutable signs of God's activity lead not only to conversions but to active hostility and persecution (for example, Acts 4:7; 5:16–17; 14:3–6).

Some scholars think that Mark wrote his Gospel for the suffering church in Rome, where Paul had written a letter a few years earlier. In that earlier letter Paul said that the Spirit joins the present suffering creation in groaning with birth pangs for a new era to come and invites us to "groan" with him (Rom. 8:22–23, 26). Thus, God works our trials for our good; prayers by the Spirit allow him to conform us to the image of his Son and to prepare us for our role in the coming age (8:26–30). In short, the Spirit makes the present bearable by reminding us that we live for another world because we belong to another world. We are here, not as citizens of this age, but as its invaders called to be faithful to the Lord of the world to come.

Conclusion

If we wish to evangelize our world today, we dare not seek to do it in our own strength. As Dawson Trotman once observed, the early church lacked all the equipment that today we assume we need to get the job done: They lacked Christian literature, mass communications, rapid transportation; they acknowledged that silver and gold they had none.[10] But because they had a radical dependence on the power of God, they turned their world upside down. God does not call all of us or equip all of us to witness in the same ways; even in Acts, different ministers were equipped to minister in different ways. Apollos could debate (18:28); Peter performed signs (5:15–16); other Christians—probably the majority, though not the focus of Acts—carried the good news of Christ as they traveled (8:4). But each of us is called to witness, and God's Spirit will not fail us if we learn to depend on him.

Sometimes God is just waiting for us to pray (compare Matt. 9:38; Luke 10:2). During my doctoral work, some friends in InterVarsity helped me recognize how strategic it was to reach international students from less open areas and prayed with me that God would open doors and help me to recognize the doors when he opened them. That very day I was able to witness to two students, one a leading scientist from China. From then on God began opening doors to share with doctoral and postdoctoral researchers from less evangelized parts of Asia, the Middle East, and elsewhere on a regular basis. Are we ready to trust God to open the doors and believe that he will empower us to do what he has called us to do?

4

The Spirit and How We Live

I have seen miraculous healings and other extraordinary signs of God's kindness, but the greatest miracle I have witnessed is meeting a Christian from a very different background whose heart reveals the same character that God has put in me. Committed Christians have different personalities and gifts and come from different cultures and church backgrounds, but when we meet, we often can still recognize the same image of our Father.

As the first two chapters emphasized, knowing God's voice requires that we recognize God's character. When we begin to recognize his character, we are transformed as sharers of that character. Moses saw God's glory and thus reflected his glory (2 Cor. 3:7–16). Someday we will see and reflect God's glory fully (1 John 3:2), but already we are being transformed into his likeness and glory by his Spirit as we get to know him better (2 Cor. 3:17–18; 4:6, 17).

This chapter addresses that process of transformation. For many people today, hearing God's voice, Spirit-empowered evangelism, and spiritual gifts are exciting topics. Oftentimes we do not consider the fruit of the Spirit to be as exciting or supernatural—as if we could manifest them on our own! But no matter how much purely human works may look like the

Spirit's fruit outwardly, the motives and power behind them are often quite different. Other people are more excited about various ethical questions of our day, but, vital as these are, ultimately we will never purify the church ethically and morally without the power of God's Spirit working in his church. For that matter, we will never achieve victory in our own struggles if we do not learn to depend on what God in Christ does in us by his Spirit.

Elsewhere in this book I address other aspects of being "Spirit-filled." Here, however, I focus on the deep work of the Spirit within us: The Spirit makes us new people in God's image; the Spirit bears the fruit of his character in our lives; the genuinely Spirit-filled person serves others; and the power of Pentecost creates a new way to live.

The Urgency of Spiritual Renewal in the Church

The revivals of Acts 2 and 4 challenge not only North American Christians' Enlightenment anti-supernaturalism (our culture's skepticism about miracles) but also our materialism (2:44–45; 4:32–37). Do Jesus and the needs of his people matter to us more than anything else? The issue is not asceticism (as if possessions were bad) but priorities and sacrifice.

I will return to the example of Acts 2 at the end of this chapter, but in the meantime, several contrasts between the early church and North American Christianity may offer some perspective. (Here I will employ some cynicism, as biblical writers sometimes do, to drive home the point of how inattentive we often are to eternal matters. My language may be strong, but I do not think it even reflects fully the tragic waste of the resources God has given us in the face of a lost world's need.) Early Christian forms of self-sacrifice sometimes could border on asceticism, which is not what I am recommending for today. At the same time, however, the zeal of such ascetics to sacrifice for Christ puts to shame our frequent unwillingness to inconvenience ourselves.

- *Entertainment:* Second-century Christians refused to go to amphitheaters with non-Christian neighbors to watch people get butchered or mauled by gladiators or animals.
- *Stewardship:* Early Christians sacrificed their resources to care for the poor so much that upper-class pagans mocked them for their lack of discernment. Meanwhile, the church was converting the poor of the

Empire who saw the Christians' love for them. Later, Anthony heard Jesus' words in the Gospels to forsake everything and committed himself to follow this command literally.

- *Evangelism:* Christians often laid their lives on the line and sometimes died for their witness.
- *Justice ministry:* Some members of the early church bought slaves, empowered them with skills, and freed them.
- *Traditional spiritual disciplines:* Christians valued prayer, learning the Bible, and fasting; some later monastic Christians spent most of each day pursuing these disciplines.

Modern Western Christians, on the other hand, reflect a different repertoire of cultural values.

- *Entertainment:* Instead of going to amphitheatres to entertain ourselves with other people's suffering, we bring such entertainment into our living rooms via television and videos. We claim we watch such movies and programs only to relax and that even though we spend hours watching violence or sexual immorality, we do not actually enjoy it. (Certainly, we insist, we do not enjoy our hours of daily television as much as we enjoy studying our Bibles, though we rarely pick up the latter.)
- *Stewardship:* The average North American Christian tithes 2.5 percent of his or her income. We may, of course, explain that given the strength of the U.S. economy, our 2.5 percent goes farther than Anthony's 100 percent.
- *Evangelism:* We try to be at least as nice as non-Christians, so that if anyone discovers we are Christians we will not have been a bad witness, in case that person ever figures out what Christians believe and decides to become one.
- *Justice ministry:* Whenever we experience unresolvable conflicts with other Christians, we sue them.
- *Traditional spiritual disciplines:* We pray before meals, and with such great faith that we can do so concisely. We have more Bibles than the early church did, but after five hours of TV, we may not have much time to *read* them. Occasionally, however, we meditate on ideas that are biblical and quote Bible verses, even if they are out of context. We fast between meals, at least when we are on diet programs to lose

the weight we acquired by consuming resources that could better have served children in famine-stricken parts of the world. Happily, we do feed the homeless in our country on Thanksgiving and Christmas, which, we assume, should tide them over for the rest of the year. (Christians who have made their peace with social Darwinism may further take comfort in the idea that starvation could be God's way of weeding out people and nations less fit for survival.)

Nominal Christians have done a remarkable job of making Christianity acceptable to our culture (though barely different from it). Such nominal Christians might invite a more relevant title than "Christian," such as "people of North American faith," or, "North Americans who happen to have some affinities at the doctrinal level with ancient Christendom." Of course, there is a wide range of Christians between those who are nominal and those who are strongly devoted. But to the extent that our priorities are not eternal, our habits should give us pause.

When Rome fell in A.D. 410, pagans complained that it was judgment from the gods due to the spread of Christianity. Augustine responded that it was instead judgment for Rome's centuries of wanton sins and that the faith of the Christians in Rome had been too shallow to stay God's judgment (compare 1 Peter 4:17). I have talked with Christians from other parts of the world who barely escaped death and saw unarmed Christian friends and family members butchered. In many cases these Christians were more faithful witnesses for Christ than are most North American Christians. If suffering should come to our nation, are we ready for the test? And if not, are we willing to begin preparing ourselves and our fellow Christians in advance?

Born and Created New

Happily, the process of transformation does not depend on our self-discipline as much as it depends on our willingness to embrace God's help. Being totally devoted to God should be second nature to us—in fact, it should be our first nature! Everyone knows that children share genetic traits with their parents and that all creatures bear after their own kind. In the same context of the Bible that teaches this truth (Gen. 1:11–12, 21, 24–25), the Bible reports that when God created humans, he meant for us, in a finite and limited way, to be his children, to bear his image. He wanted humans to reveal his moral character and wisdom in the way they governed his creation (Gen. 1:26–28). Adam fathered a son in his own "image," i.e., who bore his genetic traits (Gen. 5:3). In the same way, God created men and women to be his children, in his "image" (Gen. 1:26–27; 5:1). Graven images cannot reveal his glory, but in a limited way, his children can.

Humanity's sin marred God's image in us, but in Christ we have been "created" new in God's image (Eph. 4:24). It is not without reason that Paul speaks of us as a "new creation" (2 Cor. 5:17; Gal. 6:15). As a new creation, we are the vanguard of God's coming new world (2 Peter 3:13–14; Rev. 21:1). We are also a new creation in the sense that what God did through Adam, he has done better through Jesus Christ, the new Adam (Rom. 5:14; 1 Cor. 15:22, 45).

God promised that someday he would place a new spirit and heart within his people (Ezek. 36:26), when he would give them his Spirit so they could do his will (Ezek. 36:27). We received that new spirit when we were born again through God's Spirit (John 3:6). When we are born from God (Gal. 4:29; 1 John 2:29; 3:9; 4:7; 5:1, 4, 18), we are born with his new nature, just as we are physically born with a genetic nature (John 3:6). Thus, Peter speaks of becoming "partakers of the divine nature" (2 Peter 1:4). As Christ's body, we are his members; in modern terms, we share his moral genes. Sharing God's divine nature does not mean we become part of the Trinity, of course. Rather, by sharing God's moral character, we are renewed into his image in Christ (Rom. 8:29), who is God's supreme image (2 Cor. 4:4; Col. 1:15; Heb. 1:3). As we look at Jesus and learn of him, we are transformed into his image (2 Cor. 3:18; 4:16–18; Col. 3:10), and someday we will see him face to face and take on his character fully (1 Cor. 15:49; 1 John 3:2–3). Do we want to reflect God's glory in our lives now? As we learn to know Jesus more intimately, and like Moses spend time with God on the mountain, we will begin to reflect his glory more thoroughly (2 Cor. 3:3–18).

The New Testament takes the claim of a new birth farther than simply the beginning of our Christian life. Conception and birth begin life; God conceived and birthed us into a new and "eternal life" (John 3:3–5, 16). Depending on how we translate the phrase, Paul might even have meant that believers share the "life of God" (Eph. 4:18); we depend on him for what we are now becoming (Gal. 2:20). Likewise, it is because we are born from God that we, as his children, can trust our inheritance in him (1 Peter 1:3–4).

Having his new nature in us does not mean we can be passive about our transformation. Paul tells us to put off the old and put on the new creation in his image (Eph. 4:22–24). Through a life of obedience (Eph. 4:25–32), we conform to the model and image of God in Christ (Eph. 4:32–5:2), and the new nature becomes more and more a part of the way we live. Peter says that we purify ourselves by obeying the truth, because God has birthed us anew with his word, a seed that reflects his nature (1 Peter 1:22–25; compare Luke 8:11; James 1:21; 1 John 3:9). Peter then adds that like babies depending on their mother's milk, we continue to grow by continuing to imbibe God's message (1 Peter 2:1–2).

God uses external trials to conform us to his image (Rom. 8:18–29; compare 2 Cor. 4:10–11, 16–18), but he especially works through his Spirit in us. Discipline can help us cooperate with the Spirit (compare 1 Cor. 9:24–27; 2 Tim. 2:3–5), but we must trust God to transform us into Christ's image. Paul claims that it is Christ himself working in him who accomplishes his ministry (1 Cor. 15:10; 2 Cor. 13:3–6; Gal. 2:8; Col. 1:28–29). He also claims that it is God working in us, and Christ living in us, that brings us to maturity (1 Cor. 12:6; Gal. 2:20; Eph. 3:20; Phil. 2:12–13; compare 1 Thess. 2:13). Do we dare to believe these claims?

The Spirit's Fruit (Gal. 5:16–25)

If conversion (see chap. 7 in this book) applies to believers the saving work of Christ, the continuing work of the Spirit causes us to grow in his character. It is no coincidence that Paul wrote about the fruit of the Spirit to the church in Galatia. They were struggling to achieve righteousness on their own, instead of accepting it as God's free gift in Christ. Righteousness is a gift at the moment of conversion, but living out righteousness daily is also part of that gift (Eph. 2:8–10).

What the Law Couldn't Do

The law was a good standard for ethics, but by itself it could not save anyone. Although God had given his people a good standard by which to live, from the start, Israel repeatedly failed to keep the law. God knew his people would keep the law only if it were written in their hearts (Deut. 30:11–14). God thus promised a new covenant through which he would accomplish just that (Jer. 31:31–34). Ezekiel explains how this moral empowerment would work: God would cleanse the spirits of his people and place his own Holy Spirit within them (Ezek. 36:26–27). Paul regularly echoes this promise: The Spirit transforms us to live God's way (Rom. 8:2–10; 14:17; Gal. 5:13–6:10; compare Gal. 2:20 with Gal. 5:24–25;

Rom. 15:30; Eph. 4:25–32; Phil. 2:1; Col. 1:8; 1 Thess. 4:8; 2:13; 1 Peter 1:2, 22; 1 John 3:6, 9; 5:18).

Old Testament law, like laws in all cultures, dealt with people on the outside, but Jesus demands more than mere outside observance. The law warns, "You shall not kill"; Jesus demands, "You shall not want to kill." The law warns, "You shall not commit adultery"; Jesus demands, "You shall not want to commit adultery" (Matt. 5:21–28). Mere human effort cannot transform our hearts; it can lead us only to denial, a sort of pretend righteousness, whether we are deceiving others or merely ourselves (1 John 1:7–10).

Jesus came to save us and give us his Spirit. He came to make us new on the inside so that we would want to do what is right. Rules have their place in restraining sin, but it is Christ living in us that transforms us. As Paul points out in the context of the fruit passage in Galatians, one cannot be legalistic and walk in the Spirit at the same time (Gal. 5:16–18). Legalistic religion depends on the flesh; Spirit-filled religion depends on God and the power of his grace.

Flesh and Spirit in Galatian Christianity

In Galatia, not everyone shared Paul's understanding of God's grace in Jesus. Some Jewish Christian "missionaries" in Galatia were trying to impose Jewish customs on Paul's Gentile converts. The problem was not that these customs were Jewish. The problem was that no customs can save us, and no culture, even one formed in many respects by the Bible, should be mixed up with the saving gospel. Throughout Paul's letter to the Galatian Christians, he refutes the claims of these false missionaries. Whereas human religion appeals at best to the accomplishments of the "flesh," salvation must depend solely on God's work through the Spirit (Gal. 3:2–5; 5:5, 16–25; 6:7–8), through whom Christ lives in us (2:20).

What does Paul mean when he denies that we can depend on the "flesh"? (The NIV's "sinful nature" leaves the wrong impression if we think of an evil nature in our soul, an idea that may stem from later Greek philosophy and Gnosticism.) The Old Testament contrasts human or creaturely frailty as "flesh" with God's Spirit (Gen. 6:3; Isa. 31:3). By Paul's day, some Jewish people (such as those who wrote the Dead Sea Scrolls) thought that what is "fleshly," merely human, was weak and inadequate to stand before God. In our fallen humanity, we are susceptible to sin, but Christ living in us gives us victory. Thus, instead of struggling with sin by fleshly means, we need to dare to trust Christ's presence and lordship and let him live his character through us.

Paul warns his Galatian readers that love is the true fulfillment of the law (5:13–14) but that "fleshly," human religion leads only to spiritual competition and animosity (5:13, 15; compare 1 Cor. 3:3). Jewish people often spoke of "walking" according to God's commandments and so fulfilling them. Paul likewise declares that if we "walk" by the Spirit, we will not fulfill fleshly passions. In Greek, Paul's words are especially forceful: You cannot do the Spirit's will and at the same time do that of the flesh (Gal. 5:16). Paul then offers the reason for this incompatibility: The goals of the Spirit and the flesh are mutually exclusive (5:17).

Some Greek philosophers said that a wise person needed no external law. Here Paul declares that those whom the Spirit leads are not "under the law" (5:18). Paul undoubtedly meant that believers led by the Spirit would fulfill the moral principles of the law, such as love, because the law was written in our hearts (Jer. 31:33; Ezek. 36:27). He contrasts this Spirit-led lifestyle with a life fueled by mere human power, no matter how religious such a life might appear to be outwardly. Hypocritical religion pretends to be righteous while providing only a thin veneer to disguise its sinful passion. Using the standard ancient literary device of a vice list, he declares that the "works" of the flesh include all manner of sins (Gal. 5:19–21). Because Paul has been complaining about human "works" in religion throughout his letter to the Galatians, they would probably recognize that he implies the inadequacy of human religion here.

Instead of dependence on "fleshly works," Paul calls believers to produce the "fruit" of the Spirit. Jesus said that one would know a tree by its fruit; a tree produces according to its nature (Matt. 7:16–20). If we depend on him, Jesus said, his life within us will cause us to bear much fruit (John 15:4–5). Paul, who declares that Christians are new creatures in Christ, expects that our very nature and the presence of God's Spirit within us will of themselves produce good fruit, unless we by sinful choices deliberately repress them. The behavior of Christians should flow from our new identity, and our identity is determined not by our past but by our destiny with Christ (Rom. 6:4–5).

Paul is not telling us that we will always *feel* new but that we should accept the reality of our newness by faith and live accordingly (Rom. 6:11). Not flesh, not human effort on its own, but the transforming power of Christ and his Spirit produces good works. And since we really belong to the Spirit and not to the flesh, Paul goes on to say, we must live like it (Gal. 5:24–25).

Jesus saved us from sin by grace; in the same way we can now *live* like we are saved from sin—by faith in Christ's finished work (Gal. 2:20; 5:24; 6:14), by "reckoning ourselves dead" (Rom. 6:11). While I believe it is misguided for believers to go around "confessing" new cars and other desires, Scripture *does* invite us to tenaciously remind ourselves what God has recreated us to be in Christ. The same Spirit who made us new in Christ (Gal. 4:29; 6:15) empowers us to recognize our new identity in Christ—one determined not by feelings, not by our past, not by our circumstances, but by Christ (Gal. 5:16, 25; see also Rom. 8:13). Although Paul emphasizes this point to the Galatians, he teaches other churches in the same manner: Every good work the gospel produces in us is "fruit" (Phil. 1:10–11; Col. 1:10), which comes from understanding how to love (Phil. 1:9) and includes joyful endurance (Col. 1:11) because of our future hope (1:12).

Other Jewish people in Paul's day stressed the Spirit's work in moral purification and especially in prophetic empowerment but rarely if ever claimed that the Spirit enables us to share God's moral character. Paul stresses the fruit of the Spirit not because his contemporaries did so but because it was part of the reality he and other early Christians experienced in Christ.

Particular Fruits of the Spirit

Why does Paul list these particular fruits of the Spirit? Could he have listed others as well? Paul's other writings do indeed suggest that this particular list of the fruits the Spirit produces in the believer (Gal. 5:22–23) is probably ad hoc, as are his lists of spiritual gifts (see Eph. 5:9; Phil. 1:11; Col. 1:6, 10; compare James 3:17).

Nevertheless, the sample of fruit he lists provides a good sense of the kind of life the Spirit produces. Legalistic religion often leads to quarrels and spiritual competition; it is self-centered, empowered only by the flesh, that is, by the self (Gal. 5:13–15, 19–21). By contrast, the Spirit summons us to self-sacrificial, loving servanthood. The Spirit produces cooperation and wholesome relationships within Christ's body (Gal. 5:25–6:10). His presence and influence in our lives is evident when we begin to act toward each other as he acts toward us. Much of the fruit Paul lists involves how we treat each other.

Love

The fruit Paul lists first is the most important, both in this context (5:22; see 5:13–15; 5:26–6:2) and universally as well. Paul elsewhere lists faith, hope, and love as primary Christian virtues (Gal. 5:5–6; Col. 1:4–5; 1 Thess. 1:3), but the greatest is always love (1 Cor. 13:13). For many ancient writers, love was but one virtue among many. Early Christian writers, however, following Jesus' own interpretation of biblical law (Mark 12:29–31; John 13:34–35; 15:12; Rom. 13:8–10), agreed that love was primary.

Love is the fruit Paul most wishes to emphasize here, because it fulfills the moral intention of the whole law (Gal. 5:14; 6:2). The Galatians were concerned to fulfill the law through their own efforts, but throughout the letter Paul insists that if Christ's Spirit lives in them, they will fulfill the law's intention simply by the fruit of love. Instead of legalistic attempts at human moral achievement, they needed to depend in faith on Christ's finished work and to live out that faith by walking in love (Gal. 5:6). When we accept God's loving act to make us right with him, we are freed from a desire for personal spiritual achievement or competition and can devote ourselves to the needs of others. Many of the other expressions of the Spirit's presence relate to this fruit of love—for example, peace with one another, patience with one another, meekness (Gal. 5:22–23; 6:1). "Against these," Paul cries, "no law exists!" (5:23; see also 5:18; 6:2).

Joy

Joy is the language of celebration and worship that believers offer because we have confidence that God is with us (Pss. 5:11; 9:14; 13:5; 32:11; 35:27; 42:4; 43:4; 48:2, 11; 63:7; 67:4; 71:23; 105:43; 119:162; 132:9, 16; 149:2). Some Christians who are accustomed solely to rationally oriented worship services resent the spirit of celebration in many African American, non-Western, traditional Pentecostal churches, and other churches whose members clap with more than one hand at a time. Church services should include a rational component of teaching, and it is possible for emotion to become disorderly, but the fact that Paul puts joy second in his list of the Spirit's fruit should challenge us to reevaluate worship styles if they regularly suppress joy. Of course, our specific ways of expressing joy and praise and sensing God's greatness, whether demonstratively (for example, by dancing, Pss. 30:11; 149:3; 150:4) or more quietly (by being still before God, Ps. 46:10), are all valid; the differences are often culturally based.[1] In many traditional black Baptist, Latino Pentecostal, and other churches, people struggle in difficult jobs all week long and gather to celebrate the goodness of God in bringing them through another week.

But whether quietly or loudly, we should rejoice in the Lord as a sign of our trust in him. Although trials sometimes make joyous celebration difficult (the psalms are full of mourning as well as joy), under normal circumstances, remembering what Christ has done for us should cause us to rejoice (Phil. 4:4–7; 1 Thess. 5:16–18; James 5:13).

Peace

Peace is the opposite of what the Galatians were experiencing; it is the end of strife (see James 3:14–18). While it might occasionally mean inner tranquility (perhaps in Rom. 8:6), Paul typically uses the term *peace* to mean reconciliation or right relationship with God (Rom. 5:1; compare Eph. 6:15), with one another (Rom. 14:19; Eph. 2:14–15; 4:3; Col. 3:15; 1 Thess. 5:13), and even with outsiders (Rom. 12:18; 1 Cor. 7:15; perhaps 2 Thess. 3:16). Paul regularly regards peace with one another as a fruit of the Spirit. Christians must preserve the unity of the Spirit established among us because God has connected us by means of the bond of peace (Eph. 4:3). All his gifts are intended to bring us into deeper unity in the one body and one Spirit (Eph. 4:4–12, and esp. v. 13), a goal that is lived out by loving one another (Eph. 4:25–5:2; 1 Peter 1:22).

In a similar way, personality conflict was hurting the Philippian church (Phil. 4:2–3), so Paul's letter to them presents examples of submission and servanthood: Jesus (2:5–11), Timothy (2:19–24), Epaphroditus (2:25–30), and himself (2:16–18). In this letter Paul emphasizes unity (1:27–2:4) and notes that God's peace will guard the hearts of his people when they learn to treat one another peaceably and take their needs before God (4:2–9). Although we apply the word *fellowship* glibly today to any conversation between Christians, Paul emphasizes the "fellowship of the Spirit" (2:1; see also Acts 2:42–44; 2 Cor. 13:14; 1 John 1:3). As important as customary interpersonal bonding may be, our unity runs deeper than that: The same God lives inside all true Christians, and no one can act like a Christian while despising another member of Christ's body. We cannot help what others do to us, but insofar as it depends on us, we should be at peace with all people (Rom. 12:18).

Needless to say, if we exercise such peace, we will not divide from one another over issues secondary to the gospel—including different interpretations about spiritual gifts and hearing God's voice. Born-again Christians in the United States are deeply divided on many issues, and some have attacked the genuineness of others' Christianity not only over differences in views about spiritual gifts but also different views regarding women's ministry, the end time, or the nature of human free will. In view of the broader challenges facing us from our culture, such divisions are tragic. Unity does not mean that we agree on all details, but it does mean that we love each other and work together for the good of the gospel in spite of our differences.

Longsuffering

Longsuffering (or patience, or endurance) could refer to enduring any trial (Col. 1:11; James 5:10–11), but Paul usually applies it to relationships. Longsuffering characterizes God as he puts up with humanity (Rom. 2:4; 9:22) and represents how apostles face opposition (2 Cor. 6:1–6). Longsuffering also characterizes how we are to deal with one another (Col. 3:12–13; 1 Thess. 5:14). Paul regularly links this fruit with love (1 Cor. 13:4; 2 Cor. 6:6; Col. 3:12–14) and meekness or humility (Eph. 4:2; Col. 3:12–13).

Kindness

In Paul's letters, kindness most often represents God's kindness toward those who don't deserve it (Rom. 2:4; 11:22; Eph. 2:7; Titus 3:4). This is also the way the word is used in Greek versions of the Old Testament (reflecting language Greeks used for benevolent rulers). But kindness can also represent the apostolic model of kindness toward persecutors (2 Cor. 6:6) and the way we should show mercy to one another in Christ's body (Eph. 4:32; Col. 3:12). In Paul's view, such behavior is not natural for people until they have been made new in Christ (Rom. 3:12). This does not mean that unbelievers are never kind (compare Acts 27:3; 28:2) but rather that Christians should always be.

Goodness

Goodness characterizes the state of obedient believers (Rom. 15:14; 2 Thess. 1:11) and along with righteousness and truth can also serve as a general summary for God's work (spiritual fruit) in our lives (Eph. 5:9; Col. 1:10). Paul borrows the term from the Greek translation of the Old

Testament, where it could refer to "good things" materially (Eccles. 4:8; 5:11; 6:6; 9:18), to God's unmerited gift-giving to his people (Neh. 9:25, 35), but also to right moral action (Judg. 8:35 [some manuscripts]; 2 Chron. 24:16), the opposite of wickedness (Ps. 52:3). Perhaps Paul uses this term as a general way to cover any moral excellence not included in his other terms.

Faith

Faith, or (as many scholars translate it here) faithfulness, refers to the Old Testament idea that one shows trust in God by cleaving to him in obedience based on a relationship with him. Paul also emphasizes such trust as dependence solely on God (who alone is completely dependable) and often urges such faith(fulness) in opposition to legalistic works in Galatians. We come to Christ and the Spirit by receiving Christ's message in faith, and we continue to grow in faith by the new presence of the Spirit within us (Gal. 3:2–5; 5:5).

Meekness

Meekness means one is unassuming and loving rather than self-centered. Such a person is not timid but rather provides the sort of gentle answer that turns away wrath (Prov. 15:1; 1 Cor. 4:21; 2 Tim. 2:25; James 1:21; 3:13; 1 Peter 3:15). Paul uses Jesus as his model of meekness (2 Cor. 10:1; compare Matt. 11:29) and expects believers to treat one another the same way (Eph. 4:2; Col. 3:12). Jesus resisted injustice verbally (Mark 12:38–40; John 18:23) and sometimes even forcefully (Mark 11:15–16), but he did not grasp for human power (Matt. 12:19–20; 21:5). He was a "meek king" (Matt. 21:5); often ancient kings proved to be angry tyrants, but rulers who controlled their passions and treated subjects and enemies with kindness were called "meek."[2] Most relevant to this context, one who exhibits this fruit of the Spirit shows compassion rather than an attitude of condescension to a fellow Christian entrapped in a sin (Gal. 6:1; compare 1 Cor. 4:21).

Self-Control

Both in the Greek language in general and in Paul's writings, self-control refers to self-discipline and control over one's appetites—whether sexual (1 Cor. 7:9) or the sort of discipline required when training for athletic competitions, which provides an illustration of Christian discipline (1 Cor. 9:25). Disciplining ourselves to maintain a regular quiet time, to guard our tongue, or to say no to a habit in our lives need not depend solely on human effort (the "flesh"). Whether we recognize it or not, a Christian's success in such endeavors is the fruit of God's Spirit.

Lists of virtues were common in antiquity, and like many of these other lists, Paul's list probably represents merely a sample. Nevertheless, the fact that love is at the top of Paul's list is no coincidence (compare also 1 Cor. 13:13). We should seek to develop such qualities in our lives (2 Peter 1:4–11). Indeed, they characterize our identity in Christ and show what our life should look like as we submit to the Spirit's gentle leading from within. No spiritual gifts declare us to be people of the Spirit if we do not walk lovingly and meekly toward others.

The Spirit and Submission (Eph. 5:18–21)

Whatever else Paul might wish to tell us about a Spirit-filled life, he tells us that it affects the way we live. Whereas Acts emphasizes especially that the Spirit empowers us for evangelism, Paul tells us that the Spirit empowers us for worship and relationships with others. Paul warns us to bear the fruit of the light (Eph. 5:9) because we are no longer what we were (Eph. 5:8). Then, in Ephesians 5:18, Paul contrasts the wrong kind of inspiration that comes from drunkenness with the good kind of inspiration that comes from being filled with the Spirit.

In Greek, Paul follows the command "Be filled with the Spirit" with several subordinate clauses, like "giving thanks" and "submitting." These clauses presumably provide examples of the life that flows from being Spirit-filled. Moved by the Spirit, believers will worship God with singing and thanksgiving (5:19–20), an experience most of Paul's readers probably experienced in their house-churches. If Spirit-led worship occurred in the time of David (1 Chron. 25:1–7), we may be sure that the ideal Christian experience of Spirit-led worship is even fuller (John 4:23–24; 1 Cor. 14:26; Eph. 6:18; Jude 20).[3]

But the Spirit-filled life necessarily includes more than the sort of worship and praise we utter with our lips. It includes "submitting yourselves to one another in reverence for Christ" (Eph. 5:21). Although not all translations reflect the idea expressed by the Greek text here, this is another subordinate clause explaining what the Spirit-filled life is like. No one who beats his wife or children, spreads slander in a congregation, or harbors perpetual unforgiveness in his or her heart is full of the Spirit, no matter how many supernatural gifts he or she claims to have. Because religious people can embrace all the general principles of Scripture yet often pretend that most of the Bible's corrections do not apply to them, Paul fortunately goes on to describe just what he means by mutual submission.

Writing from a Roman jail cell, Paul was well aware of the crisis facing the early church: The Roman elite who controlled the Empire were paranoid about subversive cults undermining traditional Roman family structures and suspected Christians of being among those subversive cults. Paul instructs Christians to uphold the best values of their society, and to do so, he borrows some traditional forms used to communicate ethical wisdom. Philosophers from the time of Aristotle on had provided lists of instructions as to how the male head of the household should rule his wife, his children, and his slaves. Paul instructs wives to submit to their husbands, minor children to obey their parents, and slaves to obey their masters. In offering these instructions, Paul nowhere compromised Christian ethics. Christians should submit to those in positions of authority, and the male head of the household always exercised authority over wives, children, and slaves in that society. (For worried readers, I believe that Paul would adapt the way he applied his principles for different cultures; most Christians today agree that he would address different cultures differently, at least regarding slavery. But different views of how we should reapply Paul's teaching here today do not affect the primary point I am making.)[4]

While accommodating those Roman values that did not conflict with Christian virtues, Paul also recognized that Christian virtues went considerably beyond Roman ethics. Not only those in subordinate positions but also those in positions of authority must humbly serve others. Thus, nowhere does he merely repeat the philosophers' traditional exhortation for husbands to rule their wives, children, and slaves. Instead, Paul expects husbands to love their wives as Christ loved the church and laid down his life for her (Eph. 5:25). In our society, many boys try to become men by making babies instead of raising them, by seeking power over others rather than by using responsibly whatever power they have to serve others, by abusing women instead of respecting, honoring, and serving them. Throughout human history, those who seize power are often also seized by it, becoming oppressors of other people. The Spirit's way, however, is different. A

Spirit-filled husband must serve his wife even to the point of lovingly laying down his life for her.

In a similar way, Paul exhorts fathers not to frustrate their children by
unfair discipline. Discipline must always be for a child's good, never a product of a parent's anger (6:4). Finally, after Paul has exhorted household
slaves to obey their masters with sincerity, he calls on masters to do the
same to them, recognizing that all of us stand the same before God's authority (6:9). If taken to their natural conclusion, such instructions would abolish the abuse of authority, hence abolish slavery itself.

In other words, Paul calls us to honor the authority roles of our culture,
if we are in subordinate positions (although he encourages slaves to improve
their situation when possible, 1 Cor. 7:21). If we are in positions of authority, we are to recognize that our authority comes from God's call and opportunity to help others and not from anything in ourselves; we are responsi-
ble to serve. The Spirit-filled life is a life marked by genuine submission to
one another. Christians who cannot submit to others, cannot take responsibility, and cannot humble themselves in loving service to others are not
yielding to the full life of the Spirit. Christians who gossip, slander, and act
arrogantly or with an authoritarian attitude quench the fruit of God's Spirit.
This is true even if these same Christians are able to exercise spiritual gifts,
claim leading roles in God's work, or if others rank them highly in God's
kingdom. God will judge us for our character and obedience, not for how
much power he gave us (compare Matt. 7:15–23; 1 Cor. 3:6–15; 4:1–5).

It is not surprising that Paul defines the Spirit-filled life partly in terms
of relationships in this passage. The Christians he addresses apparently had
some problems in this area, because throughout this letter Paul emphasizes
unity (especially Eph. 4:1–16) and relationships (4:25–5:5). Yet the Spirit
affects relationships in other churches as well (Gal. 5:22–6:3). Nor is Paul
the only New Testament writer to connect the Spirit's power in our lives
with how we treat each other.

The Fruits of Pentecost (Acts 2:44–45)

Before leaving the fruit of the Spirit, we should note that even Acts,
which emphasizes the Spirit's equipping us for ministry, teaches that the
Spirit produces moral transformation. As in Ephesians, this moral transformation affects relationships; in Acts we see how it enables members of
an entire church to relate with one another.

Although the immediate sign of the Spirit's outpouring at Pentecost was a prophetic empowerment for witness, demonstrated by speaking in tongues (Acts 1:8; 2:4, 17–18), the climax of Luke's depiction of the event is the long-range impact of Pentecost in 2:41–47. The cultural diversity of the Jewish pilgrims present at Pentecost (2:9–11) anticipated the cross-cultural unity of the church and became part of a united church representing many cultures (2:41–42; 4:36; 6:1, 5). Believers grew in unity around the apostolic teaching and prayer (2:42, 46–47), and apostolic signs and wonders continued (2:43).

Besides the numerical growth of the Christian community, the community grew in its cohesiveness through the believers' commitment to one another. The Greek term for "fellowship" (2:42) could mean economic sharing as well as spending time together. When we go out to dinner with friends from our church, we often think we are doing well; and to be sure, such fellowship is better than the isolation many churchgoers feel today. But the first Christians were far more serious about fellowship in the biblical sense than we are. The believers "shared all things in common" (2:44).

"Sharing all things in common" does not mean they moved into dormitories or lived on the street together. It does mean that whenever one member of the Christian family had a need, other members sold their possessions to meet that need (2:45). No one claimed that their possessions were theirs alone; everything belonged to the whole body of Christ (4:32). While we might not trust some church leaders today to distribute the church's resources equitably (4:35; 6:1–6), the principle remains valid: People matter more than possessions. We should therefore use our resources to meet others' needs (Luke 16:9–15). Our frequent resistance to this biblical idea may suggest how difficult it is for the Spirit to get through to us when the "moral fruits" he wants to address go as deep as our wallets or purses.

Luke was not describing a practice with which he disagreed. The Greek phrases he uses to describe the church's sharing of possessions portray the ideal community; he presents the early Christians' activity in glowing terms. But while Luke uses phrases ancient writers applied to some other ideal communities such as the Pythagoreans and Essenes, the Christians' relinquishment of personal property was more voluntary than in those other circles (5:4)—it was not "communistic." We should not for this reason, however, tone it down. The point of the difference is precisely that God rather than rules transformed their hearts. By valuing one another more than their property, the Jerusalem Christians showed their concern for God's priorities. This was not a human idea; it was generated by the fellowship of the Holy Spirit. We may contrast today's standard of fellowship, by which members often do not even know many others in the church and single members often leave as lonely as when they came.

We can challenge the world's values by how we live. Since my conversion I have always endeavored to live simply, in part to make the wisest use of my resources for the kingdom. Another reason for this commitment, however, has been the desire to protest and defy by my own lifestyle the world's falsehood that possessions have anything to do with happiness. Research files dominate my one-bedroom apartment; I do have a bed, but it is rented along with the apartment. I do not have a car or a television, though I will probably need a car someday, and if I get married, I am sure my wife will demand some changes in my lifestyle. Most of my income currently goes to needs in developing countries. (Let it never be said that everyone who affirms spiritual gifts propagates a materialistic "prosperity gospel"!) I do not expect all Christians to share my current lifestyle; indeed, those with families would not be able to do so. I use it simply as an example that material abundance is not necessary for happiness. Sacrificing all our time and resources for things that matter eternally is far more fulfilling than squandering them on momentary pleasures or whims.

By collecting money for the saints in Jerusalem (2 Corinthians 8–9), Paul applied and expanded this principle of sharing modeled by the Jerusalem church. Now churches in different parts of the world would help one another. When Christians in one part of the world are in need today, more affluent parts of the body of Christ must help them. As late as the second century, enemies of Christianity continued to comment on how Christians cared for one another by sharing their possessions.

After persecution became rarer and the church could use more of its funds for church buildings rather than for caring for the poor or for freeing slaves, the radical commitment of early Christians to care for one another began to wane. Yet this commitment characterized both the first (Acts 2:44–45) and second (Acts 4:34–37) outpourings of the Spirit, and one would expect that it should accompany true outpourings of the Spirit today. It followed the renewal movements of the Waldensians, Franciscans, and Moravians. It was part of the teaching of John Wesley, Charles Finney, and others. Wesley and many other leaders in past outpourings of the Spirit emphasized hard work, thrift, and generosity. Although some who claim to be spokespersons of the Spirit today emphasize how many possessions they can get from God, true people of the Spirit emphasize how much they can give to serve their brothers and sisters and the cause of Christ.

When we dare to believe Jesus' claims, we live according to the principle that people matter more than possessions. As a lover of Christ, one cannot accumulate possessions that have no eternal value while people for whom our Lord died go hungry or without the gospel. We should not, of course, be like some early and medieval ascetics who acted as if food, drink, sleep, and other gifts of God were bad; God wants us to enjoy his creation (1 Tim. 4:3–4; 6:17). Possessions are not evil—they just have no value compared with greater human need and the work of God's kingdom. One way the ascetics do shame us, however, is that they understood at least the value of sacrifice, something most of us, especially in Western Christendom, have forgotten. If we really love Christ, we will love others. And this fruit of the Spirit is not just a mushy feeling; it requires action and commitment.

Conclusion

Dare we believe that we are actually new in Christ? Some of us trust too much in our own abilities; some of us are too consumed by our own failings; all of us must learn to depend on Christ's work in us by his Spirit. If we wish to depend on him more fully, we should begin to ask him to do his work in us (John 14:13). But we should be warned: The fruit of God's presence in our lives involves not just a changed heart but changed behavior that reveals a changed heart. It means that we must change how we relate to others, even when it costs us something.

5

Are Spiritual Gifts for Today?

I had volunteered to do the class presentation on Rudolf Bultmann in our Ph.D. seminar on biblical interpretation. (Bultmann was a major twentieth-century scholar who believed that supernatural accounts in the New Testament were edifying myths.) After summarizing some of Bultmann's positive contributions to biblical scholarship, I critiqued what I thought was a fatal flaw in his rejection of biblical miracles: "Bultmann declares that no one in the modern world believes in miracles—and thereby excludes most people today from the modern world."

I had scanned the classroom before speaking, silently counting the number of students who would likely agree that God has done miracles. "His belief that modern people cannot accept God acting visibly in history excludes from the modern world most of us around this table," I continued. "Indeed, Bultmann excludes not only orthodox Christians, Jews, and Muslims, but spiritists, traditional tribal religionists, and others who believe in supernatural phenomena—in short, everyone but Western rationalists and the atheistic Marxists who adopted some of their views. Bultmann defines the modern world simply on the basis of his mid-twentieth-century Western academic elitism—making him an ethnocentric cultural bigot."

Naturally, my erudite professor, whom we knew to be the school's last remaining Bultmannian, objected. "Bultmann has his presuppositions, but you have your presuppositions too!" he responded, appearing more than mildly irritated.

"That is true," I conceded. "When I was an atheist, I denied that miracles could happen. As a Christian, I insist that God can do miracles. But an agnostic, neutral starting point would be to ask, What evidence is there for or against miracles? To argue against miracles inductively, Bultmann would have to examine every possible claim to a miracle and show it to be false. (And even then he would not have proven that such a claim could *never* be true.) But all I have to do to begin to argue that miracles *do* happen is to cite credible eyewitness evidence."

So I started doing just that—listing instantaneous healings I had witnessed in answer to believing prayers, particularly when I had been the person healed or the person praying for another's healing. Finally, I concluded, "Now if anyone still wishes to deny that miracles can happen, the next logical step is to challenge my credibility as a reliable eyewitness." Whether out of politeness to me or for lack of a good argument, the professor quickly changed the subject.

Bultmannian professors are hardly alone in their skepticism. Although the church for most of its history believed that miracles could still occur (and sometimes was credulous enough to embrace even many false ones), some parts of today's church are skeptical about most supernatural claims. After the rise of the modern Western prejudice against miracles, some Western Christians, while acknowledging that miracles happened in the Bible, created a system that forced them to discount evidence that miracles happen in modern times. Their skepticism is perhaps understandable. This is not the first time in history that circumstances led God's people to wonder whether God might continue his powerful works in their generation (Judg. 6:13).

Many other Christians who acknowledge that God can still do miracles in answer to prayer claim that supernatural gifts have ceased, thus doubting that God does miracles the same way he did them in biblical times.[1] Given the frequent abuse and feigning of some gifts today, this position has a measure of appeal. But despite many exceptions, God most often performed his miracles in the Bible in conjunction with the prayers or ministry of servants he appointed to represent him; because this is a pattern throughout the entire Bible, one would need clear biblical evidence that at some point this pattern should change. This chapter will discuss whether the biblical evidence actually supports such a position.

Dallas Willard remarks that those who doubt that God acts and speaks today as he did in the Bible are a sort of "Bible Deists." Whereas the original Deists thought that God began the universe and then withdrew from active involvement, some Christians today act as though God withdrew as soon as the Bible was completed.[2]

Most likely the majority of Christians today acknowledge that supernatural gifts remain available, although few of us currently witness them with the same magnitude and regularity as in Acts. Yet many of us who acknowledge that miracles of a biblical scale can happen today (including some Pentecostals) would be scared out of our wits if one actually happened to us. So pervasively has Enlightenment culture's anti-supernaturalism affected the Western church, especially educated European and North American Christians, that most of us are suspicious of anything supernatural. Is it possible that God has something more to teach his church today about supernatural gifts?

Did Spiritual Gifts Cease in Early Church History?

Spiritual gifts have become a major issue of controversy, especially since the mainline charismatic renewal of the 1960s and 1970s took the experience of these gifts beyond the confines of classical Pentecostalism. (As noted in the introduction, by "charismatic" I mean those who affirm and seek to practice *charismata*, Paul's term for spiritual gifts; I am not describing a set of views. This sense of the term includes Christians from a wide variety of denominations as well as from independent churches.)

Some observers continue to maintain what is called the traditional "cessationist" position: Supernatural spiritual gifts—that is, any (or most) gifts that we cannot also explain in natural terms—have passed away. Proponents of this view usually argue their position based on 1 Corinthians 13:8–10 or Ephesians 2:20 and especially from history. But the evidence for their interpretation is hotly (and rightly) disputed by others. Those who deny that these gifts continue today must also find other explanations for charismatic phenomena among genuine fellow Christians. In the past, some attributed such phenomena to demons, but psychological interpretations are more frequent today.

Yet even if we excluded the modern Pentecostal and charismatic movements, the church throughout history continued to believe that supernatural gifts did persist or periodically recur.[3] For example, the early church fathers provide abundant evidence that gifts such as prophecy and miracles continued in their own time, even if not as abundantly as in the first century.[4] Christians in the medieval and modern periods continued to embrace these activities of the Spirit.[5] It is in fact cessationism that is not well documented in earlier history; it seems no coincidence that it arose only in a culture dominated by anti-supernaturalism.[6]

The argument that spiritual gifts ceased in history, however, would not be a very good argument against spiritual gifts today even if it were certainly true. That gifts *should* cease is not a logical conclusion based on the assertion that they *did* cease. First, signs and wonders waxed and waned from one period to another (though they were never absent) even in the Bible; they were especially prevalent in times of revival. Could they not become common again in times of revival today?

Second, the argument that gifts ceased and therefore should cease is an argument based on one kind of experience. Yet those who make this argument simply dismiss the experience of hundreds of millions of Christians today (estimated at over four hundred million—Pentecostals and charismatics may represent the largest single block of Christians after Roman Catholics). Some people's claims of spiritual experiences are inauthentic, but cessationists must be quite sure of their exegesis before they dismiss *all* of them.

Contemporary Views Concerning Spiritual Gifts

Other observers, while acknowledging that spiritual gifts could in *theory* occur today, have been understandably reticent to embrace them because of the excesses that have occurred in charismatic circles in recent decades. Some Christians approve of spiritual gifts in principle but have had little contact with them personally and find little reason to actively seek them for their own lives. Others embrace spiritual gifts personally but feel that other issues in the church are more pressing. Still others (probably representing the majority of mainline Pentecostals and charismatics) believe that spiritual gifts are critical and that the entire church should embrace them. Finally, a minority of people (mainly in traditional United Pentecostal and some Apostolic circles) believe that the particular gift of tongues-speaking is essential for salvation. (Yet I know a number of people even in those churches who do *not* hold this view.) From my own and others' observations of various sectors of the body of Christ, it appears that both extremes—the extreme cessationists (who deny miraculous gifts today) and those who require tongues for salvation—are becoming an increasingly small minority. Most Christians fall into various moderate positions between these two extremes.

Like other recent Pentecostal and charismatic scholars such as Gordon Fee and former cessationist Jack Deere, I believe the position that supernatural gifts have ceased is one that no Bible reader would hold if not previously taught to do so. It is also a position based on a modern reading of the text shaped by Enlightenment culture. At the same time, it is a possible evangelical view, in contrast to the other extreme: Adding any condition to salvation—whether tongues-speaking or anything else—distorts the sufficiency of Christ and enters the realm of heresy. Many people who hold some dangerous views in theory are fortunately not consistent with those views in practice, and undoubtedly many who claim to hold this view in theory are our brothers and sisters in Christ. But however Christian in practice some holders of the tongues-for-salvation view may be, the view itself remains a deadly distortion of Christ's gospel.

The views between these extremes not only fall within mainstream evangelicalism but differ on relatively minor points.[7] Many of us hold a somewhat eclectic position, which stands a chance of emerging as the general consensus (if a consensus emerges). We do not believe that supernatural gifts represent the most important issue facing the church today, but we do believe that they point us to a nonnegotiable, crucial issue: They call us to dependence on God's Spirit in our ministry to others. We do not believe that those who exercise particular spiritual gifts are more "spiritual" than others, but we affirm that all spiritual gifts should rightly belong to the entire body of Christ today (rather than specific gifts being segregated in specific parts of the church).

God provides gifts to serve the church not to exalt individuals. Many of us have learned from experience that there are nondivisive ways to teach non-Pentecostal churches about spiritual gifts (especially by not overemphasizing them to the exclusion of other critical issues) that can sensitize them to greater dependence on the Spirit. Many Pentecostal churches will likewise profit from a fresh examination of spiritual gifts, because among Pentecostals, as among non-Pentecostals, many of the gifts rarely function adequately.

Because the term *charismatic* has come to mean different things to different people, I reiterate that I am using *charismatic* to describe those who embrace spiritual gifts in practice, whether they belong to churches that practice them or not. In the broadest sense of the term, of course, all Christians are charismatic, because God gifted each of us with a special role and purpose when the Spirit baptized us into Christ's body (1 Cor. 12:7–13; *charisma* means "grace-gift"). But even in the narrower sense in which we employ the label here, we do not intend the specific views that have become associated with the label in some settings. Many noncharismatics rightly object to the prosperity teaching and to the way many popular charismatic ministers handle Scripture. But these practices have nothing to do with being charismatic per se and stemmed from later fashions of one wing of the charismatic movement, not from the original charismatic renewal. (In fact, some anticharismatic fundamentalist ministers have applied Scripture with equal disregard for its context, and many who disavow prosperity teaching are not for that reason any less materialistic.) We are speaking solely of charismatic views concerning spiritual gifts.

Further, while such teachings do call into question how sensitively some charismatics are functioning in the spiritual gift of *teaching*, they need not in every case negate the reality of their personal experience in the Holy Spirit. Teaching is admittedly one of the higher-ranking gifts (1 Cor. 12:28), and those whose teaching is unsound disqualify themselves from the office of pastor (1 Tim. 3:2; 2 Tim. 2:24; Titus 1:9). Nevertheless, to teach soundly, teachers must acknowledge the need for other gifts as well. We are not training only other teachers! As diverse members of Christ's body, we all need one another and need to draw on one another's gifts (1 Cor. 12:28–31). The fact that one person lacks the gift of teaching and another lacks the gift of healing is all the more reason to learn and profit from one another's gifts. When we yield to God's Spirit, he brings forth the fruit of humility so we can learn from one another (Gal. 5:22–6:2), maintaining the unity of the Spirit in Christ's body (Eph. 4:3–13). If we are humble, we are more likely to gain a hearing when we seek to bring greater truth to the rest of the church.

The Importance of Spiritual Gifts and Miracles Today

Although some have argued that miracles are limited to specific periods in biblical history, a simple survey of the Bible shows this argument to be mistaken. At the same time, however, miracles do seem to *cluster* in certain generations in history, both in the Bible and subsequently. When one examines the Bible and church history, one quickly sees that the distribution of miracles is not random. Israel would often stray far from God until he raised up servants to lead them back to his law, a process repeated throughout history. Although not all God's servants worked miracles (Gideon, Jeremiah, and

John the Baptist, for instance, did not), the raising up of true prophets especially preceded times of revival, and such activities as miracles and renewals of worship (for worship, see repeatedly in 1 and 2 Chronicles) often accompanied these prophets or times of revival.

Recognizing that God is sovereign over times of revival is not the same as supposing that we can do nothing to make ourselves more prepared for them. Our generation must seek God's face, to ask him to perform his purposes in our world today. Yet we must also be ready to allow God to do whatever must be done to answer that prayer—even if it means judgment and stripping from us the things we value, so we may learn to value what really matters. Our spiritual forebears prayed that God would embolden and empower his servants in proclaiming Christ by granting healings, signs, and wonders (Acts 4:29–30). (Although the NIV separates this into two sentences, the Greek favors the translation: "grant us boldness by stretching out your hand to heal" [compare KJV] or "while stretching out your hand to heal" [compare RSV, etc.]; see also Acts 14:3.) Signs and wonders provide a powerful attestation of God's power and interest in this world and summon attention to the gospel we proclaim.

More important and critical, however, is the prayer for the Spirit's empowerment. In Luke's Gospel, the Lord's prayer for the coming of God's kingdom and deliverance from temptation is in a context of prayer that climaxes in an entreaty for the ultimate gift: God's Spirit (Luke 11:1–13). In the broader context of Luke's emphasis on the Spirit, this is a prayer for empowerment that we may do the work that is a prerequisite for the final coming of the kingdom.

A Biblical Case Supporting Gifts for Today

Several lines of evidence suggest that miracles and supernatural gifts should continue to function in today's church. Although many other lines of evidence are possible, I seek here to provide merely a sample of the arguments that could be offered.[8]

First, Luke presents the empowerment of the church at Pentecost as a normative experience for Christians. As we noted above, this experience includes empowerment to speak by the Spirit's inspiration, especially for witness, and in Acts it at least often includes "inspired" utterances such as prophecy or tongues. (I am not arguing that these must happen in every case, only that they, like the experience they often accompanied, are for today.)

Second, the Gospel writers (in this case we will use Matthew as an example) present Jesus' miracle-working ministry as a model for disciples. This does not, of course, imply that all of us should be equally proficient in all gifts, as Paul points out. It does imply, however, that the church, through some of its members, should carry on these acts.

Third, Paul's presentation of the gifts is inseparable from his view of the church. That is, Paul believes that every member of Christ's body has a special function and should contribute his or her gift(s) for its strengthening. Paul does not envision that any of these specific functions in the body should cease to operate before the Lord's return. Indeed, he explicitly declares that our imperfect gifts will cease only at that time (1 Cor. 13:8–13). For the sake of this chapter's length, I will defer examination of the specific gifts in two of his more commonly cited lists until the following chapter, although I will explore some other issues related to gifts while examining the passages that address them.

Is the Gift of Pentecost for Today? (Acts)

Although I addressed Pentecost in chapter 3, I need to add some observations here concerning the continuance of the gift of Pentecost. Referring to the "gift of the Spirit" earlier promised to all believers (Acts 1:4–5), Peter explicitly says that "this promise" is not only for all his hearers who turn to Christ but for their descendants and "all who are far off," all whom the Lord calls (2:38–39). Perhaps unwittingly at this point, Peter speaks the language of Scripture: Those who are "far off" represent the rest of Joel's "all flesh," the Gentiles (Isa. 57:19; Eph. 2:17). Peter had also quoted, "Whoever calls on the name of the LORD shall be saved," from Joel 2:32 (Acts 2:21). He spent the rest of his sermon explaining that this invitation refers to calling specifically on the name of Jesus (Acts 2:25, 34–36). Now he finishes the line from Joel 2:32: "all that the Lord calls" (Acts 2:39). The gift of the Spirit rightly belongs to all who turn from sin and accept Jesus Christ as Lord. Acts assumes that the gift made available at Pentecost remains in force.

Further, Peter's opening quote from Joel indicates that the gift *must* remain today. Peter correctly interprets Joel's prophecy as referring to "the last days" (2:17), understanding from Joel's context (Joel 3:1) and from that of other prophets (for example, Isa. 44:3) that God would pour out his Spirit in the end time. "Last days" was a biblical expression for that period (Isa. 2:2; Micah 4:1). The outpoured Spirit signals that Christ has taken his seat at the Father's right hand (Ps. 110:1; Acts 2:33–35) and that his reign has in one sense been inaugurated. Unless God allowed the last days to begin and then retracted them—pouring out his Spirit and then taking his Spirit back, attesting Christ's reign and then concealing it—we must still be in the era of the outpoured Spirit.

More to the point, the very structure of Peter's argument requires that this gift be available throughout this present age as people are saved through trusting in Christ. When foreigners are amazed to hear disciples speaking in other languages under the Spirit's inspiration, Peter insists that this fulfills Joel's prophecy about the Spirit of prophecy being outpoured in the last days. This being the case, Peter argues, the rest of the prophecy is also in effect: Whoever calls on the name of the Lord will be saved (2:21). Salvation and the gift of the Spirit belong to the same era; indeed, those who embrace Jesus receive the gift at conversion (2:38; see the discussion above in chapter 3).

Of course, not all aspects of Pentecost are normative for all of this age. Some aspects of the first Pentecost—such as the wind and fire—were not repeated after Acts 2. But while some narratives in Acts do leave room for debate as to how *frequently* tongues accompanied the gift of the Spirit, in practice, tongues (alongside prophecy) clearly marked reception of the Spirit's prophetic empowerment (ability to speak for God) in Acts 2:4; 10:44–47; and 19:6. In fact, when Peter hears the Gentiles speaking in tongues, he marvels that they "received the Spirit in the very same way that we did" (10:47).

Acts provides a pattern that suggests that such prophetic phenomena at least *often* accompany the gift of the Spirit in the sense Luke emphasizes (see chap. 9) without ever suggesting that the pattern should change. Since (1) the gift is permanent (2:39), (2) Luke three times uses tongues-speaking to attest the reception of the gift, (3) he depicts this response as a phenomenon arising from the Spirit's inspiration rather than from human culture (2:4), and finally, (4) he nowhere implies that this phenomenon was to cease, a heavy burden of proof lies on anyone who would argue that tongues have ceased today. Luke presents a model of the Spirit's working in his narratives, and if he had wished to restrict aspects of the model that were not relevant to his audience, we would expect him to have made this restriction clear.[9] (For comments on interpretive method here, see the appendix: "What Can Bible Stories Teach Us?" Though we must be careful how we do it, the Bible is clear that we can learn principles from narrative [2 Tim. 3:16].)

Nor is the continuing work of the Spirit in Acts limited to speaking in tongues. Acts emphasizes the miracle-working ministries practiced by the original apostles (5:12), later apostles (14:3), and other Spirit-empowered

witnesses (6:8). As noted earlier, in Acts, signs and wonders remain the primary method of drawing people's attention to the gospel (see 2:5–41, 43;
3:11–4:4; 5:10–11, 12–16; 6:3, 5, 8–10; 8:6–7, 13, 39–40; 9:34–35, 40–42;
13:9–12; 15:12; 16:25–34; 19:11–20; 28:5–6, 8–10;[10] see especially 4:29–31;
14:3, 9), although well-educated Christians also engaged in public lecture
and debate forums (6:8–10; 17:2–3; 18:28; 19:8–10), and the gospel was also
passed on through the personal witness of individual Christians (8:4).

As we noted in chapter 3, the Spirit's supernatural empowerment for our
witness is a critical feature in Acts. Eyewitness testimony of what one has
"heard and seen" applies both to eyewitnesses of the risen Christ (4:20) and
to eyewitnesses of subsequent phenomena performed by his power (2:33;
compare Luke 2:20). Moreover, the "word of God" or "word of the Lord,"
which in the Old Testament referred primarily to the past or present proclamation of God's prophets, in Acts refers especially to the saving gospel of
Christ (6:7; 8:4, 14; 10:44; 13:44; 14:3; 16:32; 17:13; 19:20). Whether through
the Spirit's leading in our words, or by God answering our prayers in ways
that demonstrate miraculously the reality of his reign, the Spirit's supernatural empowerment remains essential in evangelism.

In Acts, God's Spirit empowered his church to evangelize the world,
whether by signs or with boldness to speak or both. Can anyone think that
we need his power any less to complete the task in our generation? We should
note, however, that in response to the hardships of their time, early Christians *sought* this continuing empowerment for evangelistic signs and wonders through prayer (4:29–31). If the church today often lacks such power,
it may be in part because we have not sought it or because we have sought it
only for our self-aggrandizement rather than for the evangelization of the
world.

Are Miraculous Signs of the Kingdom for Today? (Matthew)

As noted above in chapter 3, Mark portrays Jesus as the one who can
answer his people's prayers and emphasizes that Jesus empowers his followers both to do miracles and to suffer for his honor. Matthew recounts this
same point from another perspective.

Jesus' Signs

In chapters 8 and 9, Matthew provides ten specific examples of Jesus' healing power in nine accounts, interweaving these practical demonstrations of

Jesus' authority with a recurring summons to submit to that authority (8:18–22; 9:9–17, 35–38). Although the Gospel writers draw spiritual points from these accounts, most of these stories teach us something about physical healing as well.

Let us take the example of the cleansing of the leper in Matthew 8:1–4. This story teaches us about the nature of faith and about our Lord's heart toward the infirm. The leper approaches Jesus with complete trust in his authority. Though his situation is desperate, he likewise humbly acknowledges that the choice of whether or not he is healed belongs to Jesus (8:2). Acknowledging that God has the right to refuse a specific prayer need not indicate a lack of faith, as some suppose. It may simply indicate respect for God's authority (Gen. 18:27, 30, 32). Biblical faith is not a formula by which God can be manipulated but a relationship with one whose character we have come to trust. At the same time, Matthew shows us something about Jesus' character: He *wanted* to heal the man (8:3; Mark 1:41 speaks of Jesus' "compassion"). Jesus was so concerned with the man's condition that he touched the untouchable, thereby sharing the leper's uncleanness in the eyes of his own culture (8:3). Whatever God's purposes may be in a specific situation, none of us would doubt that Jesus' character and compassion remain the same today.

Another healing story includes two miracles: the healing of a woman who had been bleeding for years and the raising of a dead girl. Jesus again appears ready to heal and even to restore to life, as his response to Jairus shows (9:18–19). The bleeding woman adds a new element of teaching to the story, however. She had *scandalous* faith (9:20–21). Under biblical and Jewish law, this woman communicated ritual impurity to anyone she touched. For her to press her way to Jesus in a crowd, therefore, was scandalous. For her to intentionally touch Jesus' cloak—thereby rendering him unclean in the eyes of observant Jews—was even more scandalous. Yet she was desperate. She lived in a society in which women could not earn adequate money to survive on their own, and her condition virtually guaranteed that she could never marry. So convinced was she of Jesus' power that she acted scandalously, desperately staking everything on his ability to heal her. The narrative concludes, not with Jesus rejecting her or concealing her touch, but publicly acknowledging her condition and sharing her uncleanness in the eyes of society so that he could publicly pronounce her healed (9:22). Jesus accepted her desperation as an act of faith (9:22). That our Lord Jesus shows such mercy should not surprise us: He is the one who bore our infirmities, suffering in our place so we might go free (8:17).

Matthew emphasizes that compassion was Jesus' primary motivation for ministry to people (9:36). If his character remains the same today, we may be confident that Jesus still wishes to heal and deliver many people as he did long ago. But Jesus also explicitly declares that he needs more workers to complete the task of proclaiming the kingdom and healing (9:37–38). When Jesus came in the flesh, he could be in only one place at a time; hence, he was limited in how many people he could heal until he trained others to help with the work (9:37). So he instructed his disciples to pray for more workers (9:38). One need not read much farther to find that those Jesus taught to share his compassion became workers themselves (Matt. 10:10). Thus, Jesus multiplied his mission by means of his followers.

The Disciples' Ministry

Some aspects of this first mission, such as its limitation to Israel (10:5–6), are later specifically revoked (28:19). But for the most part, Matthew intends the mission discourse in chapter 10 as a model to teach the church how to continue to evangelize. This is clear because of the following:

1. The commission to "go" makes this passage a model for the Great Commission in 28:19 (although the emphasis there is on disciple-making through baptizing and instructing).
2. The disciples here perpetuate the kingdom message of John the Baptist and Jesus (3:2; 4:17; 9:35; 10:7), and this message of God's authority is also ours today (28:18–19).
3. The disciples are to demonstrate God's reign the way Jesus did, through healings and exorcisms (9:35; 10:8), a commission Matthew nowhere revokes (in contrast to his subsequent revoking of 10:5–6).
4. These signs fulfill Scripture and attest not simply to Jesus' earthly ministry but also to his message of the new era, the kingdom of God (11:4–6; see Isa. 35:5–6).
5. The compassion that motivated Jesus (9:36) remains operative, as does the principle of agency for those who remain Christ's representatives by the gospel (10:40–42).
6. Acts and Paul's writings show us that Jesus' commission to heal and to live simply remained the standard for early Christian missionaries.
7. Most tellingly, Matthew here includes material about the end time that comes from elsewhere in Mark. (Ancient biographers had the freedom to rearrange their sources.) Like Mark, whom we examined in chap-

ter 3, Matthew believes that Spirit-empowered ministry involves persecution (10:17–39). Plainly, his idea of God's empowerment does not
guarantee an easy life, as some Christians today hope.

Especially in view of point 7, Matthew does not just tell us about the first
disciples' commission (though he does that too); he also tells us that this mission must continue and will not be completed until the Son of Man returns
(10:23). Thus, Matthew intends this discourse as missionary instructions for
his own audience, not just a rehearsal of the past. Each of the above points
could be explained and defended in greater detail, but together they suggest
that the signs of the kingdom should continue among us today. By system-
atically excluding enough of the biblical evidence from consideration (say,
all narrative, or worse yet, all biblical evidence before the death of the apostles), one can prove almost anything. But if the entire New Testament speaks
to us, what John Wimber and others call "power evangelism" should remain
one important method of evangelism.

Gifts as Initial Evidences of Apostleship?

Before turning to the continuance of spiritual gifts in Paul's writings, we
must address one objection not included elsewhere in this chapter. Hebrews
2:3–4 indicates that God confirmed the message of the first witnesses with
signs and gifts of the Spirit, and from this some have inferred that these signs
and gifts had ceased by the time the author of Hebrews was writing. If this
argument were correct and addressed the only purpose of signs, it would actually prove too much for most of its proponents; it would suggest that God
does not perform miracles today!

But the argument is inadequate to carry even the minimum weight placed
on it. The author of Hebrews is warning that since the gospel of Christ is a
greater revelation than the law, those who neglect it will face greater penalty
(Heb. 2:1–3). God had confirmed the message with notable signs in the past
(2:4), but this no more suggests that God had stopped working signs than it
suggests that the gospel would no longer be preached. The verb for God's
bearing witness with signs is simultaneous with the verb for Christ's first witnesses preaching about him. In both cases it refers to the time when the
Hebrews received the gospel. If God's miraculous bearing witness has ceased,
one could argue in the same manner that the preaching of Christ has also
ceased. Those who believe that God provided signs to attest Christ's wit-

nesses may be right, but even if God sometimes attested witnesses, this is hardly the only purpose of signs in the New Testament. God is more often said to attest his *message*, not just the first witnesses to that message (for example, Acts 14:3), so it is reasonable to expect God to continue to use signs to confirm his message today. Nor do Paul's later letters indicate the disappearance of gifts, as some have thought (1 Tim. 1:18; 4:14; 2 Tim. 1:6). Someone not being healed (2 Tim. 4:20) was not a new phenomenon; some in an earlier period were not miraculously healed (Gal. 4:13–14; Phil. 2:27).

Are All Biblical Spiritual Gifts for Today? (Paul)

Paul treats the *charismata*, or "grace-giftings," in several different contexts, but all the relevant passages associate these gifts with members of the body of Christ—which we all regard as continuing today. Each of these passages must be seen in their larger context so we can learn more about Scripture and the gifts as well as answer some objections.

Whereas ancient culture recognized the idea that some exceptionally holy men had power with God or with gods, Paul claims that every believer has a special relationship with God and specific assignments from God. This is significant because it means that according to Paul all Christians are charismatic—endowed with special gifts to build up others. As Siegfried Schatzmann puts it, Paul characteristically "regarded all the communities of believers as charismatic communities. He did not give the slightest indication that he knew of charismatic and noncharismatic churches."[11] Neither does he provide the slightest indication that he expects the cessation of any particular gifts (as opposed to others, such as pastoring or teaching, that we all recognize must remain today).[12] Three of Paul's surviving letters address gifts, always in the context of the body of Christ (Romans 12; 1 Corinthians 12; Ephesians 4; compare 1 Peter 4:10–11).

Romans

Paul often addresses the issue of one body with many gifts to churches struggling with unity, even when diverse gifts were not part of the reason for the division. In his letter to the Christians in Rome, Paul addresses a church experiencing tensions between Jewish and Gentile Christians. He begins his letter by laying the theological groundwork for reconciliation. Jewish people believed that they were automatically saved by virtue of their descent from Abraham and that they were special because they kept the law. Ancient literature reveals that Roman Gentiles despised Jewish people due to issues regarding food and holy days. Therefore, Paul shows that

- all people are equally sinners (Romans 1–3)
- spiritual rather than ethnic descent from Abraham is what counts (Rom. 4:1–5:11)
- all people (Abraham's descendants included) are descended also from Adam the sinner (Rom. 5:12–21)
- the law by itself cannot deliver from sin (Rom. 7:7–25)
- God can sovereignly choose people for salvation on grounds other than their ethnicity (Romans 9)
- a sense of spiritual history prohibits Gentile Christians from looking down on Jewish people (Romans 11)

Having established the theological point that Jew and Gentile must approach God on the same terms, Paul turns to his pastoral concerns. Believers must serve one another (12:4–16), the central focus of the law is loving one another (13:8–10), and Gentile Christians should not look down on Jewish Sabbath-keeping and food practices the way non-Christian Greeks and Romans do (Romans 14). Both Christ (15:7–12) and Paul himself (15:15–32) become examples of reconciliation between Jew and Gentile, and Paul's concluding exhortation is to avoid those who cause division.

Thus, Paul discusses spiritual gifts (12:4–8) in the broader context of unity in the church (in this case, racial and cultural unity). Although Paul had not visited the Roman church, he writes as if he expected them to be familiar with the gifts he lists.

In view of God's mercies in history recounted in Romans 9–11, Paul exhorts the Roman Christians to act as priests offering up sacrifices. The sacrifice they are to offer is to live the right lifestyle with their bodies, directed by a choice of their minds (12:1; the Greek literally speaks of a "rational" service, not a "spiritual" one). But granted that we should choose to use our bodies for God's glory, how does one know which specific role in God's plan to choose? A renewed mind will recognize God's purposes, knowing what is good in his sight (12:2). The renewed mind thinks not of oneself (12:3) but recognizes that all of us have special functions in Christ's body (12:4–8). In other words, in this context, the living-sacrifice way to live uses the gifts God has given us to build up Christ's body and respects others' gifts no less. The gifts are essential for building up Christ's body, and as long as Christ's body needs to be built up, the gifts must continue to function for the body to be healthy.

In the Romans 12 list, Paul includes "supernatural" gifts such as prophecy (12:6, a gift Paul always ranks near the top) and "natural" gifts such as teaching (12:7). Today some people suggest that verifiably supernatural gifts have passed away but that natural gifts such as teaching continue. This distinction, however, is rooted in Enlightenment philosophy rather than in the text; it violates Paul's entire pattern of thought in this passage. The Christian worldview acknowledges that *everything* in our lives is ultimately "supernatural," because even the food on our table is a gift of God's providence. The grace-gift of teaching is not simply an intellectual exercise devoid of reliance on God's Spirit—an unsaved person could then possess the same "gift." Teaching is a special endowment of grace that is also, as 1 Corinthians 12:8–11 shows, a special empowerment of God's Spirit. I personally would hate to try to teach in either a church or a classroom without first acknowledging to God my dependence on his Spirit to help me articulate the biblical text's concepts accurately and convincingly.

1 Corinthians

Gifts may have been fresh on Paul's mind when he wrote his letter to the Romans because he wrote the letter from Corinth, a church that had some definite troubles with spiritual gifts.

MANY GIFTS, ONE BODY

Like the Roman church, the Corinthian church was divided, but in this case, the division had more to do with social class than with ethnicity. Well-to-do Christians were concerned about what their social peers would think of their teachers. These well-to-do people expected their teachers to be top-notch speakers and to depend on the financial support of their hearers. Instead, Paul embarrassed them by being a second-rate speaker—at least compared to Apollos (1 Corinthians 1–4)—and by working as a common artisan for his support (1 Corinthians 9). Paul's need to address sexual issues (1 Corinthians 5–7) may or may not reflect class tensions; intellectuals from various philosophic schools would justify free sex while avoiding marriage. More clearly, the more educated members of the church also saw no problem with food offered to idols, as long as one knew the idols meant nothing. Meanwhile, the well-to-do women saw no reason to wear traditional headcoverings to church (1 Corinthians 8–11).

But besides all its other problems, the Corinthian church was abusing spiritual gifts. Apparently some Corinthian Christians were boasting that they could pray in languages unknown to themselves or their hearers. Paul puts tongues-speaking in its place, however, noting that the purpose of any gift in the public assembly was to build up the church (1 Cor. 12:7; 14:1–5, 19). One could pray in tongues privately (14:18–19, 28; see 14:2–5), but it benefited others when practiced publicly only if someone interpreted (14:5, 13–17, 27–28). The Corinthians were also excited about wise and knowledgeable speech (1:5, 17), so Paul mentions these gifts as well (12:8). But Paul puts all the gifts in their place: If used in the public assembly, they were to be used only to serve the church.

As in Romans, Paul connects the gifts specifically to our Christian identity. We are members of Christ's body, each with our own roles as members of that body—hands, feet, and so on (12:15–26). Earlier writers had compared both the universe and the state to a body, but Paul may have been the first writer to speak of a religious group, the church, in these terms. Paul is saying that each member has its function and that we need each function. If any members are not functioning according to their gifts, the whole body suffers. One reason 95 percent of the work of the kingdom never gets done today is that 5 percent of the Christians are doing all the work, while the gifts of most of the body go unused. But if all members of the body remain essential today, all the gifts represented by those members are likewise essential.

The End of Some Gifts?

The fact that Paul assumes all gifts will continue until the return of Christ is clear from his argument in 1 Corinthians 13. There Paul argues that love is more important than the gifts (13:1–3) and that love, in contrast to the gifts, is eternal (13:8–13). Paul mentions three representative gifts of special importance to the Corinthian Christians: prophecy, tongues, and knowledge (13:8), perhaps with slight emphasis on prophecy and knowledge (13:9). In the course of Paul's argument that the gifts are temporary, we learn when Paul expects them to pass away. The church will no longer need such gifts when we know as we are known (13:12; compare Jer. 31:34), which is when we see Christ face to face (13:12).

We live now in a time when we know Christ imperfectly, but when we see him face to face "the perfect" will come. The context leaves no doubt that "the perfect" arrives at Christ's second coming. Although some older interpreters argued that Paul's "perfect" referred to the completion of the canon, such an idea could not have occurred either to Paul or to the Corinthians in their own historical context (since at that point no one knew that there would be a New Testament canon, even though Paul was presumably aware that God's Spirit was guiding his writing).[13] Evidence from the context that "the perfect" refers to the second coming, together with the impossibility that Paul could have expected the Corinthian Christians to think he meant the canon, has left few evangelical scholars who continue to use this text to support a cessation of the gifts. Richard Gaffin, a prominent cessationist, concedes that "the view that they describe the point at which the New Testament canon is completed cannot be made credible exegetically."[14]

Some have tried to use this passage to exclude only particular gifts before Christ's return, but their arguments are not very persuasive. Prophecy and tongues must pass away when knowledge does, and if "knowledge" has passed away already, how can one "know" enough to say so? (On the meaning of "knowledge" in 1 Corinthians, see the "word of knowledge" in the next chapter.) Nor can one keep knowledge and prophecy while discarding tongues. Prophecy in the biblical sense is normally no less dependent on spontaneous inspiration than tongues. It is not merely "preaching," since "sermons" in Paul's day involved especially teaching and exhortation, perhaps what Paul means by a "word of knowledge." One cannot make the verbs describing the passing of prophecy, tongues, and knowledge mean different things so that tongues must pass away quickly while prophecy and knowledge remain until the end (as some interpreters have suggested). Paul uses different terms here for the sake of variation, as he often does. But even if one were tempted to make the terms mean something different, nothing would make one term suggest that tongues had passed away earlier—nothing, that is, except the need of an interpreter to make the passage say that. Various passages in the writings of the early church fathers indicate that they were aware of the continuance of supernatural gifts in their own time, despite the decline of some public gifts as authority became centralized in institutional leadership (see, for example, Justin Martyr, Dialogue with Trypho 35; 82; 85; Tertullian, De Spectaculis [The Shows], 26).

Jack Deere, a former cessationist professor who was forced to reexamine his position when he encountered modern miracles, provides six reasons in 1 Corinthians 12–14 alone that refute cessationism. In his popular but biblically and theologically informed response to cessationism, Surprised by the Power of the Spirit, he points out that the gifts are for the common good (12:7), God commands us to zealously pursue spiritual gifts (12:31; 14:1), Paul warns us not to prohibit speaking in tongues (14:39), Paul valued tongues (14:5, 18), and spiritual gifts are necessary for the health of the body of Christ

(12:12–27). Would God place such commands in Scripture if they were relevant for only four decades, especially since during most of that time the majority of ancient Christians would not have yet had access to Paul's letter? Finally, Deere notes, Paul is explicit that these gifts will not cease until Christ's return (13:8–12).[15]

My own exegesis over the years has led me to the same basic conclusions. Deere and I have both experienced miraculous gifts, so some could accuse us both of exegetical bias. But as he forcefully reiterates throughout his book, those who argue that gifts have ceased have an experiential bias of *not* having seen the gifts—and Deere himself used to teach that these gifts had ceased. The accusation of bias can be leveled either way, but I believe that cessationism would not naturally occur to someone reading the biblical text who had not already been taught the position or did not have an experiential bias that demanded it.

Merely Correcting Abuses?

Since Paul mentions tongues only in 1 Corinthians 12–14, where he is correcting abuses, some writers think that he regards tongues negatively. To be sure, he does not regard it as the most important gift for public worship, but to treat it as negative is harsher than that. If Paul views tongues as *negative*, he would simply have to be accommodating the Corinthians' *ignorance*, for he lists it among God's "gifts" (12:10). Surely all God's gifts are good, even if some are greater than others (12:31). Admittedly, some of us have received ill-conceived holiday gifts, but who would dare say, "God gave me a *bad* gift"?

More critically, this view misses the point of Paul's argument. Paul himself prayed in tongues *privately* more than all the Corinthians, though he did not make a big deal about it (1 Cor. 14:18). Although the abuses in the Corinthian church require him to emphasize that tongues be kept in their place and be offered in proper order (14:40), he qualifies his words lest anyone overreact on the other side: He forbids the church to prohibit tongues in their public worship services (14:39). Paul would hardly add this warning against forbidding tongues if forbidding tongues were actually what he wished to do! If Paul guards against too negative a view of tongues even when he is correcting an abuse of the gift, how much less negative would he have been where no abuse existed?

Paul is instead addressing motives and public order: The public use of uninterpreted tongues is not helpful to the gathered church. Not only with regard to tongues but with regard to other gifts and practices as well, many churches today would do well to heed Paul's admonition that "the spirit of the prophet is subject to the prophet" (1 Cor. 14:32–33). Although God may allow us more of a particular gift than we need, we must be prepared to limit our expression even with the gift of prophecy (14:29–33). In the same way, I might be able to teach from Scripture for ten hours straight, but this does not mean that God always wants me to do so. Indeed, I *love* to teach for hours on end, but most students can absorb teaching for only so many hours in a row. The need of the church, rather than simply the availability of divine inspiration, should determine the use of any spiritual gift.

Although Paul corrects the abuse of tongues only in 1 Corinthians, this hardly means that tongues were practiced only in Corinth. Rather, it means only that we do not have letters addressing the *abuse* of tongues elsewhere. First, Paul prayed in tongues regularly (14:18) and seems to have regarded prayer in tongues as a special form of prayer, "praying with one's spirit" (14:14–15). Does that not sound like a positive practice he may in fact have *encouraged* elsewhere? Second, Acts suggests to us that tongues was evidence of divine inspiration in many early Christian communities, though Paul has occasion to address it only in the one congregation that is abusing the gift, Corinth. Third, we know that many of the gifts Paul lists in 1 Corinthians 12 were standard practice in Paul's other churches. Although his letters focus primarily on abuses and issues of local concern, it is clear that he expected prophecy to occur regularly (1 Thess. 5:20), even in churches he had never visited (Rom. 12:6). His expectation should not surprise us since his Jewish contemporaries believed that prophecy would accompany the restoration of the Spirit.

Finally, it is true that were it not for the Corinthians' abuse of tongues, we would know little about it in Paul's churches. But were it not for their abuse of the Lord's Supper, we would not be aware that any of Paul's churches practiced it either. Paul's letters normally address specific situations, and we read them to learn both about how Paul dealt with these situations and about the faith and experience of the earliest Christians. The latter information is often assumed rather than articulated by Paul and his audiences.

Ephesians

New Testament scholar Richard Gaffin rests his biblical case for the cessation of particular spiritual gifts almost entirely on Ephesians 2:20.[16] On the basis of this text he contends that apostles and prophets—hence the gifts of apostleship, prophecy, and tongues (the latter being subsumed under prophecy)—were foundational. Hence, they were no longer needed after the completion of the New Testament canon. (In person, Gaffin is a very char-itable example of a cessationist who is not against Pentecostals or charis-matics and has graciously mentored some in his seminary's doctoral program. I cite him at length here simply because he is one of the most articulate expo-nents of this position.)

Gaffin is correct that in this context early Christian apostles and prophets performed a revelatory function (Eph. 3:5). But Paul's apostolic ministry seems to extend beyond the initial revelation of the gospel to making it known as widely as possible (see 3:8–13). If only the apostles and prophets of his day constituted the foundation, does this necessarily preclude others who would not be part of the foundation yet would carry on the work of making the gospel known? After all, Paul here seems to refer to Christian prophets, rather than to ancient Israelite prophets, as part of the foundation (3:5; 4:11). Yet prophets had existed from early in Israel's history; we can therefore conclude that the foundation might not exhaust the full number of apostles and prophets.

Gaffin would argue that the completed canon obviates the need for fur-ther apostles and prophets. Yet Old Testament prophets certainly did much more than write Scripture. A survey of the prophets mentioned in the his-torical books of the Old Testament reveals that most of them, in fact, did not write Scripture. Further, Paul's apostolic mission did not end when he made his gospel known to *someone*; the mission was to make it known to *everyone* (3:8–9), a mission not yet completed.

And to top it all off, Gaffin seems to read too much into the foundation metaphor of 2:20. Like the authors of the Dead Sea Scrolls, Paul and Peter portrayed their community of faith by the image of a temple. But pressing chronology into the image, so that all parts of the foundation must belong to the first generation, may be making Paul's illustration more specific than he intended. Examined from a number of angles, Gaffin's hypothesis fails to prove that gifts such as prophecy must cease—hence, it proves the cessation of tongues (which he connects with this) even less.

Gaffin's argument at this critical point, though using exegesis (Bible inter-pretation), is not strictly exegetical. He starts with a logical argument, to which he then adds the exegesis of texts that would not by themselves sup-port his argument. While any "logical argument" looks consistent from within the system that supports it, it will fail to persuade those outside the system because it depends on other elements within the system to support it. This is the sort of objection that biblical scholars often raise against some sys-tematic theologians or against other biblical scholars whom they feel are too beholden to particular theological presuppositions. As Gordon Fee observes concerning the heart of Gaffin's argument for cessation:

> The logic *precedes* the exegesis. Indeed, the whole enterprise has its logical form structured by asking a question to which not one of the biblical texts intends an answer. Gaffin's overruling question is, When will tongues cease? The one text that addresses this question at all—and even there it is quite incidental to Paul's real point—is 1 Corinthians 13:10, which almost certainly intends, "at the Eschaton," as its answer. But since the answer is the one Gaffin is uncomfortable with, he sets up his logical circles to answer his own question with, "at the end of the first century." But in no case does he, nor can he, show that the answer to that question is a part of the biblical author's intent in the texts that are examined.[17]

At any rate, the analogy from Ephesians 2 provides a weak foundation for arguing that the gifts have ceased, when stronger implications of other texts, including Ephesians 4, argue the other direction.

In Ephesians 4, Paul again addresses the unity of Christ's body (4:3–5). Although he approaches gifts and Christ's body from a different angle than he did in Romans and 1 Corinthians (here the gifts are some members given to other members), he has not completely changed the subject. In this context, he still applies language familiar to us from Romans 12 and 1 Corinthians 12 ("measure," "grace"). He declares that God has distributed "grace" (as in "grace-gifts," *charismata*) to each member of the body, providing each one a special portion of the gift of Christ. Paul may mean that the members of Christ's body carry on the non-atoning aspects of Jesus' *own ministry* ("the gift of Christ" in 4:7; but see also the interpretation in the NIV, where Paul's phrase "the gift of Christ" is understood as "the gift *from* Christ" rather than "the gift *which characterizes* Christ").

After introducing the subject of the gracious gift of Christ, Paul paraphrases a psalm that speaks of a triumphant ruler receiving and distributing plunder to his followers (Eph. 4:8). In Romans and 1 Corinthians, Paul writes that God has endowed each believer with special grace. However, in this passage Paul emphasizes another kind of gift first. Here the first gifts the exalted Christ gives to his body are a special group of persons who will in turn mobilize the other members of Christ's body for their ministries.

I comment more on these specific gifts in the next chapter but should note here that apostleship and prophecy are linked with other gifts as necessary to equip the rest of the church to minister to one another (4:11–13). In so doing, they bring the church to maturity, to unity in believing and knowing

Jesus. As long as the church needs more maturity and unity, these gifts will therefore remain. It appears that just as we continue to need pastor-teachers to accomplish this maturity, we also need the other gifts Paul mentions.

Conclusion

Although I have heard of miracles such as those in Acts happening regularly in some places, I frankly confess that I have not witnessed many miracles on that scale. I could seek theological rationalizations for this lack, contending that God simply does not want to do such miracles today, but seeking an argument to validate my experience would violate my commitment to read my experience in light of Scripture. Because I affirm that Scripture is God's Word, I must submit to it rather than make it say what is convenient. As a biblical scholar who by conviction determines the meaning of the text first and then asks its implications for today, I must conform my experience to the Bible rather than the Bible to my experience. In other words, I remain committed to spiritual gifts because I am committed to Scripture, rather than the reverse (even though my spiritual experience has often helped fortify my evangelical convictions while working through formidable liberal scholarship over the years). The Bible's message does not simply confirm my own experience of miracles; it summons me to be more open to appropriate signs and wonders than I already am.

God has often increased the occurrence of miracles in times of revival, sometimes performing those miracles through individuals such as Moses, Elijah, or the apostles. God does not gift us all for the same tasks, but those of us with the gift of teaching must mobilize the body of Christ to use their scriptural gifts and not, as we have often done, merely train fellow teachers. To be sure, God is sovereign and need not do a miracle simply because we request it. But if we acknowledge God as our sovereign Lord, we must be available for him to work through our prayers if he does will to do a miracle. We must become stronger people of the Spirit whom God may empower by whatever means he chooses.

Our generation is in a desperate condition. Those involved in inner-city evangelism and other frontline ministries need firsthand faith in God's protection as the prophets Elijah or Elisha sought when facing grave dangers from mortal opposition. Some secular intellectuals have become disillusioned with their anti-supernaturalism, but many are turning to superhuman forces infinitely less powerful and benevolent than the God we serve. Perhaps it is time for us to cry with the newly empowered Elisha, "Where now is the LORD, the God of Elijah?" (2 Kings 2:14 NIV).

At the same time, we must seek the gifts with the right motives. One can pray in tongues without living a Spirit-filled life (compare the spiritually immature in 1 Cor. 14:20); one can prophesy without being saved (1 Sam. 19:21–24; Matt. 7:21–23); one can utter charismatic praise songs without giving attention to God himself, celebrating the rhythm or melody rather than God's greatness (compare the mere religious forms in Zech. 7:5–10).

One of the early pioneers in the mid-twentieth-century healing revival believes that the beginning of that revival came mostly from God's Spirit. Many of God's people had been seeking his face, and when they sought his face, he opened his hand to bless them. But this same minister has concluded that when God's people turned from seeking his face to seeking his hand, he closed it again. From that time forward, most of the "healing revival" was carried on in the flesh, with many healing evangelists jockeying for attention and losing the blessing of God's Spirit. This leader warned that he believed God would not open his hand in such a manner again until he had raised up a generation of Christians who would not be corrupted by money, sex, or power—a generation he believes is finally beginning.

If God works miracles, the miracles must be for the honor of God's name alone. God may use us in various gifts—such as teaching, healing, evangelism, charismatic prayer, and prophecy—but unless we first seek God's honor and work in conjunction with all the other gifts for the building up of Christ's church and its mission in this world, we are not behaving as people of the Spirit. May God send us a revival of signs, wonders, and spiritual gifts. But most of all, may God send us a revival of his Spirit that causes our hearts to feel God's heart, for the power of the Spirit (1 Cor. 2:4–5) lies not first of all in powerful signs but in the message of the weakness of the cross (1 Cor. 1:18; 2:6–8). It is in our weakness, our absolute dependence on him, that we become vessels truly ready for his honor (2 Cor. 11:18–12:10; 13:3–4, 9).

6

A Closer Look
at Some Spiritual Gifts

M any churches and ministries today use "spiritual gift inventories," which often tend to be interest or personality tests similar to those used in Christian counseling. While interest and personality tests are often useful and God sometimes gifts us in ways that correspond to our interests and personalities, we should not limit God's gifts to those discovered in such inventories. This is especially true when we are speaking not about gifts we are born with but those we seek from God in prayer to build up Christ's body (1 Cor. 12:31; 14:1).

On the other end of the spectrum, some Christians tend to despise natural endowments or advantages in favor of supernatural gifts. This does not follow the example of Paul, who made use of all his advantages for the kingdom, whether Roman citizenship, fluency in Greek, Aramaic, or Judean orthodoxy (Acts 21:37; 21:40–22:5; 22:25–29), even though some of these same matters counted against him in other circles (Acts 16:20–21). Even many churches that emphasize particular gifts regularly exercise only a few of them (whether the gift of tongues, teaching, prophecy, or evangelism).

In this chapter we will look at two passages (1 Cor. 12:8–10 and Eph. 4:11) that deal with the sorts of spiritual gifts Christians are not born with. The

gifts in these two passages (at least the first one) may be merely samples, but
the lists provide the opportunity to explore some gifts in further detail. In
some cases, popular ideas about what these gifts involve are based merely on
charismatic "tradition," though in other cases the popular understanding is
probably close to what Paul meant.

The Gifts in 1 Corinthians 12:8–10

Although some popular writers have argued that Paul's list of nine gifts
in 1 Corinthians 12:8–10 is a complete list of "gifts of the Spirit," we have
good reason to think otherwise. Paul uses similar language in other passages with differing lists. A comparison of Paul's various gift lists (Rom.
12:4–8; 1 Cor. 12:28; 12:29–30; 13:1–2, 8–9; 14:26; Eph. 4:11; see also
1 Peter 4:10–11) demonstrates that his lists are ad hoc—that is, he is making them up "on the spot"—and vary considerably. He could have listed
other gifts than those he listed, and even his first readers may not have
known *exactly* what each of his examples meant.

Although we learn about gifts such as prophecy and teaching in Paul's
other letters, Paul focuses in 1 Corinthians on particular gifts that are most
relevant to his readers' situation. The Corinthian culture prized speaking
and reasoning abilities; speech contests even constituted a regular part of
the nearby Isthmian Games. Naturally, Christians in Corinth prized gifts
such as "wise speech" and "knowledgeable speech." Paul's letter also informs
us that they prized tongues, perhaps because it is (at least today) one of
those gifts that comes with the least amount of work. Paul mentions specific gifts in 1 Corinthians 12:8–10 that relate to the experience of the
Corinthian Christians. He probably places tongues at the bottom of this
list (12:10) precisely because many in the church were assigning it too
important a role in comparison with the other gifts (13:1; 14:2–5).

But because so many writers and speakers have emphasized the gift list
in this particular passage, we will survey the general meaning of these gifts.
This is especially necessary given the varying ideas prevalent today about
what these gifts are. The surmises of one writer become the next writer's
information, and that writer's information becomes a movement's tradition. Although Pentecostal and charismatic scholars tend to pay more attention to what Paul actually says than do most charismatic teachers on a popular level, many charismatics have adopted ideas about these gifts that are
based on charismatic traditions rather than on sound approaches to bibli-

cal understanding. We will examine these gifts in light of clues from the context of 1 Corinthians, the same letter Paul's first readers had in front of them.

Some of the gifts in this list overlap with other gifts on the list (for example, healings, miracles, and probably faith). Paul may even have spontaneously coined the names of some of these gifts for this Corinthian list (for example, "word of knowledge"; see discussion below). He explains other gifts, however, in much greater detail. Indeed, given the Old Testament background of prophecy and healing, one could write entire books on these gifts.

The Word of Wisdom

When Paul speaks of an "utterance of wisdom" in 12:8, the Corinthian Christians probably immediately understood his point. Their city's culture emphasized speaking ability (the Greek term for "word" can also be translated "utterance" or "rhetoric") as well as knowledge and wisdom. Corinthians included speaking contests along with the athletic games they sponsored every other year. The local Christians, following their culture's lead, valued knowledgeable and wise speech, especially the lofty discourses of the sophists and the probing thoughtfulness of the philosophers. Indeed, at least part of the church was so excited about its wise and knowledgeable speech that its members preferred Apollos, the skilled public speaker, to Paul (see 1 Corinthians 1–4).

But while Paul affirms that they abound in spiritual gifts such as speaking and knowledge (1 Cor. 1:5–7), he is not impressed. The true wisdom, he insists, is God's hidden wisdom, the message of the cross. God's power was revealed in Christ's weakness, a message that matches what Jesus called the mystery of the kingdom (1 Cor. 1:18–2:16). Perhaps exaggerating the inadequacy of his speaking skills (as was the custom), Paul emphasizes that the message that saved them was neither rhetorically nor philosophically profound. It was simply God's message of salvation in Christ.

The "utterance of wisdom," then, may represent the revelation of divine mysteries, based on insight into God's purposes rather than on mere human reasoning. (Similar language for insight into God's mysteries occurs in the Dead Sea Scrolls.) Paul elsewhere says apostles and prophets provided such wisdom on a larger scale (Eph. 3:4–6), though on the local congregational level he may assume that teachers might exercise this gift as well.

The Word of Knowledge

"Word of knowledge" can also be translated, "speech with knowledgeable content." To non-Christians in Corinth, "knowledgeable utterances" might have meant the sort of extemporaneous speeches public speakers offered on a variety of subjects, primarily for the purpose of showing off. Likewise, many Christians in Corinth claimed to have special doctrinal knowledge from God that they assumed made them better than Christians who did not possess it. Paul rebuked them for their abuse of this gift (8:1–3). Like tongues and prophecy, knowledge will pass away (13:8) and is incomplete and sometimes inaccurate (13:9). Some people who rightly reprove others for being arrogant about tongues are themselves arrogant about knowledge! Arrogance is bad no matter what we are being arrogant about.

While Paul rebukes abuse of this gift, as he does with other gifts, he encourages it in its positive form (14:6; 2 Cor. 8:7; 11:6). The "word of knowledge," or ability to speak knowledge publicly, undoubtedly means imparting knowledge about God; in other words, the gift of teaching (as many other Pentecostal and charismatic scholars agree, for example Stanley Horton and J. Rodman Williams).

In more traditional charismatic usage, "word of knowledge" applies to a supernatural impartation of knowledge about some human need or situation. While this interpretation of the gift does not fit Paul's usage as well, such a gift (whatever we call it) appears frequently in Old and New Testament narratives (for example, 1 Kings 21:17–18; 2 Kings 4:27; 5:26; 6:12; Mark 2:8; Acts 14:9). Paul would probably have subsumed that gift under the heading "prophecy" or "revelation" (see 1 Cor. 14:26, 30). As a young Christian in the late 1970s, I regularly witnessed this gift of revelation in an interdenominational fellowship in Ohio called High Mill Christian Center. I always happily invited non-Christians to midweek services because the pastor regularly revealed what someone was struggling with at the time, and he was invariably right. On one occasion, a visitor who had been planning to commit suicide that evening became a Christian instead. While I doubt that this is what Paul means here by "word of knowledge," it is a valid form of the gift of prophecy (1 Cor. 14:24–25).

Faith

Faith energizes all the gifts; God provides all Christians with faith to fulfill their function in Christ's body (Rom. 12:3, 6). In this instance, however, Paul speaks of a particular endowment of faith, the sort that moves mountains (1 Cor. 13:2). Although all things are possible with God, neither Scripture nor church history reports the literal moving of mountains by Christians (except perhaps earthquakes in answer to prayer or worship; 1 Kings 19:11; Acts 4:31; 16:25–26; Rev. 6:10–12). The point, however, is simply that nothing God calls us to accomplish is impossible if Christians exercise complete faith. "Moving mountains" was a Jewish figure of speech for doing what was virtually impossible, and Jesus had promised that nothing would be impossible to those who exercised even the smallest amount of faith (Mark 11:23).

Since God is the object of our faith, possessing this faith presupposes that we are acting on God's will rather than our own (1 Kings 18:36; 2 Kings 4:28; 1 John 5:14)—that is, the goal of this genuine faith is not to get whatever we want but to carry out God's commission and what he calls us to do. This is not to say that we cannot also exercise faith for matters about which God has not spoken; God often hears these requests as well (for example, 2 Sam. 15:31; 2 Kings 20:3–6; Mark 2:4–5). It is only that sometimes in these cases God does have reasons to say no (for example, Jer. 14:11; 2 Cor. 12:8–10).

Although it would be ideal for all Christians to function at this level, Paul recognizes that some Christians are specially gifted with this kind of faith. Rather than looking down on Christians less gifted in this area, those with exceptional faith should use their gift on behalf of others in Christ's body, by their example encouraging others to grow in faith.

Gifts of Healing

The plural probably signifies, as many commentators suggest, that the Spirit develops in different Christians the faith to pray for different kinds of ailments. While this does not mean that someone cannot be gifted to pray for any kind of infirmity—most of the first-generation apostles seem to have done so (Acts 5:15–16; 28:8–9)—many Christians gifted in healing are initially able to exercise special faith only for particular kinds of infirmities. Acts 8:7 may imply this, though it may represent instead merely a concrete sample of the works performed. This limitation may suggest that the gift's continuance to the present day does not guarantee that every individual will be supernaturally healed, although God often works dramatic healings to meet the needs of his children or to draw attention to the gospel they proclaim.

Perhaps in certain settings mature Christians developed faith for this gift. Jewish Christians such as James seem to have expected elders to be ready to pray the prayer of faith (James 5:14–15). Probably in Paul's churches whoever had the gift of faith for healings was to act accordingly. In biblical testimonies about miracle-working prophets such as Elijah and Elisha, the wide diversity of miraculous acts suggests no necessary limitation to a person's faith except the assurance that the person act on God's will. Formulas do not grant this assurance; rather, it flourishes in the context of an intimate and obedient relationship with God. When God heals, he does so not because of our power or piety but because of his faithfulness to Jesus' name (Acts 3:12). We should therefore avoid the temptation to congratulate ourselves when God answers our prayers to heal someone; God alone should be praised (Mark 2:12; 5:19).

While we should trust that God will often (or even normally) answer prayers for healing and should follow our Lord's example of compassion toward the physically as well as emotionally and spiritually wounded (Matt. 9:35–36; Mark 1:41), we should also avoid assuming that anyone who is not healed is spiritually deficient (compare Job 12:5; 42:7–8). God does not always heal right away (Job 42:10; Gal. 4:13–14; Phil. 2:27; 2 Tim. 4:20), and sometimes, for whatever reason, God does not heal in this life (1 Kings 1:1; 2 Kings 13:14, 20–21; 1 Tim. 5:23).

But Jesus' willingness to heal all who came to him certainly challenges those who think healing is abnormal today, unless they wish to contend either that Jesus' character has changed or that his power in the world has declined. It is possible that we see fewer people healed today than God requires, a situation that is troubling because people's pain is real. Scripture shows that in some cases Jesus wanted people healed but his disciples were spiritually unprepared to provide what was needed (Matt. 17:16–17, 19–20; Mark 9:18–19, 28–29) or people refused to believe him (Matt. 13:58; Mark 6:3–6). That is not always the case, but hopefully, in this gift as in others, we can grow in faith rooted in an ever deeper relationship with God (James 5:14–18).[1]

Workings of Miracles

"Miracles" literally means "demonstrations of power," and the plural may signify diverse kinds of workings for different miracle workers, as in the case of healings.[2] In the Old Testament and in stories about Jesus that Paul told the Corinthians, "miracles" could include healings and presumably included acts of faith such as moving mountains (1 Cor. 13:2). This gift probably overlaps with "gifts of healing" and "faith" elsewhere in the list, but it undoubtedly includes other kinds of miracles as well, such as nature miracles. When his disciples woke him from a nap to calm an apparently life-threatening storm, Jesus reproved their unbelief. Perhaps he was demanding to know why they did not act as he had taught them, instead of waking him with their fear (Mark 4:40); certainly, at the least Jesus questioned whether they really expected the boat to sink with Jesus in it.

Similarly, another early Christian writer uses Elijah's faith to control rain according to God's will as an example for believers (James 5:17–18). At the same time, God does not always lead or authorize believers to still storms (Acts 27:24–26). James applies the example especially to faith for healing (5:14–16). Probably the term more customarily refers to a standard sort of "demonstration of power" attested to in Acts, such as exorcisms involving demonized unbelievers (Acts 5:16; 16:18).

God, who sustains the universe by his power, regularly performs works without human vessels (Exod. 3:2; John 5:17, 21), but he also often chooses to perform them through his servants. Thus, for example, a prophet confronts King Jeroboam, who, like stubborn Pharaoh of old, must be disciplined by a sign (1 Kings 13:1–6). The next recorded time Jeroboam hears a prophet, however, it is Jeroboam who initiates contact rather than the reverse, because—through God's direct judgment—his son is dying (14:1–3). God gets people's attention either directly or through his servants. For example, God often speaks through judgments (Isa. 26:9–10), but he usually sends prophets first to interpret the judgments (Isa. 48:3–5; Amos 3:7–8).

In any case, those gifted to work miracles should remember that miracles come in response to God's command (1 Kings 18:36) or the prayer of someone walking close to him (2 Kings 1:10), not simply our self-centered desire (compare James 4:1–4). Those whose desires are granted are those who delight in God and desire his will supremely (Ps. 37:3–7). Acting on a word from the Lord is not the same thing as "confessing" or "claiming" that something should happen, as if we ourselves, rather than God, have authority to speak things into being (Lam. 3:37; Rom. 4:17). We should also recognize that for the edification of the body of Christ, gifts related to God's Word are ranked higher than this spectacular gift (1 Cor. 12:28), though at the same time, miracles are extraordinarily effective in securing people's attention for evangelism (for example, Acts 14:3).

Prophecy

Prophecy involves God speaking to or through a servant who listens to his voice (or occasionally through someone who doesn't; for example, 1 Sam. 19:22–24; Matt. 7:22; John 11:51). Those who think that prophecy in 1 Corinthians 12–14 is merely preaching must treat as irrelevant the Old Testament use of the term (the background Paul shared with his Christian readers), the use in Acts, and the use in the text itself.

Prophets could, of course, "preach," but prophecy could also "reveal the secrets of hearts" (14:24–25) and could be spontaneous revelation (14:29–31). In fact, the biblical terminology for prophecy is broad enough to include any message that a prophet received from the Lord and made clear was from God. God spoke to his people through prophecy from the very start, but prophecy came in a variety of forms: visions, dreams, audible voices, ecstatic trances, and probably most often the Spirit bringing words to the heart and/or mouth of a prophet. Some texts even reveal prophets receiving messages by prophesying to themselves (2 Sam. 23:2–3; Hosea 1:2; possibly also Jer. 25:15; 27:2). Prophetic inspiration came in such a variety of forms that one could easily move back and forth between prayer or worship and prophecy (for example, 1 Chron. 25:1–8; Pss. 12:1, 5; 46:1, 10; 91:3, 14–16). In fact, worship often set the tone or provided the context for prophecy (1 Sam. 10:5; 2 Kings 3:15; possibly also Hab. 3:19).

The distinguishing feature of such prophecy is not the form used but whether the word of the Lord is being proclaimed. Although most of the Old Testament prophetic books focus on prophecies to God's people or to other groups, prophets also delivered countless prophecies to individuals. Due to their focus, the Old Testament books often record personal prophecies to kings, but less prominent persons also received messages (for example, 1 Kings 17:13–14; 2 Kings 4:3–4). Texts such as 1 Samuel 9:6–10 indicate that individuals also customarily inquired of prominent prophets. Acts records personal prophecies to Paul (Acts 21:4, 11; compare 20:23).

Before the exile, most prophets who recorded their prophecies prophesied in poetry; after the exile, most prophecies were in prose (for example, most of Haggai and Malachi). Prophecies by nature do not need to be only spontaneous, as some have argued. Often biblical prophets received a prophecy at one time but delivered it later (Jer. 28:12–17), and a prophet could even record his prophecy and allow another to read it later (Jer. 36:4–8).

While all inspired speech is "prophetic speech" in the broadest sense of the term (compare, for example, Acts 2:4, 16–18; Rev. 19:10), by "prophecies" Paul specifically means revelatory words, in this case spoken in a congregational setting. He does not confuse the gift with teaching (expounding Scripture or the implications of the gospel), although one may learn from prophecies (1 Cor. 14:31). Nor does he confuse it with "exhortation" as a discrete gift (Rom. 12:8; Paul uses the gift in Rom. 12:1), although prophecy likewise could include this function (1 Cor. 14:3).

In teaching, God's authority rested in the text or other prior message and was appropriated by the teacher to the extent that the teacher accurately expounded it. In prophecy, God's message was in the prophecy itself to the extent that the prophecy accurately reflected what the Spirit was saying (although New Testament prophecy, like Old Testament prophecy, often reflected the language of earlier biblical prophecies). In prophecy, one was inspired to speak directly as God's agent, essentially declaring, "Thus says the Spirit" (Acts 21:11; Rev. 2:1; 3:1).[3]

Although Paul seems to have known of experienced prophets who spoke God's message (Acts 11:28; 21:10; Eph. 4:11), in 1 Corinthians he employs the term *prophet* more broadly to describe all those who prophesy (1 Cor. 14:29–32). In theory, at least, because all Christians have received the Spirit, all Christians can prophesy (14:5, 31; compare Num. 11:29; Acts 2:17–18), though in practice not all will do so (1 Cor. 12:29). Prophets may, however, function on different levels. We may appreciate prophecies of encouragement, which seem common today, but unfortunately there remains a dearth of prophets who will stand for God's ideals of justice against the oppression of the poor, the unborn, and other powerless elements of society. Reflection on this emphasis in biblical prophecy (for example, Isa. 1:15–17; 58:1–14; Jer. 22:13–17; Amos 5:7–24; James 5:1–6) might broaden the scope of contemporary prophecy.

Discernment of Spirits

Although modern readers employ this phrase in a variety of ways, the context indicates that Paul means especially the gift of evaluating prophecy accurately. This is not to say that the ability to detect error in nonprophetic situations is not from the Spirit. I have on occasion met persons and known by the Spirit that they were in a particular cult or false teaching before they provided any tangible indication of it. On one of these occasions, I had gone out witnessing and felt led to take a tract challenging errors of the cult known as the Way International. The only person I ran into that evening appeared to be a Christian, but the Lord led me to ask if he was in the Way. He was, so I gave him the tract and followed up afterward. Another time I felt uncomfortable listening to a speaker and afterward asked if he knew of Sam Fife (leader of a cult in the 1970s), without rational reason to do so. The speaker turned out to have been his friend and a member of the group he started.

But by this phrase Paul more than likely specifically refers to evaluating prophecies. He later uses the same Greek word for "discerning" in this manner (14:29) and elsewhere speaks of "spirits" in conjunction with prophecy (14:32; see also perhaps Ezek. 13:3; 1 John 4:1–6; Rev. 22:6).

Discernment in regard to prophecies is important. In the Old Testament period, experienced prophets often mentored the prophetic development of novices (1 Sam. 19:20; 2 Kings 2:15; 4:38). Among first- and second-generation Christians, however, maturing prophets had to mentor one another by evaluating one another's prophecies (1 Cor. 14:29). Like our teaching, our prophecies are not perfect or complete, for we all "know in part and prophesy in part" (1 Cor. 13:9). Feeling moved by the Spirit with the burden of God's message is not the same thing as writing canonical Scripture. (That prophecies do not automatically constitute Scripture is clear from Scripture—most prophecies in biblical times were not recorded in Scripture; see, for example, 1 Kings 18:13.) Further, human error can interfere with our prophecy—for that matter, even apostles could be mistaken in some assertions or actions (Acts 11:1–2; Gal. 2:11–14), or need further insight (Acts 15:6).

But God builds a safety mechanism into the church's use of prophetic gifts by warning us that human error can distort them and by requiring us to test all our finite assurances that the Spirit is speaking to us. That is why prophecies must be tested (1 Thess. 5:20–22) not quenched (1 Thess. 5:19). Both those who do not evaluate the claims of people who say they've heard from God and those who uncritically reject all supernatural revelations equally disobey Scripture (1 Cor. 14:39–40).

Some people who prophesy today simply use stereotypical phrases and proof texts out of context; some may simply be trying to prophesy without first developing a relationship with the God of Scripture. In other cases, perhaps those who prophesy this weakly feel the Spirit's inspiration but are not yet full enough of biblical revelation to translate those feelings into a more accurate understanding of what God is saying. Rather than always assuming that they have no evidence of the gift of prophecy, we should encourage them to immerse themselves in Scripture and be mentored by the prophecies of God's Word interpreted in their proper context and with sensitivity to their cultural background. The language of the biblical prophets is rich with allusions to earlier prophets and especially to the Mosaic covenant. Perhaps even the false prophets of Jeremiah's day could have been turned to the truth and led others in that direction had they genuinely learned to hear God's voice and proclaim the unpopular message God had for his disobedient people (Jer. 23:21–22; compare 1 Tim. 1:12–13, 20). Though there were exceptions (Acts 8:13; 2 Tim. 2:25–26), fully false prophets usually admit their error too late (1 Kings 22:24–25).

All prophecy must be tested by Scripture and, where that is impossible because of the subject matter of the prophecy, by other mature and Bible-centered prophets sensitive to the Spirit (1 Cor. 14:29). The most sensitive believer still has more to learn about sensitivity to the Spirit's voice and must submit to Scripture—understood in context. That is why Scripture is the "canon," the "measuring stick," hence, the final arbiter of revelation. To fail to evaluate our claims to hear the Lord is arrogance and invites the discipline of the Lord. Can we possibly think that any one of us hears God accurately if we contradict the apostles and prophets God inspired through the centuries, whose prophecies were tested by time and were fulfilled? When those who prophesy apply Scripture according to teachings circulating only in their own charismatic circle rather than according to the Scripture's context, our guard should go up. (We discuss this matter further in the final chapter.)

Tongues

Both because Paul treats tongues at significant length in 1 Corinthians 14 and because many questions surround the gift today, I will examine several facets of this gift.

Tongues as a Gift for Worship

The main recorded public function of tongues, like its private function, was prayer and praise (1 Cor. 14:14–17; see also Acts 2:11; 10:46).[4] Whether in a language one did or did not know, Paul regarded prayer as too important to be done without the Spirit's inspiration and empowerment (see also Eph. 6:18; Jude 20). Biblical evidence for tongues functioning as a message from God, perhaps to an individual (1 Cor. 14:28), is possible yet remains inconclusive. This is not to say that God might not sovereignly use public utterances in tongues differently today than he did in the Bible, even if this meant choosing to accommodate human tradition to communicate his will. Pentecostal scholars still debate the matter among themselves, but I see no reason why God could not at least on occasion do so. The biblical emphasis of tongues, however, is clearly on Spirit-led prayer.[5]

Although Paul thinks that tongues would be good for everyone, he insists that prophecy would be better (14:5). Tongues is valueless except for the person whose spirit is praying, unless that person or someone else interprets and makes tongues intelligible for the gathered body (14:13–19). Of course, the principle that Paul applies here extends beyond tongues. In the gathered assembly, we should make sure that any contributions we bring—whether supernatural gifts or a song or a sermon—are worth the time of those who listen to us. If what we bring is for our good alone, we should offer it in private.

Paul does not prohibit interpreted tongues, but he restricts uninterpreted tongues entirely to the context in which his own use of the gift occurs: private prayer (14:28; compare 14:18–19). Perhaps Paul would not have objected to a prayer meeting in which many speak under inspiration simultaneously, similar to the experience described in 1 Samuel 10:5–6 and 19:20, but he objected to anything that would distract the assembly from its chief purposes for gathering: edification, exhortation, and evangelism (14:3, 23–25).

Although in 1 Corinthians 12–14 Paul focuses on gifts for the building up of the church (hence, his insistence that tongues in public be interpreted), we will briefly digress to investigate the private use of tongues. Those of us who usually minister in churches in which the public use of tongues would probably divide more than edify tend to focus more on the private use of tongues. Nevertheless, according to Paul, tongues is a valid public gift, when interpreted, once churches understand and appreciate its function.

Paul indicates that tongues is prayer with one's spirit (14:14–16) and that it edifies the person praying (14:4). Edifying oneself is not a sub-Christian goal, even if it is not the goal of ministry in the church (see, for example, Jude 20). Do we not pursue personal prayer and Bible study partly to strengthen our own relationship with the Lord?[6]

Paul would not mind if everyone prayed in tongues, though prophecy is more valuable because it edifies the entire church (14:5). Although in public, uninterpreted tongues serve no function, and Paul seems reticent to pray publicly in tongues, he nevertheless prays in tongues quite a bit—undoubtedly in his private devotional life (14:18–19). He may also have chosen to interpret these utterances in order to edify his mind (hence, "praying with the understanding" in the context of 14:13–16).

At the same time, tongues is not the ultimate goal of the Christian life or the pinnacle of Christian experience (a view that Pentecostals are sometimes accused of holding, though most Pentecostals I know do not hold it). Each of us is experiencing just a foretaste of God's glory and just a measure of God's power; we should not criticize others' measure.

TONGUES AS LANGUAGE

In contrast to some Pentecostals, I believe that "tongues" in both Acts and 1 Corinthians refers to genuine languages, albeit languages unknown to the speaker. I believe that biblical tongues should be the same today, though I should qualify my statement before I proceed. Vern Poythress and D. A.

Carson may well also be right about the "encoding" of the language in many cases of tongues,[7] and I do not deny that God could work through something on a lesser level than the biblical gift. Nor would I suggest that Pentecostals should supervise one another to make sure the words *sound* like a genuine language; I have heard real foreign languages that sounded like gibberish to me. We also have to allow those who are young in a gift to mature in their use of it, as with prophecy or teaching or any other gift. The speaker's focus should be on sincerely praying with his or her spirit to God, allowing the Holy Spirit to make sure the words come out right.

Yet some tongues-speakers seem to perform their "gift" out of habit or rote, rather than by cultivating sensitivity to the Spirit. When one hears a particular phrase (for example, "shonda ma kee") repeated ten times and followed by a much more lucid "interpretation," one is tempted to be rather skeptical concerning the "tongue." Believing in the reality of the genuine gift does not require us to accept as genuine all purported manifestations of the gift. Jonathan Edwards warned of spiritual counterfeits during genuine times of revival, and William Seymour argued that one who focused on signs more than on God and his holiness would get a counterfeit. Because my concern is pastoral, I hope that this observation moves us to seek a deeper sensitivity to the Spirit rather than leads sincere but insecure seekers to doubt the reality of their spiritual experience. As prophecies of even accepted church prophets had to be tested, as teachers may mature in their gift, as we "know in part and prophesy in part," tongues-prayers presumably may grow more fluent and Spirit-led as well.

Thirteen years ago, when I was experiencing the deepest crisis I had ever faced as a Christian, a family took me to a charismatic church. During prayer someone came up and started praying for me, making a buzzing sound like a bee, which I supposed he thought was tongues. I did not want him to pray for me; I wanted him to go away and allow me to pray undisturbed! Perhaps noting my perplexity, he explained, "I felt that the Lord showed me you were going through something and I should come and pray for you." I allowed him to pray but was so annoyed by his buzzing that I did not tell him I was in fact facing a crisis. Afterward I complained to one of the people who brought me that the buzzing was certainly not tongues. "He has a bee-anointing," she explained. Then I was even more annoyed! I did not and do not believe he was praying in biblical tongues. Yet the man had enough sensitivity to the Spirit and concern for a brother to pray for me. While I am sure he didn't have a "bee-anointing," I also think it likely that he was my brother in Christ, probably doing the best he knew to follow the Spirit's leading.

Praying with One's Spirit

Today some segments of Christendom emphasize the mind to the exclusion of other aspects of the human personality; other groups emphasize emotion to the exclusion of reason. Tongues are not primarily rational; those of us who emphasize rationality in other aspects of our faith may especially need the kind of emotional release tongues provide. To illustrate the value of "praying with one's spirit" (1 Cor. 14:14–16), even when one does not immediately comprehend what one is praying, I offer the following account known to me.

A North American seminary student got into a loud debate with his Bible interpretation professor over the interpretation of a verse in Philippians, and for the rest of the day he felt incomprehensibly threatened. He knew he needed to apologize to the professor for losing his temper, but why was the debate bothering him so much? He began to pray in tongues, and as his spirit prayed, his mental defense mechanisms were no longer in a position to suppress his true feelings. As he poured out his heart in tongues, the Spirit also began to provide the interpretation for what he was feeling. He realized that he felt threatened by authority figures because he had always felt threatened by his father (the one authority figure he had known in his formative years). As long as he could remember, his father had always ridiculed whatever he said, no matter how hard he sought to defend himself with valid arguments. As the buried feelings continued to pour forth, he realized something else he never would have verbalized: He had felt hatred toward his father. As he continued to pray, however, he began to weep, realizing how much he also had always loved his father.

The next day he apologized to his professor, who also apologized to him and declared, "But now we'll be better friends for it." But the seminarian still had to deal with his father, who was not a Christian and with whom he had never had an intimate conversation. He began praying about resolving his relationship with his father, and that summer, for the first time in a few years, he traveled to see his father. One afternoon, when the other family members were out of the house, he found his father reading a newspaper. "Dad, may I speak with you?" he asked. Even trying to open the subject was difficult.

"Sure, son," his father responded, the newspaper still in front of his face.

"Dad, what I'm about to tell you—I'm not saying that you were like this, just that this was my perception of you when I was growing up. Dad, I never felt I could talk with you about anything. I felt like you never listened to anything I had to say, and I felt I hated you for that. But I want to let you know that I'm really sorry for having felt that way, because I really love you now."

With the paper still in front of his face, his father responded, "That's all right, son. That's how every kid feels about his dad." But the young man knew that he himself had done what was required of him.

Later, the seminarian's mother asked him what he'd spoken with his father about that day. "He's been acting differently ever since then," she observed, noting that he was now spending time with his youngest son, who remained at home. When he told his mother what his father had said, she responded, "That's how he felt about *his* father, but he never made peace with him before he died." Today, the father and son freely express their love for each other.

Because of a prayer from his spirit, the seminarian was able to resolve some emotional conflicts that he might never have admitted he had. He was able to break a transgenerational cycle of pain because his spirit could be honest about feeling something his mind had not wanted to admit.

The Gifts in Ephesians 4:11

Many Christians employ Ephesians 4:11 today, especially in circles that emphasize the "five-fold ministry." (The Greek wording is probably fourfold rather than fivefold, but the basic idea that the church needs all the gifts remains valid; see the context of 4:11–13 and the discussion in the previous chapter.)

Christ provides ministers of his Word in various forms. Most of those listed in Ephesians 4:11, except evangelists, deliver God's message partly (apostles) or primarily (prophets and pastor-teachers) to his church (4:12); given the context, even evangelists seem to serve the church in some way here.

These four designations do not necessarily exclude one another. Paul may have functioned as a prophet and teacher before beginning his apostolic mission (Acts 13:1; commentators debate the grammar). Long afterward he continued to function as a prophet (1 Cor. 14:37–38) and a teacher (1 Tim. 2:7; 2 Tim. 1:11). At least in the early church of Antioch, prophets and teachers seem to have filled the role of overseer (pastors; Acts 13:1), and in later Pauline churches, at least some elders (pastors) were prophetically endowed (1 Tim. 4:14). Timothy is both teacher (2 Tim. 2:24) and evangelist (2 Tim. 4:5). And one cannot read Acts 13–28 without recognizing that Paul is as much an itinerant evangelist as Philip had been in his earlier days. Obviously, these ministry callings can overlap. Nevertheless, we will attempt to summarize the basic aspects of each office.

Apostles

First, Paul speaks of apostles. I address this designation at somewhat greater length than the others because of its importance but also because the New Testament nowhere specifically defines it, requiring closer investigation. Many people like to claim the title in some circles today, but not all are aware of the biblical price involved in this calling.

Paul never restricted the use of God's apostles to the Twelve or to the Twelve plus himself (Rom. 16:7; 1 Cor. 15:5–7; Gal. 1:19; compare occasionally even in Acts 1:26; 14:4, 14). Given the need for apostles in bringing Christ's body to maturity (Eph. 4:12–13), Paul would presumably assume that this gift, like the others he mentions, would continue to function until Christ's return. (Some limit apostles to those who saw Christ based on 1 Cor. 9:1, but Paul asks four distinct questions there, including, "Am I not free?" Others object to apostles continuing because they think apostles write Scripture—though most biblical apostles didn't. But whatever apostles could specifically mean, Scripture as canon is by definition closed. As we argued earlier, believing that apostles and prophets could continue after the first century does not mean that anyone is still writing Scripture. No orthodox charismatics today believe that Scripture is still being written.)

Many Christians today see New Testament apostles as missionaries, but although Paul was certainly a missionary, the mission to the Gentiles was his specific call. New Testament evidence for most other apostles is inconclusive; despite later Christian traditions about their effective missionary work later in life, most of the first apostles apparently remained in Jerusalem nearly two decades after Jesus' resurrection (Acts 15:4). The most we can say from such evidence is that some apostles were missionaries, "master builders" who strategized and laid the foundations for churches in new regions (1 Cor. 3:10). I know some missionaries today who fit this category.

Based on an examination of every use of the term *apostle* in the New Testament, I concluded that some features regularly characterized apostles, though apostles were otherwise diverse (Paul and the Twelve were very different in many respects). First, apostles seem to have broken new ground, originating a ministry. Beyond this, they diverge on the kind of new ground: The Twelve founded the church in Jerusalem by passing on Jesus' message, then remained there. Paul, eager not to build on another's foundation (2 Cor. 10:15–18; 11:5–6; compare Rom. 15:17–20), planted small Bible study groups across the Mediterranean world that gradually multiplied. He remained in contact with them but could not be with them most of the time; still, they were the proof of his ministry (1 Cor. 9:1–2; 2 Cor. 3:1–3). God could call apostles to specialties (or peoples; Rom. 11:13; Gal. 2:8–9; 1 Tim. 2:7). Apostles were like imperial legates, representing the authority of the one who sent them, but Paul and his colleagues broke more new ground than the Twelve.

Second, apostles apparently exercised an authority generated by their ministry role, not by the church's institutional structure. The Twelve in Jerusalem exercised a special authority as the appointed overseers of Jesus' message (Acts 4:35–37; 5:2). This authority, however, was not a purely administrative authority. Rather, the Twelve willingly shared with the seven (Acts 6:6) and especially with local "elders" in the Jerusalem church (Acts 15:2, 4, 6, 22–23; 16:4). They were willing to recognize God's work in others' leadership (Acts 8:14) and listen to other Christians (Acts 9:27).

True apostles must be servants, never people who pull rank (compare Acts 15:22; 1 Cor. 4:9–16; 2 Cor. 11:5–15; Col. 1:24–25). Paul occasionally—though only when necessary—pulled rank and commanded his churches (1 Cor. 4:17; 5:3–5; 2 Cor. 2:9; 13:1–3, 10; as a prophet, 1 Cor. 14:36–38). More often, though, he reasons with them (2 Cor. 1:24; 8:8) and provides an example of humble service (2 Cor. 1:3–7; 4:15). He continually reaffirms his love for his church people, even when he needs to reprove them (for example, 2 Cor. 4:15; 5:13; 6:11–13; 7:3; 11:2, 11; 12:14–15, 19); he emphasizes that they should be able to be proud of him (2 Cor. 5:12) as he is of them (7:4, 14; 9:2). He turned down their money because he was committed to look out for them like a father for his children (1 Cor. 4:14–16; 2 Cor. 12:14). He wants to spend and be spent for them (2 Cor. 12:15) and would rather suffer than let them suffer (13:9; compare 4:12; Eph. 3:13; 1 Thess. 2:18). The Lord gave him authority mainly to build them up, he notes; he would tear them down only if they forced him to do so (2 Cor. 13:10; compare 12:19). This is the language of a loving relationship, not pure institutional authority. Apostolic authority seemed to flow from apostles' special message, a message often more authoritative than that of prophets (Acts 2:42; 4:33; though compare Luke 11:49; Eph. 3:5).

Third, both signs and sacrificial, simple living characterized apostolic ministry. When Jesus sent out ("apostled") his agents the first time, he commissioned them to work signs and to travel lightly (Matt. 10:1–2; Mark 6:6–10, 30) and warned them to expect persecution (compare Matt. 10:16–39). The Jerusalem apostles appear to have suffered (Luke 11:49; Acts 5:18, 29, 40; 12:2), continued to live sacrificially (Acts 3:6), and certainly performed signs (Acts 2:43; 5:12; 8:18; 14:3–4). Scripture is clear that Paul lived sacrificially, a lifestyle he could associate with his calling as an apostle, a calling he suggested required special suffering (1 Cor. 4:9–13; compare 2 Cor. 11:12–13).

He also performed signs, especially in some periods of evangelistic ministry (Acts 19:11–12; Rom. 15:18), and could speak of these as proof of his apostolic calling and ministry (2 Cor. 12:11–12).

But though Philip traveled lightly, founded the church in Samaria, and performed signs, he is called an "evangelist" rather than an apostle, perhaps because he does not exercise apostolic authority. The New Testament never defines apostleship, but it seems to assume a particular authority, albeit one validated through sufferings. It is also a calling that God alone may choose (Mark 3:14; Rom. 1:1; 1 Cor. 1:1; 2 Cor. 1:1). (He may invite volunteers for various ministries, as some texts suggest, for example, 1 Cor. 14:1; 1 Tim. 3:1. But in the end God decides whom to appoint and exalt. It is therefore important to remember that no Christian should feel second-class based on his or her calling; God ultimately evaluates us not on the calling he gives us but on our embracing it and our faithfulness to it.)

The term *apostle* and its usage may tell us something more about the role. Although Paul sometimes uses the term in a more general sense ("apostles *of the churches*," 2 Cor. 8:23), when used by itself the term represents special envoys or ambassadors of God. An apostle is literally a commissioned "messenger," similar to the ancient idea of a herald or the Jewish custom of the *shaliach*. As an appointed agent of the one who sent him, a *shaliach* was backed by the full authority of the one who sent him (to the extent that he accurately represented his commission).

Jewish people sometimes viewed the biblical prophets as God's *shaliachim*, and the Greek version of the Old Testament often uses the verb related to apostle for God commissioning Moses and the prophets. The New Testament probably builds on this idea but uses apostle in a somewhat more specific way. The only specific Old Testament model cited for New Testament apostleship is Moses (John 1:14–18; 2 Cor. 3:6–18; 2 Tim. 3:8). Although God had authorized the prophets to speak for him, God's mission gave special authority to some prophets such as Moses, prophetic judges (Deborah, Samuel), and leaders who raised up prophetic movements (Elijah and Elisha). (God also anointed the first kings, Saul and David, prophetically, indicating that he desired in leaders a special combination of spiritual insight and administration—1 Sam. 10:10–11; 16:13; Acts 2:30. Unfortunately, to some extent power corrupted both of them, especially Saul.) Christ apparently commissions Christian apostles (in the specific sense of apostleship) with a higher rank than normal prophets in order to strategize and act with authority.

Prophets, Evangelists, and Pastor-Teachers

Second, Paul addresses prophets, who focused on the prophetic message God had given them. The term *prophet* applied in general to anyone who spoke for God. In the broadest sense (as in Acts 1:8 with 2:16–18) it could apply to all witnessing Christians (Rev. 19:10). But in Ephesians, Paul often couples prophets with apostles as contemporary expositors of God's mysteries found in the Bible (2:20; 3:5). Thus, by prophets here, Paul may mean more than merely those who offer prophecies of encouragement (1 Cor. 14:31) or who tell people where their lost donkeys are (1 Sam. 9:6–9, 20).

He may refer in this case to those who provide divine direction and strategies for Christ's body in the world, revealing God's purposes so God's people can influence their generation in the wisest way. He probably refers to an office of recognized prophets (Acts 11:27; 13:1; 21:10) rather than to anyone who occasionally prophesies. If the church should receive the message of true prophets, it is only because they have been thoroughly tested and found faithful to the message of previous generations of apostles and prophets in the Bible. Although they held less administrative authority than apostles, the prophets' mission of revealing God's purposes left them second only to apostles (1 Cor. 12:28).[8]

The third group, evangelists, focused on the saving gospel. An evangelist was literally a "herald of good news," a "gospelizer." Evangelists thus served the church by announcing the word that brought people into the church to begin with (Eph. 1:13). They were frontline warriors, because the one piece of armor specifically designed for advancing into enemy territory and the one offensive weapon are both related to the gospel (Eph. 6:15, 17).

By their example, these gifted gospelizers probably also stirred or mobilized others in the church to witness, thereby continuing to build up Christ's body (4:11–13). In contrast to the use of the term in some church traditions, biblical evangelists are not simply people who go from church to church stirring up church members for a week. Evangelists are those who take the gospel directly to the streets, to the nursing homes, to the campuses, and so on, bearing the saving message of Christ (Acts 21:8; compare 2 Tim. 4:5). If some of them do travel from church to church stirring up church members, it is probably not simply to teach them that they should witness but also to show them how to witness, for instance by taking them out to the streets. There may be other forms of this gift as well (musicians who can draw crowds and share Christ with them, mass evangelists, and so on), but the basic heart of the calling involves preaching the gospel.

Fourth, Paul notes pastor-teachers, who would expound Scripture to their congregations. Paul's language in the Greek refers to pastor-teachers as a single calling, and their focus was to expound the word that God had already provided in the Old Testament and the traditions about Jesus (now recorded in the New Testament). While all the above gifts can overlap, pastors by definition must be teachers of God's Word. The word *pastors* means "shepherds," those whom God has appointed to watch over the sheep and care for their needs, as with Israel's spiritual leaders (Ezek. 34:2–4). These shepherds are also called "overseers" (KJV: "bishops") and "elders" (Acts 20:17, 28; Titus 1:5–7; 1 Peter 5:1–4).

Just as one could seek other spiritual gifts (1 Cor. 14:1), one could desire the office of an overseer (1 Tim. 3:1), provided one met the qualifications for being above reproach in the local community where one functioned as a church leader (3:2–7). (In the first generation, such leaders were often raised up in the local congregations—Acts 14:23—hence, started with a working knowledge of their community.) Scripture reading and exposition became standard in churches as they had been in synagogues (1 Tim. 4:13), because they were necessary for perseverance to salvation (1 Tim. 4:16; 2 Tim. 3:14–4:4). Church leaders had to depend on God's gift (1 Tim. 4:14; 2 Tim. 1:6). Pastor-teachers apparently focused on explaining God's Word and applying it to the needs of their church members.

The Purpose of These Gifts

Most strikingly, Ephesians 4 indicates the purpose of these ministers of the Word: They were to equip all God's people for the work of ministry, so that by evangelism, teaching, and inspired guidance the church would become all it should be (Eph. 4:12–13). The most important function of these ministers of the Word, therefore, was to mobilize the rest of Christ's body, because *all* Christians are called to be ministers. The places in which Christians work and study and reside are their parishes. If we could mobilize all Christians to minister where they live, we would have a spiritual army to proclaim Christ, to meet the needs of our society, and to lay a better foundation for our society's ethics. Can we imagine the impact on the church, and thus on the world, if these ministry gifts began functioning the way they should? As long as this work remains incomplete in any generation, we will continue to need the apostles, prophets, evangelists, and pastor-teachers who Paul says are called for this purpose (4:11–13).

If you feel drawn to any of these gifts, you should begin asking God for more specific direction as to how to pursue them. It is also wise, when possible, to learn from others. The first generation of Christians had teachings direct from those who knew Jesus; we have to study those teachings and learn about the culture and settings they first addressed. Calling is what starts us out, but equipping us also takes time (especially for some gifts), whether through years of suffering (Joseph, David) or waiting (Abraham and Sarah, Paul; compare Acts 9:30; 11:25; 13:1–2; Gal. 1:18; 2:1). Educational equipping is often helpful (Acts 7:22; 17:28; 18:24; 22:3); still, neither Bible college nor seminary can make one a man or woman of God; only God can do that, and we desperately need his gifts and calling.

Pursuing Gifts

Whatever other reasons many of us do not experience any particular gifts, one reason may be because we do not pursue them as Paul commands (1 Cor. 12:31; 14:1). To be sure, Paul wants the church as a whole to seek gifts, so his exhortation may not mean that God will necessarily grant every gift that every Christian desires (12:11). Also, Paul surely does not imply that all Christians should exercise all gifts (12:28–30). But God often grants prayer requests, especially when Christians offer them for his honor. Paul gives us some guidelines for what kinds of gifts God may be most eager to give us.

Some translators render the verb in 1 Corinthians 12:31 as a statement ("you desire") instead of a command ("desire"). But the same word occurs in 1 Corinthians 14:1 (where it is clearly a command, as in 14:39), forming a literary frame around chapter 13. The chapter between these two commands defines which gifts are the "best" ones we should seek: those that build up the church by love. In churches in which prejudice against the gift would not create division, prophecy certainly contributes to the building up of the assembly and is thus among the "best" gifts in such settings (14:1). (In some churches and denominations today even prophecy creates division, so at least in the short run it might not be the "best" gift there. We would at least need to prepare the groundwork with teaching about the gift, its proper use, and be ready to exercise discernment.)

Some writers object by saying that the Bible does not give us models of people who seek gifts. But just as I argue elsewhere in this book that we should embrace the teaching of narrative on matters that Paul's letters do not directly address, so we should accept here Paul's letters on a matter even if narratives do not address it. We do not have much narrative to look to on the subject. The Book of Acts is the only book of New Testament narrative outside the Gospels, and it provides no examples of seeking gifts in a godly way (when tongues came, they came spontaneously with the Spirit). It contains few examples of anything outside Luke's purview and shows gifts mainly in their use in evangelism rather than in the church. (We do get a couple negative examples of people trying to get apostolic gifts of power without going to God for them—8:18–24; 19:13–19.)

But there are some biblical models of seeking empowerment from the Spirit. In the Old Testament, Elisha cleaved to his mentor, seeking Elijah's empowerment, even if Elijah did not guarantee it to him (2 Kings 2:1–14). And in the New Testament, when the Samaritans did not receive the gift of the Spirit immediately, two apostles went to make sure they received it (Acts 8:14–17). These and similar experiences serve as a model (see appendix), implying that we should seek the same empowerment the early church had if we lack it (compare Luke 11:13). One disciple of Jesus even requests the opportunity to learn miraculous faith and, though imperfect, walks on water longer than most of us, his critics, have (Matt. 14:28–31).

The fact that God is sovereign over the distribution of gifts (1 Cor. 12:7) is no reason not to seek the gifts. God is sovereign over our food too, but though he desires to provide it for his children (see Matt. 6:25–34) and wants us to seek his kingdom first (Matt. 6:9–10, 33), he expects us to pray for him to provide our food (Matt. 6:11; 7:7–11). Those who argue that we should never seek gifts, that God will give them whether we ask for them or not, may be sounding a note of false piety, like some complacent American churchgoers in the eighteenth and nineteenth centuries who reasoned, "God will save us if he has predestined us, so there is no point in us trying to do anything about it." The Bible teaches both God's sovereignty and our responsibility to pray. If God has stirred a passion for him in our hearts, our act of seeking God is also a gift from him. God does not grant every request, but that is not a reason not to ask.[9] Even in the seeking we learn more of him, and often if we persist in faith, God does begin to equip us with that gift or with others in its place.

Gifts and beyond Gifts

The very diversity of the gifts Paul mentions summons us to be open to more of God's work than just the way he has worked among us in the past.

While we should not play down the significance of any gift God has for us, it is easy to focus so much on one gift that we are unaware of entire areas of spiritual experience in the Bible that are unrelated to that particular gift. Paul not only prayed in tongues (1 Cor. 14:18) but also experienced deeper revelations in the Spirit (2 Cor. 12:1). However, he preferred to reserve such experiences mainly for his private devotion and boasted instead in his sufferings and weakness in which God alone was glorified (2 Cor. 12:1–10).

Some of us are content simply to pray in tongues or employ some other gift without considering that there may be more we could learn from God's Spirit. When Ezekiel saw the awesome majesty of the Lord, he was so overwhelmed that he fell on his face before God (Ezek. 1:28), but the Spirit empowered him to withstand the glory of the revelation and so to receive what God had to say (Ezek. 2:1–2). The Spirit here both reveals the majesty of our God and equips us with God's message to our generation.

The diversity of the Spirit's work should not surprise anyone who has read the Old Testament. Although God's Spirit was active in the whole creation (Gen. 1:2; Pss. 104:30; 139:7; perhaps Job 33:4; Isa. 34:16; 40:7), the Old Testament especially associates the Spirit with prophecy (Num. 11:25–29; 24:2; 1 Sam. 10:6, 10; 19:20, 23; 2 Sam. 23:2; 1 Kings 22:24; 1 Chron. 12:18; 2 Chron. 15:1; 18:23; 20:14; 24:20; Neh. 9:30; Isa. 61:1; Micah 3:8; Zech. 7:12), revelations (Ezek. 2:2; 3:12, 14, 24; 8:3; 11:1, 5, 24; 37:1; 43:5), other speaking for God (Isa. 42:1; 44:1–5; 48:16; 59:21; see 43:10), and perhaps prophets' empowerment to do miracles (2 Kings 2:9, 15; compare 1 Kings 18:12).

Yet the Old Testament also shows the Spirit empowering people for various skills, including art and architecture devoted to God (Exod. 31:3; 35:31; see 28:3) and military and political leadership (Num. 27:18; Deut. 34:9; Judg. 3:10; 6:34; 11:29; 13:25; 14:6, 19; 15:14; 1 Sam. 11:6; 16:13–14; Isa. 11:2; Zech. 4:6; perhaps Ps. 51:11). Sometimes prophetic empowerment evidenced empowerment for leadership (Num. 11:17, 25–26; 1 Sam. 10:6, 10). Paul reflects the same emphasis on the diversity of the Spirit's works, although, as in the Old Testament, various forms of prophetic speech predominate.

Conclusion

God has provided many gifts for building up his church. The treatment above, though only a sampling, should demonstrate the wide range of diverse gifts God has for his people. We should learn to be confident in the gifts and calling God gives us for his work, because we are confident in the God who gives them to us. We dare never either demean or exalt our particular gifts. God gives each of us different tasks and judges us by whether we are faithful to our task, not by how dramatic our task appears. At the same time, Paul also calls us to consider what gifts are most necessary for the church in our time. Having considered them, we should ask God to give those gifts to his body and be open to him using us if he chooses.

We must seek to cultivate especially those gifts that most build up the body of Christ. We must accept and encourage one another's gifts, and in our pursuit of gifts, honor the unity of Christ's body. The gifts should not be segregated into "charismatic" parts of the church; they belong to the whole body of Christ, a reality that many believers, both charismatic and noncharismatic, have often failed to appreciate.

Yet the bottom line of the Spirit's work in our lives is not power to perform miracles but a transformed heart that learns how to love. Spiritual power without love is dangerous, but love without some degree of spiritual power to carry forth its designs is impotent. Once our hearts are attuned to God's heart in love, we can seek various spiritual gifts for his glory, for serving our brothers and sisters in Christ, and for changing the world around us that desperately needs transformation by Christ's power. We can pray together for the establishment of God's kingdom rather than our own kingdoms and be the gifts for each other that God called us to be.

7

The Spirit and Salvation

As we noted above, when discussing the fruit of the Spirit, the greatest work of the Spirit in this age is transforming us into new creatures in Christ. I speak of this work as the greatest because it is in keeping with God's greatest act of power, raising Jesus Christ from the dead (Eph. 1:19–23; 2:1, 6). When God spoke the world into being, that was an act of power. The new creation to come, however, reflects a greater expression of God's power, and the power of that new creation, inaugurated in Jesus' resurrection, continues in us (Eph. 3:16, 20; 4:22–24). Few of us recognize the greatness of God's power at work in us!

The fruit of the Spirit reflects God's continuing creative power in our lives. But it is also important to recognize the beginning of that creative activity in our lives, when we acknowledge Jesus Christ as Lord, when God himself enters us and transforms us into new creations. We need to focus not merely on what God is enabling us to become but on the transformation he already began in us.

Different Aspects of the Spirit's Work

For readers tempted to skip to the next chapter, thinking they already know everything about a matter as basic as conversion, I recommend that you read this chapter anyway. Even if you understand everything about conversion, you will find intriguing the discussion of some biblical passages that introduce it. Although many Scripture passages testify to the Spirit's work in transforming us in salvation, in this brief chapter I will focus on just two examples. Both of these examples are necessary prerequisites for the following chapter on baptism in the Holy Spirit.

Because Jewish people used water baptism to symbolize purification, conversion, and transformation, it provided a useful analogy for a purification and transformation by the Spirit at conversion. We will look at this theme as developed most fully in the Gospel of John but also as articulated in the preaching of John the Baptist. In the next chapter we will examine some examples in Acts that can be used to support a subsequent experience, possibly a "baptism in the Holy Spirit." The present chapter examines two examples that can be used to support a baptism in the Holy Spirit at conversion.

I will save discussion of most of the issues for the next chapter, but here I will briefly emphasize the Spirit's work in conversion. Pursuing a more specific focus than some other parts of the New Testament, Luke-Acts emphasizes the Spirit's work in empowering us to speak for God (see chapter 3 on the Spirit and evangelism). But while most other New Testament writers also connect the Spirit with speaking for God (perhaps especially John, for example, 15:26–27), they also emphasize the Spirit's role in our conversion.

If the phrase "baptism in the Holy Spirit" applies to the entire work of the Spirit in our lives, then it is perfectly reasonable for different passages to apply it to different aspects of his work in our lives. Some differences are largely semantic: Most Christians agree that the Spirit transforms us at conversion but continues to work in us and that we may encounter special experiences with the Spirit after conversion. Therefore, I urge readers who are committed to either side in the baptism in the Spirit debate to hear me out through both of these chapters. Before Christians can work toward consensus, we need to lay out all the evidence useful for both sides in the discussion.

Purified by the Spirit

Jesus introduces the theme of the new birth in his discussion with Nicodemus (John 3:3–5; compare 1:12–13; Gal. 4:29; Titus 3:5; 1 Peter 1:3, 23). This conversation about being "born again" is well known, but many Christians are unaware that John speaks of spiritual purification far more often than in just this one passage.

One way John describes this new birth is being born "of water" (3:5). This mention of water reflects a theme that runs through John's Gospel: The washing that God offers us is more than ritual; it is a transformation by his Spirit![1]

Born of Water and the Spirit (John 3:3–5)

When Nicodemus comes to Jesus by night, Jesus informs him that he must be "born again" (John 3:3). While we understand today that Jesus referred to spiritual rebirth, a miraculous transformation of our character by God's Spirit, such a concept eluded Nicodemus. He assumed that Jesus meant he had to reenter his mother's womb and be physically reborn (3:4). The alternative was simply unthinkable to him. The only kind of spiritual rebirth Nicodemus knew about was appropriate only for pagans, not for religious Jewish persons such as himself. Jewish people generally believed that a Gentile converting to Judaism needed to be baptized. Because Gentiles were impure, they needed to wash away that impurity when they converted to Judaism. After a Gentile converted, some Jewish teachers regarded the person as "a newborn child," with a new, "clean" legal status.

Nicodemus, like the religious people John the Baptist admonished in Matthew 3:9, could not imagine that he needed to become "newborn" in this sense; such a baptism of repentance was for Gentiles only! So Jesus makes the concept of being born again more explicit: A person must be born "from water and from the Spirit." The "water" should have immediately reminded Nicodemus of the baptismal part of the Jewish ceremony used for Gentiles who are being legally "reborn" as Jews. If Nicodemus grasped the comparison, he would have been unhappy with it, for Jesus was suggesting that even a teacher of Israel needed to repent in order to become a child of God.

But Jesus was not asking Nicodemus merely to be baptized in water according to the Jewish ritual, as embarrassing as that would have been for him. Jesus wanted Nicodemus to be born of spiritual water, to be spiritually converted by the "water of the Spirit." In Greek, one preposition governs both "water" and "Spirit." Because of this, the expression "from water and the Spirit" could also be translated, "from the water of the Spirit." Lest we doubt that this is the likely meaning here, we should note that later in this Gospel, Jesus uses water as a symbol for the Spirit (John 7:37–39). This symbolic use of water carries on a biblical comparison that remained popular among some of Jesus' contemporaries (Ezek. 36:25–27). Thus, Jesus goes on to speak simply of "that which is born from the Spirit" (John 3:6). Natural birth was utterly inadequate for God's kingdom unless supplemented by Spirit rebirth; rebirth by God's Spirit is the beginning of an eternal life (3:16).

Developing the same kind of comparison, the rest of John's Gospel emphasizes that Jesus' spiritual "water" is better than any of the kinds of ritual "water" offered by human religion. John the Baptist declares that whereas he baptizes merely with water (which is good), Jesus will baptize in the Holy Spirit (which is better, John 1:31–33). Similarly, in Cana Jesus honors a friend's need more highly than traditional Jewish water rituals. Although weddings typically lasted seven days, running out of wine at one's wedding was so humiliating that Jesus' friend would have been the laughingstock of Cana for years to come. So Jesus has attendants fill with water six waterpots that had been reserved for the ceremony of purification (John 2:6). To transform that water into wine profaned the normally holy purpose of the pots as far as Jewish tradition was concerned, but Jesus was not concerned about ritual purity or tradition. He had higher priorities than honoring merely ritual uses of water.

Wells of Water (John 4)

In chapter 4, Jesus meets a sinful Samaritan woman. Jesus crosses three barriers to reach this woman, although she initially does not understand his intention. First, she was a woman, and many Jewish teachers considered it immoral to speak with women in public (even the disciples were surprised— 4:27). That she was a Samaritan made matters worse; many Jewish teachers considered Samaritan women unclean from the time they were babies. Worst of all, Jesus was speaking with a sinner: Everyone would know that a woman forced to come to the well alone must be isolated from other women because of her sinful behavior (at the very least, currently living with a man she was not married to, 4:18).

The meeting place may have made Jesus' kindness seem more ambiguous: Jacob, Isaac's steward, and Moses all found wives at wells, and some Jewish teachers recognized that wells remained a good place for finding marriage prospects. It is thus not surprising that the Samaritan woman initially misinterprets him: "I'm not married," she suggests (John 4:17). Jesus' response gets the discussion back on track. She eventually not only comes to faith but leads her people to Jesus as well (4:28–42).

Jacob's well, water holy to the Samaritans, forms the backdrop for this story. It represents another side to religious ritual: Ancient peoples often felt that one could meet God particularly in special holy sites. (If this sounds superstitious to us today, we should remember how many nominal Christians similarly seek to meet God in church on Sunday mornings after they have ignored him during the week.) Jesus is greater than Jacob and greater than Jacob's well; he gives the water of eternal life, the Spirit (4:14). He is thus not only greater than John's baptism or ritual waterpots but also greater than water considered holy to Samaritans.

Healing Water (John 5:1–9; 9:1–7)

Jesus is not only superior to the good washing of John (1:31–33), the washing of regular Jewish purification (2:6), the water of Jewish proselyte baptism (3:5), and the water of Jacob's well (4:14). He is also superior to the water of ancient healing shrines, including, perhaps, the pool of Bethesda. Ancients often sought healing at sacred pools. If archaeologists have the right site for the pool, some archaeological evidence suggests that the pool of Bethesda may have functioned as a healing shrine even in later centuries, after Gentiles had resettled Jerusalem.

One lame man at the pool had failed for thirty-eight years to find healing there. Jesus, by contrast, provided him healing instantly (John 5:5–9). John compares and contrasts this man with another whom Jesus healed by a pool in John 9. The man in John 5 became ill in punishment for his sin (5:14), but the man in John 9 was born blind without sinning (9:3). Both are cured at pools, but the first man essentially betrays Jesus to the authorities (5:10–16), whereas the second man grows in his commitment to Jesus despite being punished for it (9:24–39). The two healed men illustrate contrasting responses to Jesus transforming our lives: We can continue to pursue him, or we can turn away from him.

In John 9, the pool is the Pool of Siloam, which had been used for special rituals during the Feast of Tabernacles just then ending. For the first seven days of the feast, priests would march in procession from the Pool of Siloam to the temple. On the eighth day they would recite ancient prophecies that someday rivers of living water would flow from the foundation stone of the temple, bringing life to all the earth (Ezek. 47:1–6; Zech. 14:8).

Rivers of Living Water (John 7:37–39)

On the last day of the Feast of Tabernacles, Jesus stood in the midst of the assembly in the temple and called out a promise of the Spirit to those who were listening (John 7:37–39). But from whom does the Spirit flow in this passage? The earliest Greek texts included no punctuation, so scholars are divided over how to punctuate the text. Many follow the traditional English reading: "Let whoever is thirsty come to me and drink. Of the one who believes in me, the Bible says, 'From his innermost being rivers of living water will flow'" (John 7:37–38). The NRSV even reads this view into the text: "out of the believer's heart."

But in this context, I think the other ancient view, held by many Greek church fathers, concerning the punctuation may be more likely: "Whoever thirsts should come to me; let them drink, whoever believes in me. As the Bible says, 'From his innermost being rivers of living water will flow.'" The difference is that the latter punctuation helps us to see that Jesus himself is the foundation stone of a new temple, the source of living water for the believer. A believer may have a well of water springing up inside (4:14), but Jesus is the source of living water, and this text says that those who believe in him would receive the Spirit, not give it (John 7:39). The priests had just read the texts about living water flowing from God's temple in the end time; we may be Jesus' temple, but he is the foundation of this new temple. Either way we punctuate the text, this much is clear: Jesus is the source of water.

John informs us that the Spirit could not be given until Jesus was glorified (John 7:39)—that is, until he was "lifted up" on the cross (John 12:23–25, 32–33; see also 8:28; 17:1–5). Later in John's Gospel, he vividly illustrates this giving of the Spirit once Jesus is crucified. Narratives, unlike more prophetic books such as Revelation, do not usually contain much symbolism. Among narrative books, however, John is sometimes an exception; for example, in view of Jesus' symbolic use of "night" (9:4; 11:10), it is not surprising that the Gospel mentions "night" in cases of cowardice (3:2) or evil (13:30).

After Jesus had died on the cross, John describes an event that the other Gospels do not report, because this event has special significance for his readers. When a soldier pierced Jesus' side with a spear, not only blood but water flowed out (19:34). Whatever the medical reasons for the water, John's illustrations about water elsewhere in his Gospel lead us to see the climax of a theme here: The water from Jesus' side represents the gift of the Spirit, finally available after Jesus' death. From the throne of God and of the lamb flows the fountain of the river of life; let the one who wills come and drink freely (compare Rev. 22:1, 17).

This theme of purification by Jesus' water of the Spirit, as opposed to merely ritual water, runs through the entire Gospel. When we read the story of Nicodemus, then, we should recognize how central is the message of 3:5: True proselyte baptism, true conversion, is accomplished only by the Spirit. Our self-discipline, emotions, or intellectual persuasion did not transform us when we became believers; God's Spirit entering us did. We should recognize by faith the decisive work that God accomplished in us "the hour we first believed."

The Continuing Work of the Spirit (John 14–20)

Jesus gives the Spirit like living water to his people, a gift that we embrace at conversion (John 4:13–14; see also 1 Cor. 12:13). But the new birth is the beginning, not the end, of our experience with the Spirit. The Spirit continues to flow like the fresh water of a river (compare John 7:37–38). True partakers of eternal life are those who continue to eat and drink of Christ (John 6:53–71; compare 8:31 with 8:59). Jesus promised that after he went to the Father, the Spirit would continue to empower his disciples both to understand his message (John 14:26; 16:12–15) and to testify about him (John 15:26–16:11). This section of John's Gospel emphasizes Jesus' continuing presence with us by the Spirit (14:16–23) and our continuing dependence on him for fruitful spiritual life (15:1–7; see further chapters 1 and 2).

Although Luke provides a fuller version of the complete empowerment by the Spirit that happened some time later, John 20:19–23 ties together the earlier mentions of the Spirit as far as John's Gospel is concerned. Because John ends his Gospel before Jesus' ascension, he does not include Pentecost. Thus, he emphasizes the ways this promise of the Spirit began to be fulfilled already shortly after the resurrection. He therefore includes an incident that happened shortly after Jesus rose from the dead when Jesus came to impart his Spirit to his disciples, breathing on them as God first breathed the breath of life into Adam (Gen. 2:7; John 20:22; see Job 27:3; Isa. 32:15; Ezek. 37:5–14; John 3:8). Thus, the disciples were "born anew" with new life and were also equipped for mission: "As the Father sent me, I have sent you" (John 20:21).

"He Will Baptize in the Holy Spirit and Fire" (Matt. 3:11)

Many Christians today speak of being fire-baptized as if it were pleasant, but that is not how John the Baptist meant it. By contrast, everyone agrees that baptism in God's Spirit is positive. How can we be sure of the meaning of "fire-baptized"? In contrast to Mark's abbreviated introduction to his Gospel (treated earlier), Matthew and Luke describe in greater detail John the Baptist's wilderness proclamation about the Spirit. From the context in Matthew, one gathers that he offered this promise of fire baptism to a largely unfriendly crowd.

In John's day most people thought that prophecy was rare and that prophets were rarer. Many people believed that the arrival of true prophets in the wilderness prefigured the coming of God's kingdom. Thus, when John the Baptist began prophesying in the wilderness about God's coming kingdom, people began to stream out to him from across the land. Because John was dressed like Elijah of old (2 Kings 1:8; Matt. 3:4), many of his followers probably considered him to be a new Elijah. The prophets had, after all, promised that Elijah would return just before the time of the end (Mal. 4:5–6). John's diet also showed that he was serious about his mission (Matt. 3:4). While some other Jewish people also ate locusts, a diet completely restricted to bugs and natural sweetener showed serious commitment.

Of course, John did not have a great deal of choice about his diet or location; outspoken prophets are rarely welcome within established society. When true prophets like John the Baptist begin to speak in modern society, we usually chase them out just as our ancient counterparts did. (Imagine how we might react if a prophet overturned the communion table in church on Sunday morning and asked us how we could claim to be disciples of Christ when we are materialistic, or how we could partake of Christ's body while attending a deliberately racially segregated church in a racially segregated community.)

Not only was John unwelcome in much of society, but he even denounced some of his listeners! Observing the crowds (Matthew zeroes in on the religious leaders who had come to check him out), John labels them "offspring of vipers" (Matt. 3:7), an even nastier insult than modern readers might suspect. In John's day many people thought that vipers ate their way out of their mother's wombs, thereby killing their mothers. Since ancient people considered parent-murderers the most morally reprobate people possible, calling someone the child of a viper was even worse than calling them a viper. Undoubtedly, the religious people were not amused, but John does not stop with that insult. Religious people then, like most religious people today, felt secure in their salvation. Jewish people generally thought they were saved because they were descended from Abraham (Matt. 3:9). But John warns them that only genuine repentance will spare them from the coming wrath (Matt. 3:7–8).

Rather than leaving "coming wrath" ambiguous, John explains to his hearers just what kind of wrath they may expect. He compares them to trees and warns that if they neglect the fruit of repentance, they will be cut down and hurled into the fire of judgment (Matt. 3:10). The coming one will gather his wheat into the barn, but he will burn up the chaff with unquenchable fire

(Matt. 3:12). When farmers harvested wheat, they hurled the wheat into the air, allowing the wind to blow out the chaff, a light substance that was useful only as cheap fuel that burned quickly. John tells his listeners that those who do not repent and produce the behavioral fruit of repentance will be cast into a fire that never ceases to burn: the fire of hell.

This is the context of John's prophecy concerning baptism in the Holy Spirit. The promised time of the kingdom and the restoration of Israel was coming (Matt. 3:2). God was preparing to gather his servants and to burn up the wicked with fire. In different passages "fire" may symbolize different things, but in this context (as most frequently in the Bible) it symbolizes judgment (Matt. 3:10, 12). Not all John's listeners will repent. Some will be wheat, others will be chaff. Some will be baptized in the Spirit, others will be baptized in fire.

Thus, when John announces that the coming one will baptize in both the Holy Spirit and fire, hearers would recognize that his announcement was not entirely good news. In this context, baptism in fire can only be a negative promise of baptism in judgment for the wicked, whereas baptism in the Spirit is a positive promise for the righteous. (My students sometimes lament that this means the denomination called the Fire-Baptized Holiness Church is misnamed. What most fire-baptized churches mean by their name, though, is holiness, something we all affirm. The question is whether we should base the title on this passage.)

What did John mean by "baptism" in the Holy Spirit? Undoubtedly, he was thinking of the Old Testament prophecies about God "pouring out" his Spirit like water on his people (Isa. 44:3; Ezek. 39:29; Joel 2:28). Thus, he might have thought of both prophetic empowerment, as in Joel and possibly Isaiah (Isa. 42:1; 44:8), and purification, as in Ezekiel (Ezek. 36:25–27). The former emphasis is related to what most Pentecostals (and, I believe, the Book of Acts) seem to mean by baptism in the Holy Spirit; the latter is related to what most Baptist and Reformed thinkers (and Paul in 1 Cor. 12:13) mean by Spirit baptism. But John's prophecy about the outpoured Spirit must at least include conversion, because he explicitly contrasts it with a baptism of judgment for the wicked.

Perhaps more importantly, John viewed baptism in the Spirit, like baptism in fire, as an end time baptism—that is, an event that belonged to the impending end of the age. He predicted a baptism in the Spirit that was as imminent as the kingdom and God's fiery wrath that he was proclaiming. John did not understand, of course, that Jesus would have a first and second coming; thus, he had no idea that the kingdom would come in two stages (note his confusion in Matt. 11:2–3). But we can look back and understand that the King who will someday come to reign has already inaugurated his reign among his followers, although that reign's beginnings seemed as obscure (compared to the future kingdom) as a mustard seed before growing into a huge plant (Mark 4:30–32).

We recognize, though John may not have, that different aspects of his prophecy were fulfilled at different times. As we noted early in this book, Jesus' followers have tasted the power of the coming kingdom (Eph. 1:13–14; Heb. 6:5). The King who is yet to come has already come once, hence, has invaded history with his rule. Whereas most people define their identity in terms of their past or their present, the gospel summons believers to define their identity in terms of what we shall be, in terms of what God has called us to be. Empowered by the Spirit, we are to represent the future kingdom in the midst of the present evil age.

Conclusion

The Bible is clear that the Spirit is involved in conversion. Interpreters divide today not over whether the Spirit is involved in conversion, however, but over the specific meaning of the phrase "baptism in the Holy Spirit." Some apply this phrase to what occurs at conversion; others use it to describe an experience after conversion.

Because John the Baptist contrasts baptism in the Holy Spirit with hell-fire, he apparently applies it to all true believers. In John 3:5, where Jesus seems to speak of being born from "water and the Spirit" as a "spiritual" proselyte baptism, he seems to describe the new birth as a "baptism in the Holy Spirit."

There are, however, some passages in Acts in which Christians appear to experience the Spirit's empowerment after their conversion, in ways identical to what some passages in Acts call being "baptized in the Holy Spirit." Is it possible that both views are biblical? Is it possible that baptism in the Spirit refers to the entirety of the Spirit's work in our lives, perhaps initiated at conversion but also discovered in aspects of the Spirit's work sometimes demonstrated afterward? To this question we turn in the next chapter.

8

When Are We Baptized in the Spirit?

The Bible has more to say about the baptism in the Holy Spirit than what Christians today often debate. Thus, in the midst of current debates about when and how one is baptized in the Spirit, we often lose sight of *why* the Lord baptizes his followers in the Spirit. This is why we focused on power for evangelism, the fruit of the Spirit, and other aspects of the Spirit's work before coming to this more controversial issue.

Now, however, we must address this often-debated issue. The Spirit transformed me at my conversion, but I experienced what seemed to be an even more overwhelming encounter with the Spirit two days later, when I better understood the nature of the commitment I had made. Which of these experiences was the "baptism in the Holy Spirit"? Are we baptized in the Spirit at conversion or afterward? Or does the Bible challenge us to go beyond even these two alternatives?

A Matter of Semantics

If we could get past some semantic debates in our discussions about the timing of the baptism in the Holy Spirit, we would have more time avail-

able for the more practical questions surrounding the Spirit's empowerment. Nearly all Christians agree, for example, that all Christians have
the Spirit by virtue of being born again. We also agree that we all should
regularly experience a Spirit-filled life, walk in the Spirit, depend on the
Spirit's power in our behavior and witness, and be open to experiences
from God's Spirit subsequent to conversion. We want to cultivate a deeper
daily dependence on God's Spirit and understand how deeply we need the
Spirit for our service to God in this world and for living the Christian life.
In practice, we agree on most matters that deeply affect us. In other words,
some of the most significant areas of disagreement today may be merely
semantic.

This is not the only example of Christians dividing over words or phrases
rather than the issues behind such language, even on matters that involve
the Spirit. For example, some noncharismatics have reproved charismatics for using terms such as *revelation* and *inspiration* for something other than
Scripture, yet they agree that God's Spirit can lead our daily lives, which
is what most charismatics mean by the terms. Undoubtedly, it is helpful to
distinguish our experience of the Spirit's guidance from the Bible, which
is the measuring stick for all other claims to hear God. Yet we should not
condemn others for using terms in ways that our own Bible translations do.

As in the example above, we all agree that the Bible is the standard for
evaluating claims that the Spirit is leading us; the Bible is the ultimate written "revelation." Yet whereas some limit the term *revelation* to the Bible
alone, the biblical term translated "revelation" is not limited to Scripture.
It can refer to a Damascus road–type encounter with Christ (Gal. 1:12, 16)
or to information revealed in prophecy (1 Cor. 14:26, 30; compare perhaps
Gal. 2:2 with Acts 11:28–30).

Likewise, many Christians apply the term *sanctification* to the biblical
concept of maturing in Christ. But while maturing in Christ is a biblical
notion, surveying a concordance shows that the New Testament almost
never uses the term we translate "sanctification" to describe that idea. If
we scan New Testament references to sanctification, we will discover that
most texts refer to being set apart for God at conversion. However, other
texts do indicate that we should learn to live as God called us to live at our
conversion (some calling us to "be holy," the adjective that relates to the
verb *sanctify*). Do we really need to fight about the particular terms we use
to describe it?

We often assume particular working definitions of terms that are not
shared by everyone else. By adopting some fairly neutral terms and phrases

such as "conversion" and "being filled with the Spirit," we could deal with the main issues with much less conflict. Consequently, when I teach publicly, I usually bypass the semantic issue and emphasize the practical matter of seeking God's power to do his work. After all, the Bible forbids us to argue over semantics (2 Tim. 2:14).

This practical solution does not, however, solve what the Bible means by phrases such as "baptism in the Holy Spirit." Can different interpretations of that expression possibly be semantic differences too? I will propose that they are—although the biblical pool of evidence on the phrase is small enough that I must also admit that other proposals are also feasible.

Different Views on the "When" Question

The controversy about when baptism in the Holy Spirit occurs in a believer's life has been around for some time and shows no sign of abating. Indeed, although some speak as if only Pentecostals hold to a definite work of the Spirit after conversion, the idea was common for well over a century before the birth of the modern Pentecostal movement.

John Wesley and many of his followers became convinced that the Bible taught a second work of grace in a believer's life after conversion, in which the Spirit brought a believer to a higher level of inward purity.[1] Richard Baxter and other Puritan and Reformed sealers also envisioned a subsequent work. Pursuit of this deeper experience of holiness became a common feature in North American revivals of the mid to late nineteenth century. Some came to employ the title "baptism in the Holy Spirit" for the subsequent empowerment. By the late nineteenth and early twentieth century, some Reformed ministers, such as R. A. Torrey, superintendent of Moody Bible Institute, Baptists such as A. J. Gordon and others also emphasized the baptism in the Spirit as a second work of grace, as did Andrew Murray and F. B. Meyer. Indeed, some of history's most effective evangelists, including Charles Finney, Dwight Moody, and Torrey, viewed baptism in the Holy Spirit as an empowerment for service that was subsequent to conversion.[2]

The first Pentecostals thought they had found a third experience in the Spirit (subsequent to both conversion and this second experience of sanctification), although other Pentecostals (today probably the majority) concluded that their experience was a second and final one, the baptism in the Holy Spirit. While no one should fault another Christian for seeking God's holiness more passionately, many other Christians doubt that the specific expression "baptism in the Holy Spirit" applies to such a postconversion experience of God's Spirit. Many believe it applies only to conversion itself.

Today's most effective evangelistic movements appear on either side of the debate; most Southern Baptists, for example, identify "baptism in the Spirit" with conversion, whereas most Pentecostals identify it with a subsequent empowerment. I recount this contrast to point out, before proceeding, that God has abundantly used and continues to use Christians with different views on the matter. In light of God's blessing on Christians with different views, it appears that actually being empowered by the Holy Spirit matters more than what we think about *how* the Spirit empowers us. That is not to suggest that the subject does not matter or that you should skip the rest of this chapter. Rather, such an awareness puts the larger question in perspective.

Different Starting Points

Most evangelical Christians today think of baptism in the Spirit in one of two ways: Either Christians receive the Spirit completely at conversion (the typical Reformed position), or Christians receive a special empowerment after conversion (the usual Holiness and Pentecostal position). Those who emphasize the Bible's theological statements (such as Paul's comments) rather than narrative examples (such as stories in Acts) usually identify baptism in the Spirit with conversion to faith in Christ. Those who emphasize Acts over against Paul usually believe that baptism in the Spirit can occur after conversion.

Each tradition builds its case on Bible texts—just different ones. I will argue that both traditions may have correctly interpreted their favored texts—that both groups of interpreters are in fact largely right about what they affirm. It appears that the New Testament teaches both views—because different texts appear to employ the phrase "baptism in the Holy Spirit" in different ways. The fact that the phrase "baptism in the Spirit" could emphasize a different aspect of the Spirit's work in different biblical passages is not difficult to affirm once we recognize that these different emphases are all part of the work of the same Spirit. Before someone is tempted to think that such an approach is too convenient to be correct, I will offer reasons why I think this is the fairest way to read the biblical texts on their own terms.

In view of John the Baptist's use of the phrase (contrasted with fiery judgment), he probably assumed that the Spirit's work involved a number of aspects, including salvation and any subsequent empowerments. When Jesus tells Nicodemus to be born from "the water of the Spirit," he is calling Nicodemus to undergo a "spiritual" proselyte baptism, i.e., a baptism in the Holy Spirit. Similarly, whenever New Testament writers write about believers receiving the Spirit, they invariably speak of the Spirit coming at the time of conversion (for example, Acts 2:38; Gal. 3:2). Christ's work is complete (Col. 2:6–23) and we cannot add to what God has provided for us in conversion (Rom. 5:5; Gal. 3:2–5). We made this case in slightly more detail in the previous chapter.

Yet full access to God's transforming power at conversion need not imply that each of us has appropriated all that power in our daily lives. I suspect most of us will admit that in practice we may later yield more of our lives to the direction of God's Spirit. In narratives in the Book of Acts, examples indicate that believers embraced some aspects of the Spirit in an experience after their conversion (2:4; 8:15–16; 9:17; 19:4–6, treated below).

Meanwhile, other passages rarely cited by either side in the debate show us that the work of the Spirit not only means more than conversion but also more than any single subsequent experience. Acts indicates that believers may receive empowerments subsequent to their "second experience" (4:8, 31; 13:9). Paul likewise speaks of living a Spirit-filled life (Eph. 5:18), walking by the same Spirit one has already received (Gal. 5:16–23)—passages that surely deserve more emphasis in the way most of us live.

These passages suggest that the whole sphere of the Spirit's work becomes available at conversion, but believers may experience some aspects of the Spirit's work only subsequent to conversion. Once we lay the traditional semantic debates aside, this New Testament picture makes good sense in most of our personal lives. One may compare other teachings in the New Testament about regularly appropriating Christ's finished work. For example, Paul teaches that believers become dead to sin at conversion, yet few of us dispute that we must learn to appropriate that reality in our daily lives. (Terrible as this may be, most Christians I know have sinned since their conversion.) Those interpreters who emphasize our completeness in Christ and the sufficiency of spiritual resources provided us in salvation are correct: When the Spirit enters our lives, God makes us new and gives us complete access to the Spirit's resources. At the same time, it is also biblical to emphasize that we need to draw on that empowerment in practice and that all Christians, no matter how full of God's Spirit, can grow to seek God more deeply.

Before we survey New Testament teaching about baptism in the Holy Spirit, we should survey the background of the way Jesus' contemporaries thought about God's Spirit. Because they emphasized certain elements of what the Old Testament said about the Spirit, the first Christians could take for granted some ideas about the Spirit without always explaining them. Once we understand some ideas that the New Testament writers took for granted, we will be ready to delve into New Testament perspectives on the baptism in the Spirit.[3]

What Did the Phrase "Baptism in the Holy Spirit" Mean to First-Century Hearers?

The phrase "baptism in the Holy Spirit" self-evidently includes two primary elements: "baptize" and "Holy Spirit." "Baptize" is the easier of the two elements to summarize: Jewish people baptized Gentiles who wished to convert to Judaism by having them immerse themselves in water. The image of baptism thus connoted two ideas to ancient Jewish hearers: conversion and immersion. Those who identify baptism in the Spirit with conversion may support their case from the first idea; those who identify it with a second work in which the Spirit overwhelms the believer (immersed in the Spirit) may appeal to the latter.

The second element of the phrase is the "Holy Spirit," which Jesus' Jewish contemporaries saw as God's way to purify his people or (far more often) to empower them to prophesy. The former image may support the idea that baptism in the Spirit occurs at conversion; the latter, that it reflects a subsequent experience of empowerment. Hence, the phrase by itself is not precise enough to solve the chronology question above.

Nevertheless, what first-century hearers knew about the Holy Spirit helps explain how Jesus' first disciples would have understood his promise, the chronology question aside. The Bible tells us that the prophets of ancient Israel experienced the Spirit (1 Sam. 19:20–23; Ezek. 3:12; 1 Peter 1:10–11; 2 Peter 1:21); many of them must have wished that all their people would experience the Spirit more fully (Num. 11:29). By the early seventh century B.C., Isaiah began to announce that God was going to make his Spirit more widely available. After judging his people, God would save and restore them and pour out his Spirit on them like water on dry ground (Isa. 44:3; compare 42:1; 59:21). During the exile in Babylonia, the prophet Ezekiel made the same announcement: God would wash his people with the pure water of his Spirit (Ezek. 36:26–27), revive them by his Spirit (37:14), and pour out his Spirit on them (39:29). The prophet Joel announced that God would pour out his Spirit on his people—again using the image of the Spirit as water—and they would prophesy like the prophets of old (Joel 2:28–29).

But a few centuries before Jesus, many Jewish people decided that this full restoration of the Spirit and prophets belonged entirely to the distant future. They came to believe that prophets had ceased in their own time (although they allowed that prophecy occasionally continued) and that the Spirit was usually no longer available to individuals. A few groups, such as the Essenes, who wrote the Dead Sea Scrolls, believed that the Spirit remained active among them, but most Jewish people believed the Spirit had been quenched to a large extent in the present era. They longed for the future era when God would restore his people and pour out his Spirit.

Although all Jewish people were familiar with Old Testament teachings on the Spirit, different Jewish groups emphasized different aspects of the Spirit. The two most frequent emphases were the Spirit of purification and (more commonly) the Spirit of prophecy. Some interpreters, especially the Essenes, recited Ezekiel's promise that God would purify his people from sin (Ezek. 36:26–27; see also 18:31; 37:14). Nearly all Jews (including, to a lesser extent, the Essenes) associated the Spirit with prophecy, an even more common emphasis in the Old Testament (Num. 11:25–29; 2 Sam. 23:2; 2 Chron. 15:1–7; 18:23; Micah 3:8). Jewish thinkers on the whole rarely commented on some ideas that became common in the New Testament—such as continual moral empowerment or God's presence within the individual believer. But Jewish readers of the New Testament would have readily recognized early Christian emphases on the Spirit of purification (being "born of water and the Spirit") and prophecy (the Spirit enabling Christians to prophesy or engage in other forms of strongly Spirit-led speech).

Many New Testament passages assume that readers understand the association of the Spirit with prophecy (Matt. 22:43; Luke 1:17; 2:27; 4:18; Acts 11:28; 21:4; 1 Cor. 7:40; 12:3; 1 Thess. 5:19; 1 Tim. 4:1; 1 Peter 1:11; 1 John 4:1–6; Rev. 1:10; 2:7; 3:6; 4:2; 14:13; 17:3; 19:10; 21:10; 22:17; compare 2 Thess. 2:2). These associations include empowerment to speak for God in evangelism (Matt. 10:20; Acts 1:8; 6:10; 8:29; 10:19; 11:12; 16:7; 2 Cor. 3:3–8; Eph. 6:17), revelation of the true understanding of the gospel

(1 Cor. 2:10–14; Eph. 1:17; 3:5), and apostolic miracles (Rom. 15:19; perhaps 1 Cor. 2:4). Other texts assume that we understand the import of the Spirit in giving life and in transformation (John 3:5–8; 1 Cor. 6:11; Gal. 4:29; 5:17–18, 22–23; 6:8; Jude 19). These two emphases to some extent represent the basic ideas about the Spirit over which many modern Christians have divided: the Spirit's role in conversion and the Spirit's role in empowering believers for speaking moved by the Spirit (tongues, prophecy, witness, etc.).

One, Two, or More Works of Grace?

As noted earlier, many Christians in the Wesleyan, Holiness, and Pentecostal traditions have argued for a second work of grace that frequently occurs after conversion. In such circles, the work is sometimes called "sanctification" or "baptism in the Holy Spirit." Some groups also distinguish between sanctification and baptism in the Holy Spirit, thus providing three works of grace. With some notable exceptions (such as many Puritan writers), the Reformed tradition normally argues that one receives everything at conversion.

As we have also noted, both traditions are largely correct in what they affirm. Most Christians, in fact, agree on the basic issues: The Spirit transforms us at conversion, but God can subsequently fill Christians with the Spirit in special ways and for special tasks. The disagreement over terminology stems primarily from the different ways the New Testament writers themselves speak about the Spirit. Because of the variety in the Spirit's work, Paul may refer to one aspect of the Spirit's work by the phrase "receiving the Spirit," while Luke may use the same phrase to refer to a different aspect. These writers do not contradict each other; God led them to emphasize different issues.[4]

Paul's Theology of the Spirit

Paul is clear that one receives all of Christ's provision at conversion. Those who try to add to the finished work of Christ, whether they be circumcizers in Galatia or mystics in Colosse, undermine the gospel itself. At conversion we were "sealed" in Christ for the day of redemption (Eph. 4:30); those who do not have the Spirit are simply not Christians (Rom. 8:9).

Some Christians who dispute this conclusion have tried to argue that "sealing" with the Spirit in Ephesians 1:13 occurs after believing the gospel, for the verb tense used here usually implies subsequence. The problem with this argument is that it focuses on a grammatical pattern rather than on context and the writer's style; exceptions to this typical grammatical pattern are abundant. Only a few verses later, where Paul uses the same construction, it cannot imply subsequence because if it did, it would mean that God exerted his mighty power in Christ *after* resurrecting him, rather than by resurrecting him (Eph. 1:19–20; compare Rom. 1:4). More importantly, the text indicates that this seal of the Spirit is a down payment guaranteeing our future inheritance at the redemption of our bodies (Eph. 1:13–14). If this sealing is subsequent to conversion, then conversion is inadequate to guarantee us a place in God's kingdom! We were sealed by the Spirit "for the day of redemption" (Eph. 4:30).

Paul is no less clear in other texts about receiving the Spirit. Whatever Luke means when he speaks of disciples "receiving the Spirit" (see below), Paul clearly means conversion. The Galatians want to earn their spiritual experience by coming up to the cultural standards of law-keeping Jewish-Christian missionaries. Thus, Paul emphasizes that they "received the Spirit" by faith, not by obeying the law (Gal. 3:2; compare 1 Cor. 2:12). The Spirit always comes as a gift rather than as something we earn (Rom. 5:5). Even in Ephesians 5:18, the command to be "filled with the Spirit" is passive, which might suggest receptivity to divine action. If the beginning of their life in the Spirit (conversion) was a gift, how could the Galatian Christians possibly hope to complete their Christian life by legalistic works (Gal. 3:3)?

In 1 Corinthians, Paul divides humanity into two groups: those who have the Spirit ("spiritual") and those who do not ("fleshly," or "natural"; 2:10–16). Of course the finished work of Christ does not force us to live according to the Spirit. Even though the Corinthian Christians were Spirit-people by virtue of their conversion (1 Cor. 6:11), by dividing and competing spiritually they were acting like the world. Paul uses two Greek expressions—one meaning "fleshlike," the other meaning "as if you were fleshly" (1 Cor. 3:1–3). Sometimes we don't act like the Spirit rules us, but Paul still balks at calling genuine Christians completely "fleshly."

Romans 8

Romans 8, which mentions the Spirit of God more than any other chapter in the Bible, makes the same point. To understand Romans 8 most fully, we should start in the previous chapter, the much debated Romans 7. Christians debate whether or not it depicts Paul's experience as a Christian; I am inclined to argue that the context and depth of sin depicted here exclude that approach. I would thus argue that the present-tense verbs are for vividness (like historical presents in the Greek of the Gospels). But if I am wrong (and I may be), we can all agree on this much: The focus of the chapter is life under the law (7:5–14).

The extent to which our lives resemble Romans 7 (if they do) is due to the fact that we struggle to achieve our own righteousness rather than accept and simply live out God's gift of righteousness in Jesus Christ. To counter some Jewish Christians' view that the law gave them a spiritual advantage, Paul insists that he too had once lived life under the law (7:9–14). Yet whereas most Jewish teachers felt that the law empowered people to overcome the evil impulse within them, Paul declared that for him it simply brought evil more into focus, until it controlled him. One could not achieve righteousness by depending on one's ability to fulfill the law. One died to sin only through Christ—through accepting the finished work of Christ and continually reaffirming it by faith (Rom. 6:1–11). Under the law, Paul said, he found that he was "fleshly," "sold into slavery to sin" (7:14). In Christ, however, he was "not in the flesh" (8:9) but had been redeemed from slavery to sin (6:18, 20, 22).

No longer was the law simply a death sentence. Now, written in the believer's heart, the law was the moral guidance of God's own Spirit (8:2; compare Jer. 31:33–34; Ezek. 36:26–27). No longer would sin dwelling in the person control the person (Rom. 7:17–18). Now the Spirit lives in the believer, and any professed believer who does not have this Spirit does not belong to Christ (8:9).

This does not mean we have arrived at our "promised land" yet, but we have certainly started on the way! In Romans 8, Paul borrows images relating to the time when God first saved his people Israel and applies these images to Christians: Like Israel, we "groan" because of our slavery (Exod. 2:23; Rom. 8:23); God has begun to free us from that bondage (Exod. 2:24; Rom. 8:15); God has adopted us as his children (Exod. 4:22; Rom. 8:14–16); he leads us on our way in the present time (Exod. 13:21; Rom. 8:14); and he has a future inheritance for us (Num. 33:53–54; Rom. 8:17), so that the fulfillment of our redemption awaits that future promised inheritance (Rom. 8:23).

From start to finish, Christians are people whose future hope is guaranteed by God's Spirit within them (Rom. 8:9–11, 14–16, 23, 26–27), just as God's presence with Israel was their guarantee of victory. Clearly anyone who does not have the Spirit in the Romans 8 sense is not yet saved. And if Paul believes in receiving the Spirit as a second work distinct from this work, he gives not the slightest clue here or anywhere else in his writings.

Is the Spirit Only Past Tense for Paul?

At the same time, Paul recognizes that believers can avail themselves of a continued "supply" of the Holy Spirit (Phil. 1:19).[5] He summons them to "remain filled with the Spirit" continuously (Eph. 5:18), and he expects them to walk in the Spirit and produce the fruit of the Spirit (Gal. 5:16–23)—a matter on which he exhorts them precisely because they were falling short. Perhaps his view that God continues to "give" (present tense) his Spirit to the Galatians also implies a continuing supply of God's power (Gal. 3:5). (Although it could refer to the continuing experience of welcoming newcomers into the community, Paul nowhere else in the letter has newcomers in view.)

In other words, although all God's fullness becomes ours in Christ at the moment of our conversion, we still have to actualize that fullness in our daily lives. Returning to our analogy, it is one thing to be dead to sin in Christ—that is accomplished at conversion (Rom. 6:3–4; Col. 3:3). It is quite another to live like we are dead to sin (Rom. 6:11–14; 8:13; Col. 3:5). Any Christian who has sinned since his or her conversion recognizes this difference. Likewise, any Christian who has faltered in his or her witness or sensitivity to God's leading recognizes the need for a greater dependence on the Spirit's power, to which God has given us full access in Christ.

Christian Experience of the Spirit in Acts

When God's Spirit inspired the Bible through chosen people obedient to his leading (Rom. 1:2), he worked through their distinctive styles and modes of expression. That is why Isaiah reads different from Jeremiah, Jeremiah from Ezekiel, and so on. God even had a special nickname for Ezekiel—"son of man," or "human one"—which he did not apply to most of his prophets. These differences reflect the very nature of language—there is more than one way to say something. This is one reason we dare not jump to the conclusion that a particular phrase means the same thing in every passage or for every writer. Sometimes it plainly means something different. That is why James and Paul do not contradict each other even though they say very different things about faith; they are using their terms differently (Rom. 4:5; James 2:14). By "receiving the Spirit," John or Paul may refer to a particular aspect of the Spirit's work, while Luke may refer to a different one.

We noted earlier that Jewish people in the first century held various views about the Holy Spirit. Whereas John and Paul blend two of these emphases together (new birth and prophetic empowerment: compare 1 Sam. 10:6, 10), Luke's writings focus almost exclusively on prophetic empowerment. Thus, being "filled with the Spirit" normally results in some sort of prophetic speech (Luke 1:15, 41–42, 67; Acts 2:4; 13:9–10) or witness (Acts 4:8, 31; only 9:17 lists no effects, and 13:52 alone appears to constitute an exception).

Whereas one might think, from reading Paul's writings, that baptism in the Spirit and receiving the Spirit occur at conversion (but filling afterward), Luke seems to identify this initial filling of the prophetic Spirit with the baptism in the Spirit (Acts 2:4 fulfills 1:4–5; see 2:33, 39) and "receiving the Spirit" (2:38–39). The Spirit could "come on" believers (as he came on the prophets of old) when they "receive" him (10:44, 47; 19:2, 6), an experience identified with the Pentecost experience of the first disciples and called being "baptized in the Holy Spirit" (10:47; 11:15–17; note also the expression "poured out" in 10:45). Thus, the Samaritans could be converted yet not have "received the Spirit" in the sense in which Luke means the phrase (8:15–16; see discussion below).

Even for Luke, however, conversion is the only prerequisite for receiving the Spirit (Acts 2:38). On the level of direct theological statements, Luke probably would have preached exactly the same message as Paul or John: You receive the Spirit when you accept Christ as Lord and Savior. But on the level of experience, he seems to indicate that at least some people encounter a fuller prophetic empowerment of the Spirit after conversion. We dare not underestimate the significance of Luke's testimony, because Acts is the only New Testament book that directly depicts early Christian experience (although we may infer other aspects of that experience from letters that address it). Rather than interpreting half of the examples in Acts in a way that harmonizes them with Paul, perhaps we need to look at Acts to understand how the New Testament's theological statements function in practice. Luke apparently intends us to interpret his direct statement in Acts 2:38 and his narrative examples in light of each other.

I must add one caveat. I am employing phrases such as "receive the Spirit" and "be baptized in the Spirit" interchangeably. Technically, Luke explicitly employs the expression "baptized in the Holy Spirit" in only two instances: with reference to Pentecost (Acts 1:5; compare 2:1–4) and in Peter's description of the conversion of Cornelius's household (Acts 11:15–16; compare 10:44–47). Some of my colleagues therefore argue that the expression applies only to conversion. I would respond that Acts uses a variety of synonymous expressions that it identifies with one another (as I noted a few paragraphs above) and that it applies these to the experience of empowerment whether or not it happens at conversion (as noted below).

Thus, I would apply the expression to the whole sphere of the Spirit's work and think that Luke focuses on a particular aspect of that work that is not always simultaneous with conversion. But my primary interest in this chapter is the experience and its effects, rather than the precise terminology. What I hope will persuade all my readers at the least is that Luke shows us that experiences of empowerment by the Holy Spirit are desirable, even after conversion. Luke emphasizes this special empowerment for crossing cultural boundaries and evangelizing the world, and I believe that he reports Christians sometimes experiencing this empowerment after conversion.

Examples of Receiving the Spirit in Acts

Sometimes the Spirit came at conversion, even in Acts. Although some have argued that Cornelius and his household (Acts 10:2) were believers before Peter preached, the evidence of the text argues otherwise. Acts elsewhere testifies that God sent Peter precisely so that these Gentiles could hear the gospel, believe, and be saved, having their hearts cleansed by faith (11:14; 15:7–11). Peter had earlier declared that all who repented and were baptized would receive the gift of the Spirit (2:38), and the conversion of Cornelius's household fits this promise perfectly, except for the matter of sequence. Hearing the gospel, they immediately were baptized in the Holy Spirit, even before they had received water baptism (10:44–48; 11:15–17). (It was a good thing it happened this way too, or Peter's companions may have wanted to circumcise them first.) Here the theology of the Spirit worked out in practice exactly as it did in theory (in 2:38): A person received the Spirit in his overwhelming fullness through faith at the moment of conversion.

Yet does the principle always work this easily in practice? Most Christians, for instance, do not experience an equally dramatic overwhelming of the Spirit at conversion as this text describes. On that point, at least, we do not make this passage a universal model but allow for some variety in experience. The gospel declares that we died to sin when we accepted Christ, which means that the normal Christian life should be sinless (including perfect thoughts and attitudes). Yet most Christians I know did not begin living such "normal" Christian lives immediately at conversion (or do so even now), although deliverance from sin is implicit in our conversion. It is the standard we should look for, but we should not declare a conversion inauthentic if all its anticipated fruits do not sprout forth at once. Baptism in the Spirit may provide another kind of delayed action.

Other examples of conversions in Acts that mention the Spirit's coming are not as simple as Acts 10. Some examples do not explicitly mention the Spirit at all, offering no evidence in either direction. In other cases, Luke notes only an encounter with the Spirit after conversion. Paul appears to have accepted Christ's lordship before being filled with the Spirit for the first time (9:17). In Acts 9:5 Paul acknowledges Jesus' identity. Some writers may overemphasize Paul's understanding of Jesus at this point, suggesting that his entire Gospel was implicit in this revelation. Nevertheless, Paul apparently had made at least the basic acknowledgment necessary to be a Christian. Once he recognized that Jesus was Lord, he submitted himself to obey whatever Jesus said (Acts 9:5–6, 8; 22:10; 26:15–16). In contrast to what some writers suggest, Paul's "Lord" here hardly means merely "sir"; the character of Jesus' revelation to him was similar to Old Testament manifestations of God's glory and would leave Paul little doubt what Jesus' lordship actually involved.

True, Paul may not "officially" have been a Christian until his baptism (22:16), but this does not mean he had not yet made his inward commitment to Christ. Jewish people had Gentiles baptized as an act of conversion to Judaism, so Jewish people would understand baptism as an act of conversion. This understanding should not suggest, however, that the Spirit waits to transform the repentant heart until water is applied to the body. The New Testament picture of baptism can be explained by the analogy of an engagement ring: A man may ask a woman to marry him, but usually she wants more than his request—she wants to see the ring. Baptism makes it official, as a public testimony of one's commitment to Christ, but baptism is the result of (rather than the cause of) one's inward commitment. If my understanding is correct (and I did hold this understanding of baptism before I became a Baptist), Luke shows us that Paul had already submitted to Christ's call three days before being filled with the Spirit.

Whether or not one agrees that Paul's faith in Christ preceded his empowerment by the Spirit, most readers will agree that believers can be "filled" with the Spirit after conversion. It is the language of "receiving" the Spirit (which does not appear in this passage) that bothers some people. So we must look at two other passages. "Receiving" the Spirit appears in some form in 1:8; 2:33, 38; 8:15–19; 10:47; 19:2; the Spirit is called a "gift" in 2:38; 8:20; 10:45; 11:17. These passages seem to apply specifically to initial reception of prophetic power, more narrowly than being "filled" with the Spirit, which can happen more than once (2:4; 4:8, 31; 9:17; 13:9, 52). (Luke also used "filled" to describe sin or other negative behavior, 5:3, 17; 13:45; 19:28–29.)

Acts 19 speaks of "certain disciples" receiving the Spirit. "Disciples" refers to Christians elsewhere in Acts, including the description "certain disciple(s)" (9:10, 36; 16:1), as classical Pentecostal scholars point out.[6] At the same time, these particular disciples had only received John's baptism and had not yet heard that the Holy Spirit had come, which suggests that they left Palestine before Pentecost and were not in fellowship with Christians. In other words, scholars who argue that these particular disciples were probably disciples of John, rather than Christians, are probably right.

Nevertheless, they do not receive the Spirit in the Lukan sense at the exact moment of their fuller faith in Christ or their Christian baptism; they receive it afterward when Paul lays hands on them (19:6). How long it took them to reach water for baptism is uncertain; perhaps they could have used fountains or public baths or the nearby river. We might guess that this took at least half an hour, but without knowing where they were located in Ephesus (near a synagogue? near the agora, or marketplace, where Paul worked?) we cannot be sure. In any case, these disciples were converted *at least* a few minutes before their baptism. Otherwise, did they receive the Spirit in conversion through the laying on of hands? (If that is what the text teaches, we would definitely have to adjust the way we do altar calls, at least in Baptist churches.) Conversion often involves a process, as some argue, but unless we believe in spiritual purgatory, surely faith and not the laying on of hands is the point at which one passes from spiritual death to spiritual life.

162

The Samaritans in Acts 8

Acts 2 speaks of believers receiving the Spirit after they have already been following Christ, but many interpreters consider this example an exception. Although I suspect that Luke intends it in many respects as a model rather than as an exception, for the sake of argument I will turn instead to Acts 8, where people apparently are converted and then afterward receive the Spirit.

Some interpreters, such as John MacArthur, consider Acts 8 another exception, due to the transitional period covered by Acts. But interpreters who treat examples of subsequence in Acts as exceptions should honestly acknowledge what their approach implies. If only reception of the Spirit at the moment of conversion (Acts 10) is normative, we must explain as exceptions instances in which believers received the Spirit in some sense after conversion (anywhere from a few minutes to a few days; see Acts 2, 8, 9, and 19). When four of our five biblical examples are "exceptions," however, one is tempted to question the validity of the "rule."

Acts is history, but very few Acts scholars today would ignore that Luke teaches theology through his history, a fact that I. Howard Marshall, Charles Talbert, and Robert Tannehill among others have forcefully demonstrated. Paul believed that we could derive theology from history (1 Cor. 10:6, 11; 2 Tim. 3:16; see also this book's appendix). While not every example is a positive or universal one, examples of God's working that do not fit our paradigms may require us to adjust our paradigms.

Luke does not address all early apostolic history, but he emphasizes those features that advance the themes that will equip his audience. Given that ancient writers normally expected readers to draw morals from their narratives, the burden of proof rests on those who contend that Luke's history does not teach theology, rather than on those who contend that it does.

To be sure, most of the events Luke reports are exceptional in some sense, narrating the carrying forth of the gospel (with the attendant Christian baptism and the gift of the Spirit) to different groups of people. But this hardly means that Luke wants us to think that patterns he establishes among different groups ceased in his own day. Rather, he wants us to recognize that this pattern follows all Christians regardless of their background. Being filled with the Spirit should be a normal part of all Christians' lives.

Acts presents Philip, like Stephen, in an unambiguously positive light (6:3–7; 8:4–5), for, unlike the apostles, he was ready to begin crossing cultural barriers from the start. The inhabitants of a leading Samaritan city, perhaps ancient Shechem, responded with joy to Philip's preaching and

healing ministry (8:6–8). This kind of joyous response also characterized Paul's ministry (13:48, 52), although most of Paul's audiences also
included hostile responses alongside the receptive ones. The description
of signs and wonders sounds like those God worked through other of his
servants in Acts (2:43; 3:6–7; 4:30; 5:12–16; 6:8; 14:3; 19:11–12). Philip
was preaching "Christ" (8:5) and "the good news of God's kingdom"
(8:12), just as Paul later did (20:25; 28:31). One would think that Philip
understood the gospel, understood what was essential for conversion,
and knew better than to baptize those who had not yet committed themselves to Christ.

The text also tells us that the Samaritans "believed" (8:12)—a term
applied elsewhere in Acts to saving faith (for example, 4:4; 10:45; 11:17;
14:1–2; 15:7, 9; 16:1; 17:12, 34; 19:18), especially when accompanied
by baptism, as here (16:31–34; 18:8). The text indicates that they
believed "Philip proclaiming the good news of the kingdom"; that is,
they embraced the gospel. Everywhere else in Acts where followers of
Jesus offer baptism, it is because those being baptized have accepted the
gospel (2:41; 9:18; 10:47; 16:33; 18:8; 19:5). They "accepted God's word"
(8:14), language that throughout Acts normally refers to conversion
(2:41; 11:1; compare 17:11). If these baptized believers who received
God's message with joy were not converted, is anyone in the entire Book
of Acts converted?

Some object that Luke does not mention the Samaritans' repentance.
Repentance seems to be assumed as a part of faith and baptism; after 2:38
it is mentioned (11:18; 13:24; 14:15; 17:30; 20:21; 26:18), but rarely in
descriptions of conversions. If we doubt all conversions in Acts in which
repentance is not explicitly mentioned, very few converts in Acts may be
accepted as true converts. Luke generally includes the notion of repentance
in his descriptions of faith and baptism, whether or not he states it explicitly. Similarly, baptism is often assumed in the term *believed*; here, however,
it is explicitly mentioned, providing clearer testimony of conversion than
some other examples of conversion in Acts.

Yet these new Christians still need to "receive" the Holy Spirit (8:15),
although this is the same expression Acts 2:38 promised in response to conversion (10:47; 19:2). The promise was available upon conversion but apparently had not yet been appropriated. Whether the early Christians regarded
this delay as normal or not—the apostles do seem to have been concerned
about it—a delay is plainly in view. Even if abnormal, such a delay would
count as evidence that delays can happen, for whatever reason.[7]

Responses to Acts 8

Is there any other way to explain the postconversion reception of the
Spirit in Acts 8? Indeed there is. James Dunn, whose excellent classic work
on the New Testament's teaching about the baptism in the Spirit is in most
respects quite helpful, argues that the Samaritans were not genuinely converted. In contrast to many scholars before him who suggested that the
Samaritans must have received the Spirit earlier with the manifestation
coming later (John Calvin, F. F. Bruce, G. R. Beasley-Murray), or that this
account refers to a second reception of the Spirit (most Roman and Anglo-
Catholics [for confirmation] and Pentecostals), Dunn contends that the
Samaritans were not converted until, in effect, the Jerusalem apostles came
to lay hands on them.[8]

If Dunn's interpretation of the text provided a model of conversion, it
would suggest an extraordinary precedent (one that, fortunately, Dunn
himself does not draw): People may receive God's Word with joy, may
believe, may receive Christian baptism, yet may still require apostles to
lay hands on them to complete their conversion! Worse yet, the text
would call into question Luke's usual terminology for conversion and leave
one wondering if baptism and faith in the gospel of Christ are sufficient
for salvation.

Dunn seeks to avoid this conclusion by presenting Luke's use of the terminology in Acts 8 as exceptional. But a survey of Luke's use of terminology (below) indicates that the variations are too subtle for the average pre-
Dunn reader of Acts to catch them. Since most of Luke's first audience
would have simply heard Acts read in church services, Dunn's overly subtle case would have surely eluded them. Instead, I believe they would have
read this text largely as Pentecostals do.

Dunn's thesis, based on other New Testament passages, does not permit
him to accept a postconversion experience with the Spirit here:

> The problem of Acts 8, long the chief stronghold of Pentecostal (baptism in
> the Spirit) and Catholic (Confirmation) alike, centres on two facts: the
> Samaritans believed and were baptized; they did not receive the Spirit until
> some time later. The problem is that in the context of the rest of the NT
> these facts appear to be mutually exclusive and wholly irreconcilable.[9]

But must one force the details of Acts 8 (as I believe Dunn does) to fit
"the rest of the New Testament"? Or might a more plausible explanation
exist? As Clark Pinnock puts it, referring to Dunn's own belief that vari-

ous New Testament writers might articulate their message in different ways, "Ironically, at this point at least, there is greater diversity in the New Testament than even Jimmy Dunn is prepared to grant!"[10]

Dunn argues that the Samaritans' conversion was not genuine by appealing to what he thinks are special irregularities in the narrative.[11] He contends that Samaritans were superstitious and easily misled by magic. But ancient texts tell us the same about most other ancient peoples, not least the people of Ephesus (Acts 19:18–19), where some people also believed and received the Spirit (Acts 19:1–6). He further argues that the way the Samaritans "believe" here constitutes only intellectual assent, in contrast to saving faith, because Luke uses a Greek case called the dative. If this argument sounds strong to those who do not know Greek, one should keep in mind that Dunn provides only two examples of "believe" with this dative meaning, neither of which is clear. Luke usually employs the dative with "believe" when the object of faith is a person, with absolutely no indication that the faith is defective (for example, Acts 16:34; 18:8; 27:25). Because few "rules" in first-century Greek functioned without exception, arguments from grammar may be helpful but must always be examined carefully.

Further, apostolic baptism always presupposes faith in Christ (22:16), and the apostles accepted Philip's baptism of the believing Samaritans as legitimate. We know that the apostles accepted the Samaritans' baptism because, in contrast to Acts 19:5 (a defective baptism by John alone), they do not rebaptize the Samaritans.[12] Dunn is correct that Simon the sorcerer's initial faith did not seem to prove as enduring as that of the Samaritans (8:18–24), but Luke (no less than the rest of the New Testament) requires perseverance as well as an initial profession of faith (whether to prove one's salvation, as some hold, or to keep it, as others hold). As Ervin points out, Simon proving a false or apostate convert tells us no more about the reality of the Samaritans' faith than Judas's apostasy tells us about that of the Twelve (Acts 1:17).

Gordon Fee is a Pentecostal scholar who, like Dunn, does not differentiate baptism in the Spirit from conversion; rather, he regards baptism in the Spirit as the experiential dimension of conversion. Nevertheless, he also finds Dunn's case in Acts 8 weak. He thinks that the point in Acts 8 is not subsequence, which admittedly does not appear to be the ideal for the Christian experience. (Note that the apostles sought for the Samaritan converts to receive the Spirit as quickly as possible.) Rather, this passage emphasizes "the experiential, dynamic quality of the gift of the Spirit" that completes the conversion experience. Fee believes that the church in later centuries largely abandoned this experiential dimension of conversion through not expecting it. He is not implying that those who lack the experience are unconverted but (if I have understood him correctly) that most Christians have settled for less than their spiritual birthright as Christians.[13]

My approach, which emphasizes prophetic empowerment more than an experiential dimension of conversion, appears somewhat different from Fee's (though it seems closely related in practice). Though Fee is correct that in Acts it was quite normal for Christians to experience the full working of the Spirit at conversion, in my view Acts 8 does allow that this experience of prophetic empowerment (implicitly available in conversion itself) may occur after conversion. (My own experience actually fits Fee's view as well as my own, but it does not fit that of most other committed Christians I know. In the final analysis, of course, our experience may be helpful but is not the ultimate norm anyway.)

In any case, however, much of the disagreement on the relationship of "receiving the Spirit" (in the Lukan sense) to conversion is semantic. Unless one takes Dunn's view here, these Christians plainly experienced something that the apostles considered essential for Christians, and experienced it after conversion. Such delay may not have been the ideal either then or today, but Acts shows us real Christian experience, not just the theological ideal. Real Christian experience is where the church usually lives, even if we are seeking to experience the ideal.

Only Two Experiences in Acts?

While Christians in Acts sometimes entered this new sphere of spiritual experience shortly after conversion (Acts 8:14–17; 9:17; see also 1:4–5; 19:5–6), sometimes they experienced it during or almost simultaneous with their conversion (Acts 10:44; 11:14–15; almost simultaneous, 19:4–6). What may surprise some readers, however, is that Spirit-empowerment did not stop with what some call a "second work of grace," even among those who had undoubtedly received a full "dose" of the Spirit by that point.

For example, Peter and John were unquestionably among those who received the Spirit on Pentecost (Acts 2:1–4, 14), but they later received additional power for a special circumstance, power reminiscent of God's Spirit "coming on" his prophets or other servants in ancient Israel (Acts 4:8; see Judg. 6:34; 13:25; 14:19; 1 Sam. 10:6; 19:20). Likewise, Paul was filled with the Holy Spirit shortly after Acts 9:17, but God filled him anew for a special situation in Acts 13:9. (The terminology of "filling," at least, provides no clear distinction between the filling in 13:9 and what we might call his initial filling in 9:17 or the church's initial filling in 2:4.) Whole assemblies of people also experienced outpourings of the Spirit in fervent prayer meetings (4:31 and 13:52). Other experiences with the Spirit undoubtedly occurred; Luke merely provides samples of the Spirit's works, usually encountered during prayer or ministry of the Word.

In other words, Acts, like Paul, is not simply calling us to a second (or third, or fourth) spiritual experience. As D. A. Carson says, "Although I find no biblical support for a second-blessing theology, I do find support for a second-, third-, fourth-, or fifth-blessing theology."[14] Acts summons us to a Spirit-empowered life, by whatever initial and continuing experiences we are introduced into it. That is, the one book of the New Testament that most vividly portrays early Christian experience does not allow us to settle for a purely intellectual, rational examination of faith. While we do need the rational aspect of the faith (for example, Acts 19:9; Titus 1:9), the very Bible we rationally study invites us also to *experience* God's power in and through us.

On the one hand, Acts challenges many Pentecostals and charismatics who are satisfied to pray in tongues but neglect God's power in other ways (especially power for witness). On the other, it challenges many non-Pentecostals who are satisfied with a static devotional life devoid of real passion or power. That is, Acts challenges *most* of the church to a deeper encounter with God's Spirit. If my observations of today's church are accurate, I suspect that those most clearly experiencing God's power like that found in Acts are those living on the cutting edge of evangelism—Christians challenging the powers of darkness on their own turf by reaching unevangelized and often hostile people with the gospel. When those who are born of the Spirit enter crisis situations in obedience to God's call, they learn dependence on God's Spirit.

Second-work Pentecostals and their theological cousins in the Wesleyan and Holiness traditions have brought a gift to the rest of Christ's body by reminding us that we all need an experiential empowerment of the Spirit, just as other traditions have rightly emphasized the need to depend on the finished work of Christ. Whether we think of that empowerment as implicit in our conversion, in our water baptism, or in a second or third special work, we recognize that in practice we must yield more fully to God's grace and power in our lives.

The primary issue in Acts, however, is not subsequence or lack of sub-sequence. Although it was theologically ideal to receive the full impact of the Spirit at conversion, whether people had the experience of empower-ment was more important than when they received it. Have we yielded ourselves the way God wants us to, either at conversion or afterward, to the overwhelming direction of the Spirit in uttering praise, prophecy, or witness? That the apostles laid hands on the Samaritan Christians to make sure that they received the Spirit shows that they regarded receiving the Spirit in this empowerment sense as normative, something Christians need to have.

Luke nowhere suggests that we need this particular work of the Spirit for salvation or spiritual virtue; it is a special empowerment for evangelism and the work of the kingdom. People differ over whether all Christians receive complete access to this power at their conversion (I believe they do receive full access, though not always the full experience); they also debate what kind of manifestations may accompany the believer's experi-ence of this empowerment (we discuss one of these debates in the follow-ing chapter). But aside from these issues, the fact remains that in practice we need the Spirit's power. The Spirit is not just something we *have*; the Spirit is someone whose power we need to embrace and depend on. Because we seek to cultivate an intimate relationship with God, we can seek him for his power and activity in our lives. If Luke wrote Acts to teach us any-thing in particular, he expects the missionary church to be a Spirit-empow-ered church in experience, not just in theory.

Conclusion

We are complete in Christ and dead to sin, but in practice that means neither that all of us always live accordingly nor that we always appropri-ate the power of the Spirit that enables us to do so. Conversion gives us access to all we need, but neither conversion nor a single experience after conversion frees us from the need to seek God's empowerment in practice. That means we seek not a single experience but a continuing relationship, daily encountering our master in the power of his Holy Spirit, living out of the power already imparted to us when we became followers of Jesus Christ. But if we become more yielded to his power in our lives through such expe-riences as Acts describes, then by all means we should be ready to encounter God in such ways.

All Christians must cultivate a deeper dependence on the Spirit's power in our daily walk of obedient faith in God. I am sure that I, at least, would not dare to face my calling and the conflicts that my calling entails without the Spirit's help. Whether I am offering outreach lectures on secular campuses about the historical reliability of the Gospels or lecturing to ministry students in my seminary classes about matters of faith and obedience, I need the Spirit's strength, guidance, and boldness.

While much of the contemporary church has divided over whether baptism in the Spirit occurs at or after conversion, we have often neglected the sense of exactly what this baptism in the Spirit means for our daily lives in Christ. Whichever view we take concerning the chronology of Spirit baptism (some readers may, with us, opt for both), all believers need to know what the Spirit means in practical terms for our relationship with Christ.

What is baptism in the Holy Spirit? Aside from debates about how much of God's empowerment occurs at what point in a believer's life, the baptism in the Holy Spirit includes God's empowerment for the mission he has given us, his church. I have summarized some of the diverse emphases about this power earlier in the book (in the chapters on evangelism, the Spirit's fruit, and salvation). God has made us new by his Spirit and now enables us to live holy lives and build up our fellow believers by the Spirit's fruit and gifts (Paul). God has washed us, causing us to be born from him with a new character (John). Through the empowerment of God's Spirit, we are called to take Jesus' message both to those around us and to the ends of the earth (Acts). Through the empowerment of God's Spirit, Jesus prepares us to face the conflicts involved in our mission, confronting and defeating the devil at the point of human need (Mark). The Spirit transforms us when we come to Christ; from that point forward we must continue to depend on his power to carry out the mission Jesus gave us.

9

Tongues and the Spirit

When I was a graduate student at Duke, Julie, a Catholic undergraduate working with Young Life, asked me curiously about prayer in tongues. I talked with her about the subject, and she sounded intrigued but assured me that it would never happen to her. About a month later, however, she was praying quietly with a group of other Young Life staff, and her quiet prayer began to come out in another language.

One day I was talking with Missy, the Episcopalian treasurer of our InterVarsity group, when Julie walked up. Julie and I started discussing her new experience. I suddenly realized that we might be scaring Missy. "Missy, is this disturbing you?" I inquired, trying to be sensitive.

"Oh, no, I pray in tongues," Missy responded.

I smiled. "A number of people in the InterVarsity chapter have told me they do it privately," I remarked, "but none of them wants me to tell anyone else. They think people will think them strange if others find out."

"Does Derek pray in tongues?" Missy inquired. Derek was the Southern Baptist large group leader. I hesitated. Derek didn't want anyone to know.

"You'd better ask Derek," I suggested. At that moment, Derek appeared out of nowhere; West Campus is fairly large, so this was a significant "coincidence."

"Hey, guys, what's up?" Derek asked.

"Derek, do you speak in tongues?" Missy pressed immediately. Derek paused, lowered his face, and quietly admitted it. "I do too!" Missy declared.

"You do?" Derek rebounded happily. We decided to go up to Missy's room and have a little "charismatic" prayer meeting to celebrate. As we were preparing to do so, however, Alison, a Presbyterian freshman from the group, walked up.

"Hey, guys, what's up?"

"Ah, we're going to pray," Derek responded nervously.

"Oh, cool. May I join you?" she asked.

"Of course," we responded, starting to march up the stairs of Missy's residence hall. Before reaching Missy's room I decided I'd better check whether it would bother Alison if anyone prayed in tongues.

"Oh, no, I pray in tongues too," Alison replied. After that the Christians who secretly prayed in tongues started coming out of the closet.

For Somebody, Anybody, Everybody, or Nobody?

In this chapter I will try to represent fairly the best arguments for both the traditional Pentecostal position and that of those who affirm the gifts but doubt that tongues always accompanies baptism in the Spirit. The arguments for each side are better than the other side usually gives them credit for.

Before discussing the issue, however, we should place it in perspective. Variously gifted parts of Christ's body can help one another by sharing their gifts rather than by negating others' gifts, whether the gift be tongues or wisdom or knowledge. Those who have never experienced particular gifts can learn much from the experiences of those who have experienced them. Similarly, most Christians can learn more about how to read the Bible from those who know and understand it best, about God's concern for the broken and wounded from those who have been through pain and learned to share others' pain, and so on. We are one body, and we need one another's gifts. If Satan's kingdom cannot stand if divided, we must also question whether the church serves Christ best when members divide from one another. We are members of one another and should bring all our gifts together to build up his one body (Rom. 12:4–8; 1 Cor. 12:7).

The Controversy Today

Tongues is not listed among the fruits of the Spirit, nor is it the most dramatic gift of the Spirit. It remains, however, the most controversial gift of the Spirit today; hence, it warrants special treatment in this book. We discussed tongues briefly in the chapter on spiritual gifts, but in this chapter we discuss its proposed connection with baptism in the Holy Spirit.

Although a consensus seems to be emerging on many points about the Spirit, differences of opinion on tongues remain. The extreme and relatively rare view that tongues-speaking is mandatory for salvation is currently declining, even in circles that officially hold it. Beyond this, however, many divide. Some affirm that tongues is a valid gift for today and is useful for those who practice it, but it is not necessary for everyone. Most Pentecostals and many independent charismatics, however, see it as the initial physical sign of baptism in the Holy Spirit.

I will begin the discussion assuming that most readers accept tongues as a valid gift for today. Even most of those who do not affirm that tongues occurs today believe that those who do pray in tongues can be committed Christians, and they are willing to work with these Christians in the cause of Christ. Christians who refuse all fellowship with Pentecostals are, at least in the parts of Christendom I know, usually out of fellowship with most other parts of Christ's body as well.

The fact that tens of millions of Christians believe that tongues must accompany baptism in the Spirit (and tens of millions of other Christians do not) is reason enough to continue open dialogue about the issue in Christ's body today. There seems to be less middle ground on this issue than on some other matters, and readers from varying perspectives who find most of this book agreeable may disagree with my argument here. Not all readers will agree with all of my conclusions, but I hope to present the arguments for various positions clearly and fairly enough to further dialogue. My hope is that if Christians who hold different positions can at least hear one another's arguments clearly, we can understand why others hold their positions and work together more charitably. Christians need not agree on every matter, but we cannot afford to disrespect or mistrust one another.

Tongues-Speaking and Baptism in the Holy Spirit

The assertion that tongues-speaking always accompanies baptism in the Spirit may represent the major, irreconcilable difference between traditional Pentecostals and those who disagree with them, as D. A. Carson notes:

> If the charismatic movement would firmly renounce, on biblical grounds, not the gift of tongues but the idea that tongues constitute a special sign of a second blessing, a very substantial part of the wall between charismatics and noncharismatics would come crashing down. Does 1 Corinthians 12 demand any less?[1]

One can pray in tongues yet avoid the controversy. In the circles in which I move, most believers—including those of us who pray in tongues—treat tongues as simply one gift among many and as a useful resource for prayer (see our discussion of tongues in 1 Corinthians 14, under spiritual gifts).

Traditional Pentecostals and many charismatics, however, typically associate tongues with baptism in the Holy Spirit in Acts, and this position deserves a fairer evaluation than it usually receives outside Pentecostal circles. Whether or not we wish to connect tongues with that experience, we cannot avoid the fact that in Acts at least sometimes, and probably several times, the connection is made. The primary debate today is what *we* should make of that connection.

It is easiest to speak about tongues simply the way Paul does (a way of praying with one's spirit); most people who agree that the gift is for today find little offense in Paul's description. But we must also be fair to Luke's apparently more "Pentecostal" perspective in Acts. A central practical question is whether Luke provided a model that he expected all subsequent believers to duplicate. I believe that Luke did provide a model (see the discussion in the appendix as to what we can learn from accounts in the Bible); exactly what that model teaches us, however, is a more complex question.

Three times when believers in Acts "receive the Spirit," they speak in tongues; in at least two other cases, speaking in tongues is not expressly mentioned. Because we focus here on the evidence in Acts, I will concentrate on clarifying two positions: (1) the belief that tongues always accompanies the Spirit's empowerment depicted in Acts and (2) the belief that it is normal and not surprising, but also not mandatory, for tongues to accompany the Spirit's empowerment depicted in Acts.

My Experience with Tongues

It is helpful to readers if those who write about spiritual gifts share their background—whether charismatic, noncharismatic, or anticharismatic—since past experiences may shape how we approach the issue. My experience with tongues is so much a part of my Christian life that I must allow you to take it into account as you read how I address this issue.

Although I pray in tongues, my initial experience with tongues came entirely unexpectedly. I first heard the gospel on the way home from high school one day, and after arguing for forty-five minutes with the fundamental Baptists who shared it with me, I walked home trembling. Although I had been an atheist and found their intellectual arguments unconvincing, the Spirit was pressing me for a decision and would not stop pressing until I surrendered or told him to leave me. Within an hour I fell to my knees on my bedroom floor and acknowledged that, though I did not understand it, I accepted God's claim that Jesus died and rose to save me. "But I don't know how to be saved," I confessed. "God, please save me yourself." Instantly I felt something rushing through my body that I had never felt before, and I quickly jumped to my feet, wondering what was happening.

Though I had long doubted what little I knew of the claims of Christianity, I had also decided that if I ever did discover that Christianity was true, I would serve my creator with everything I was and had. I had even clandestinely asked God, if he was there, to reveal himself to me. I had wanted empirical evidence, but that day God confronted me first with the evidence of his presence. The power of his presence was so strong that I resolved to be a Christian henceforth, although I was not yet certain of exactly what details this commitment entailed. On Sunday I went to a church, and a pastor prayed with me to turn my life over to Christ. Assured now that I had accepted Christ "properly," I felt the same overwhelming presence of God I had felt two days before and this time decided to yield to it fully.

In a moment I was so overwhelmed with the awesome majesty and presence of God that I understood that only he could provide me adequate words with which to praise him. And because I intuitively understood that God knows all languages, it somehow did not surprise me when the Spirit gave me another language in which to praise him. For an hour or two I worshiped God in tongues—often punctuated with deep, cathartic laughter (which has recurred on occasion since)—experiencing a joy I had never known before. When I finished, I was convinced that the purpose in life I had long sought must be to promote the glory of Jesus Christ alone.

Over the years God provided other experiences (including learning how to read the Bible in context) that made this experience of prayer in tongues one experience among many, but it remains an important part of my personal prayer life. Having never read the Bible before that day or been exposed to speaking in tongues, I did not know "tongues" existed, nor did I hold preconceptions about what tongues should involve. God simply granted me the gift as an act of grace to a completely unchurched convert who desperately needed an overwhelming experience of his presence.

I recognize that everyone's experience is different, but I offer my own story as an example of how God might provide an experience similar to the ones in Acts for a person who had not been taught anything pro or con about tongues. I also mention it so you may evaluate how my experience may have shaped my perspective in ways of which I am not aware. I ask only that you be equally honest about how your own experience or nonexperience may shape the way you approach the biblical evidence.

Because the circles in which we move may affect the way we approach issues, I should also acknowledge that my personal experience is intensely pervaded by gifts such as tongues and prophecy, but many or most of my circles of fellowship and teaching are outside circles in which these are practiced. In addition, many of the charismatics with whom I currently fellowship are the sort of charismatics for whom speaking in tongues is a "normal" (common) but not "normative" (mandatory) evidence of the Spirit's work.[2] Other charismatic friends who believe it is "normative" nevertheless prefer to emphasize other distinctives they feel are more important.

Tongues comes up rarely in my work as a biblical scholar (it appears clearly in only six chapters in the Bible); further, none of my close friends who do not pray in tongues, including cessationists, have objected to me doing it, giving me little personal reason to make an issue out of it. As mentioned earlier in the book, many or most of my closest ministry colleagues, people I trust minister in the power of God's Spirit no less than I, do not pray in tongues. I think of Dr. Danny McCain, a friend in Nigeria whose ministry touches millions of lives; I dedicated a book to him, and his ministry looks "apostolic" to me in most ways. He affirms those who pray in tongues, but as of the time of this book's writing, he has not done it himself. I think of another friend in Africa who has given her life to working among the poor, especially to reaching and transforming prostitutes. She literally sacrificed all her possessions for the kingdom, holds back nothing from God's work, and strikes me as "apostolic" in some sense as well. (In her humility, she did not want me to use her name!) But though she also affirms tongues as a good gift, she has not yet received that gift herself. Would tongues refresh and strengthen them? They themselves may be open to that idea. But it is difficult for me to doubt that the Spirit empowers their ministries more powerfully—for the things God called them to do—than that of very many people who pray in tongues.

At the same time, I often see young believers pray in tongues when I pray for them to experience the empowerment described in the previous chapter. In these times of prayer, the vast majority of people I pray with dramatically sense the overwhelming presence of God's Spirit, many in ways they have never sensed before. Often (though not always) they begin to pray in tongues at that time; many others (though not all) end up doing so later (including some who insisted they never would!).

If I wanted to argue purely from my experience, it would probably push me toward the general consensus that tongues are useful but not a valid way to measure someone's spiritual commitment. Our experiences, however, are limited, so the question remains: What does the Bible teach?

Tongues as Evidence of the Spirit in Acts

Some texts appear to fit the traditional Pentecostal model better than many non-Pentecostals acknowledge. Although Luke's focus for baptism in the Spirit is evangelism rather than speaking in tongues (Acts 1:8), tongues clearly functions as the initial sign of baptism in the Spirit in Acts 2.

In that chapter, the hearers who recognize the languages demand, "What does this mean?" (2:12 NIV). Others in the audience charge the disciples with drunkenness (2:13). Peter responds to these comments in reverse order: The charge of drunkenness is absurd (2:15). Conversely, what this means (2:12) is clear: This is what Joel meant when he said the Spirit would be poured out and God's people would prophesy (2:16–18). And if that part of Joel's prophecy is fulfilled, then the time of salvation has also come (2:19–21). Peter regarded tongues as evidence that the Spirit had come, as evidence of the prophetic empowerment promised by Joel. Acts 2 thus becomes a model for the Spirit-empowerment of the church in Acts.

Does Luke intend for other Christians to follow this model? Interestingly, unlike some aspects of the Pentecost model, tongues are repeated later in Acts (Acts 10 and 19). Tongues-speaking evidences the reception of the

178 Gift and Giver

Spirit in Acts 10:46–47 ("they received the Spirit the same way we did"). It accompanies prophecy as evidence of prophetic empowerment in Acts 19:6 (perhaps suggesting that other kinds of inspired speech can serve the same function). Tongues-speaking is not mentioned at the initial reception of the Spirit among the Samaritan converts in Acts 8 or by Paul in Acts 9. However, many scholars point out that something tangible happened in Acts 8 (Simon saw and wanted it), and 1 Corinthians 14:18 indicates that Paul at some point did begin praying in tongues.

Because the narrative in Acts 9 predicts (but does not describe) Paul's reception of the Spirit, one cannot conclude from Luke's silence that tongues-speaking did not occur on that occasion. Still, one may conclude that whether or not it occurred, Luke did not seek to emphasize it at that point. Some Pentecostal scholars have argued that tongues accompanies baptism in the Holy Spirit the way water baptism accompanies conversion: Luke does not mention baptism after every conversion, but he expects the reader to infer it from the cases in which it is stated. Perhaps the experience of tongues was so typical in Luke's circle of Christianity, they argue, that readers simply assumed tongues accompanied baptism in the Spirit, even when tongues was not mentioned.

Conclusions from This Pattern and Objections

Traditional Pentecostals find in such observations a confirmation of their belief that speaking in tongues provides the initial physical evidence of baptism in the Holy Spirit. According to one version of early Pentecostal history, Charles Parham in December 1900 instructed his students to determine inductively and independently the evidence of baptism in the Spirit in Acts. When all the students independently arrived at the conclusion that tongues was evidence of baptism in the Holy Spirit, the group decided to pray for the gift. God initiated a revival movement, especially launched under William Seymour's direction at Azusa Street, that now counts over four hundred million Pentecostals and charismatics around the world. Seymour himself was so convinced that speaking in tongues was biblical that he began preaching it months before he experienced it himself.

Most traditional North American Pentecostals argue that tongues-speaking *always* accompanies Spirit baptism. Yet some Pentecostals disagree (especially Pentecostals in some other parts of the world, such as Chile and Germany), as do a significant percentage of nondenominational and mainline charismatics, including those of the growing Vineyard movement.

Given the evidence above, many of those who believe the gifts of the Spirit continue today concede that tongues often accompanied baptism in the Holy Spirit in Acts and fail to be surprised when the two occur together today. For reasons supplied in our appendix, "What Can Bible Stories Teach Us?" many concede that Acts provides models for the Spirit-filled church (especially where the Spirit himself acts directly), not solely a description of an early stage of the church.

But despite these concessions, noncharismatics, many charismatics, and some Pentecostals today point out that Luke's use of narrative to teach does not automatically guarantee consensus concerning what Luke wished to teach. Thus, British New Testament scholar James D. G. Dunn traces the initial reception of the Spirit through Acts and concludes that in every instance in which reception of the Spirit is described, Christians seem to have spoken in tongues. Thus, "the corollary is then not without force that Luke intended to portray 'speaking in tongues' as 'the initial physical evidence' of the outpouring of the Spirit." But Dunn goes on to note that while Luke focuses on such tangible evidences of the Spirit's presence, he also clearly includes praise (10:45–46), prophecy (19:6), and boldness (4:8, 31); and if Luke wished to emphasize tongues as the necessary evidence, he would have mentioned it more explicitly in Acts 8.[3]

Those who believe in tongues but who doubt that it always accompanies baptism in the Spirit thus can raise important objections to the view that tongues invariably accompanies baptism in the Holy Spirit. The question is not whether Luke is teaching something through his narrative (2 Tim. 3:16; see appendix); the question is simply *what* he is teaching. Because tongues is a form of inspired speech, Luke could often use it to inform readers that people in his narrative had received prophetic empowerment. Saying that genuine manifestations of tongues guarantee that prophetic empowerment has come need not, however, imply that prophetic empowerment always is accompanied by tongues. That is, because genuine tongues-speakers are baptized in the Spirit, this need not imply that all Spirit-baptized people must speak in tongues. (In the same way, one might reason that all true apostles are Christians, but not all true Christians are apostles.)

Luke's intention, as well as we can infer it from his text, is to demonstrate that the outpouring of the Spirit on Pentecost continues to mark the advance of Christianity to all peoples. Each stage in the expansion of the gospel in Acts is marked by prophetic empowerment empirically demonstrated, as in the church's first experience, with tongues. That is, Luke teaches us about the transcultural spread of the Spirit's work by means of the evidence of tongues, rather than about tongues by examples of people receiving the Spirit.

Why would Luke emphasize tongues more than other gifts or signs he could have mentioned? Remember that his central theme is Spirit-empowered cross-cultural witness (Acts 1:8). What more crucial sign could the Spirit offer that he is empowering us to cross cultural barriers? In this case, Luke might mention tongues at every available opportunity. If so, it is possible that when he does not mention it, it may not have occurred, at least not at that time.

Whatever one might wish to infer happened in the cases in Acts in which tongues are not explicitly mentioned, most readers note that the fact that Luke did not mention their occurrence suggests he is not intentionally *teaching* that tongues always accompanies Spirit baptism. And if he is not teaching it, they note, we lack a single New Testament passage that explicitly teaches the doctrine.

Round Two: Objections to Objections

Classical Pentecostals may respond, however, that this caveat does not settle the case against tongues accompanying baptism in the Spirit. Some have argued that even if the Book of Acts does not explicitly teach this doctrine, it may nevertheless serve as a window into early Christian experience. At the very least, Acts indicates a pattern in which tongues often accompanied the experience it describes. (This much is difficult to dispute; the pattern is in the text, even if Acts is too short to provide us many examples.)

Given the brevity and narrow focus of Acts, we can assume that the Spirit worked in many ways for which little clear record remains. Many important early Christian doctrines appear in the New Testament writings only because controversy surrounded them (for example, the Lord's Supper in 1 Cor. 11:17–34). The New Testament is not a doctrine manual written by a symposium of theologians but a collection of essential inspired writings from the earliest Christians commissioned by our Lord. Thus, claiming that no texts in the Bible *conclusively* prove the Pentecostal position is not the same as saying that this disproves the Pentecostal position. The usual classical Pentecostal view that tongues-speaking necessarily and immediately accompanies baptism in the Holy Spirit could still be true, attested to by some other means such as Pentecostal experience. Further, the close connection in Acts between tongues and baptism in the Spirit would have made the most sense to an audience who saw that the two frequently occurred together.

Non-Pentecostals will, however, also respond to this Pentecostal objection. If early Christians did not acknowledge that baptism in the Spirit had occurred unless the person began speaking in tongues, it is surprising that the rest of the New Testament does not preserve more testimonies to such a central evidence. Further, it is questionable whether even modern Pentecostal experience proves that tongues must always accompany baptism in the Spirit, at least immediately (unless one argues circularly that a powerful charismatic experience is not genuine Spirit baptism without tongues). Statistics suggest that a large percentage of Pentecostals do not speak in tongues! (Some argue that this is over half of all Pentecostals.[4] The Pentecostal argument from Scripture at this point is stronger than their argument from experience.) Some charismatics I know consider it presumptuous to insist that tongues accompanies baptism in the Spirit, as presumptuous as declaring that God heals without exception if we have enough faith.

Further, one may argue, most Pentecostals do not hold God to every other pattern in Scripture. Although in both Acts and 1 Corinthians tongues seems to be used only in prayer (see the discussion of tongues among spiritual gifts), some Pentecostals justify a "message in tongues" by insisting that God can do whatever he wants. I would accept this response; God can provide a "message in tongues" if he wants, whether because he has long done so or because he is willing to speak to us in a way that we expect to hear him.

Yet if the normal biblical pattern does not hold in all situations (God can, after all, do anything that does not contradict his nature), must God always confer tongues when baptizing his children in his Spirit? For instance, would God withhold the empowerment of his Spirit from those who had been taught to fear tongues? Would he wait to empower them for evangelism until they had overcome their fear of this specific gift? Most of us who move in noncharismatic circles have many Christian friends who live deeply Spirit-led lives without tongues, some of whom act more empowered for holiness and witness than many who speak in tongues. The addition of tongues might strengthen their prayer life still further, but they already have some greater gifts to offer the rest of Christ's body. Noncharismatics also point to Paul's claim that not all speak in tongues (1 Cor. 12:30). In the context, Paul is arguing that although we need all the gifts in the body of Christ, one should not regard one's own gifts as superior or inferior to the others.

Pentecostals usually respond to this argument in one of two ways. First, they traditionally argue that Paul here refers to the public gift of tongues rather than to private prayer language. (The context may support this distinction, though it may have more to do with the way the gift is being used than with an intrinsic difference between the two forms of tongues themselves.) Second, some Pentecostals also cite 1 Corinthians 14:5 to suggest that even if not all Christians speak in tongues, Paul thinks that it would be a good idea for them to do so. Whether one interprets 14:5 in light of 1 Corinthians 12:30 or the reverse, however, often depends on the view with which one begins, stalemating the arguments for either side on this point.

Differences among Pentecostals

Some charismatic writers have pointed out that the traditional Pentecostal position is not completely monolithic; some classical Pentecostals in fact rejected the position. Agnes Ozman (the first person to speak in tongues at the beginning of the twentieth-century Pentecostal revival), F. F. Bosworth, and other prominent early Pentecostals questioned whether tongues always accompanied Spirit baptism.[5] Indeed, even today it is mostly a shared experience rather than a common way of formulating that experience that connects those who pray in tongues in Pentecostal and various independent and mainline churches.

Perhaps most significantly, William Seymour, leader of the Azusa Street Revival, ultimately denied that tongues was "the evidence" of the baptism in the Holy Spirit. Seymour had originally accepted Charles Parham's teaching that tongues represented the initial sign of Spirit baptism, but when confronted with Parham's own behavior—reportedly including his white racist rhetoric directed against Seymour, who was black—Seymour reportedly came to question whether Parham was even saved, since he lacked the fruit of the Spirit in his life. Although Seymour continued to affirm the importance of tongues-speaking, he rejected the doctrine that tongues must always accompany Spirit-baptism. Considering it a false doctrine that bound God, he regarded it as a form of idolatry.[6]

Some others who affirmed supernatural empowerment also stressed that the Spirit's fruit is a clearer sign of the Spirit's work than tongues. Wesley accepted revelations, prophecies, healings, and so forth among his followers, but he emphasized that the true evidence of the Spirit was maturation toward Christian perfection. Some early Pentecostals also stressed love as the primary evidence. For instance, Pandita Ramabai, the leading figure in a major early-twentieth-century outpouring of the Spirit in India, stressed that while tongues was one sign of baptism in the Spirit, the essential and inevitable sign was love.[7]

Classical Pentecostals usually respond that the Spirit's fruit is an essential sign of his presence, but tongues-speaking is (as noted above) the most frequent mark of the initial experience depicted in Acts, a pattern most Pentecostals believe is normative.

Here is where the biblical evidence in the debate between many Pentecostals and non-Pentecostals ends: Acts shows that tongues often accompanies one's first filling with prophetic empowerment, but Acts by itself is hard-pressed to prove that it always must do so. Most non-Pentecostals therefore remain skeptical about whether we can conclude that someone is not filled (even in the Acts sense) because he or she has not spoken in tongues. Beyond this, the debate often becomes one of which side bears the burden of proof, because each side has often felt that the other side dismisses their side's spiritual experience.

Nevertheless, all those sensitive to the text should at least appreciate traditional Pentecostal scholars for bringing to our attention an inescapable feature of the accounts in Acts: In Acts, tongues frequently accompanies being filled with the Spirit for the first time, sometimes in conjunction with other Spirit-anointed speech such as prophecy.

Although Christians continue to dispute whether tongues occurs in every instance in Acts (and even more so whether it must regularly occur today), Luke uses tongues far more than any other sign to indicate that believers have received the Spirit's prophetic empowerment. By pointing to tongues, Pentecostals have reminded us that being filled with the Spirit in the Lukan sense is empowerment to speak God's message (Acts 1:8), an ability to speak with special sensitivity what the Spirit puts in our hearts (Acts 4:31; compare Eph. 5:18–20). I believe that Luke also intended us to see in this gift a sign that God has called his church to evangelize all peoples and cultures.

Whether by praying in tongues or by other means, all of us can profit by inculcating deeper sensitivity to the Spirit's leading in our words. Some of us who pray in tongues have found that spiritual sensitivity developed during prayer in a language we do not know has helped us pray and witness more effectively in the languages we do know. But ultimately, all Christians will agree that prayer and witness are more important than whether they are done in an unknown language.

Considering the Practical Issues

Entirely aside from the above questions, both charismatics and non-charismatics agree that our spiritual quest should emphasize the Spirit, not tongues. When we ask God to empower us to pray in tongues, should we be asking him for "evidence" that we have had a spiritual experience or for a fresh way to pray and worship him? Even if one believes that tongues was evidence of Spirit-reception in Acts (and in three cases Luke does mention it for that purpose), Acts does not suggest that Christians should *seek* tongues for this purpose.

I recall friends who went on long fasts, experienced visions, or witnessed boldly but who later rejected the Christian faith. Ultimately, any focus—no matter how good in itself—that replaces allegiance to Christ will become a counterfeit. Tongues, as every other gift, functions best when Christ rather than the gift summons our attention. I like to worship God in tongues for the same reason I like to worship him in English: God merits our worship, and our hearts are most at home when turned to him.

This book will not be able to reconcile the two positions on tongues and baptism in the Spirit that differ as much as do the classical Pentecostal and non-Pentecostal positions. Nevertheless, I hope that Christians in both groups will be able to understand why other Christians hold different views and recognize the depth of their spiritual commitment. We should not use the negative examples on either side to caricaturize an entire movement. Further, on the central issues, both sides can have more biblical common ground than differences. Biblically we should acknowledge that tongues often accompanies a spiritual experience described in the Book of Acts. We can also agree that what is most important about the experience is not tongues-speaking itself but empowerment for mission.

In practice, some of the traditional discussion may be less about initial evidence than about other concerns. One of the standard pragmatic reasons offered for traditional Pentecostal insistence on maintaining the "initial evidence" doctrine has been the concern that Pentecostals will stop seeking the ability to pray in tongues if the doctrine is abandoned. As long as traditional Pentecostals and charismatics believe they are the only people seeking the gift, many may continue to feel the pressure to make sure as many as possible of their number function in that gift. Yet if (as I suggest in my comments on spiritual gifts) tongues is a useful gift for private prayer and one may approach God in prayer for spiritual gifts, "necessary evidence of Spirit baptism" is not the only reason for seeking the gift. (Indeed, I have heard some Pentecostal scholars suggest that it is more Pentecostal to promote spiritual experience, not only gifts but other openness to God's Spirit, than to promote the fine points of this doctrine.)

Praying in tongues, like other forms of prayer, can add a new dimension to one's prayer life. Few of us would claim to be proficient in all forms of prayer, and most of us desire more help from the Spirit when we pray. This emphasis may also make immediate results seem less urgent, help us avoid the temptation to grade people spiritually on the basis of whether they speak in tongues, and prevent despair among those who have long sought the gift and not received it. (This is not to say that advocates of the tongues-as-evidence position want people to feel second-class because they have not spoken in tongues; yet I have known Christians who have felt this way).

I do not here propose a pragmatic test of truth that decides the genuineness of the classical Pentecostal position based on results. Pentecostals could as easily point to their success in worldwide evangelism as a pragmatic proof that their position has God's blessing (I suspect that at least their emphasis on the Spirit's empowerment does have God's blessing). My point is that one can maintain a strong appreciation for the gift yet articulate it in ways that will commend it to a wider cross-section of the body of Christ, ways that may actually lead to more people sharing the gift even if they do not share all details of classical Pentecostal theology.

Because most Christians today are not against speaking in tongues, as was the case in earlier eras, some Pentecostals have begun to feel that it is less important to focus as much attention on defending the doctrine as it was previously. Many other Christians, having learned from what Pentecostals offer, seem ready to move beyond the controversy over tongues and begin to explore all that God's Spirit has for the church (including, but not limited to, prayer in tongues).

Conclusion

I have tried to present both sides fairly. Since my own convictions do not fall exactly into any of the traditional "camps," I have tried to learn from the best biblical arguments of each. In my view, in Acts, God often demonstrated that he had empowered his people to speak prophetically across cultural barriers by enabling them to speak in tongues. The pattern in Acts suggests that we should not be surprised when God empowers his people in similar ways today. Luke does not report the pattern in every case, however, and we should therefore not claim that he was "teaching" it as mandatory for every case. Tongues are a good gift and helpful for prayer, but we dare not claim that some Christians lack a special empowerment of the Spirit simply because they do not pray in tongues.

When in doubt, most Christians fall back on denominational views, hopefully without disrespecting Christian brothers and sisters in different denominations. I believe, however, that most readers can agree on some practical issues clear from the New Testament witness: (1) Speaking in tongues is a biblical evidence of the Spirit's empowerment for evangelism (even though many of us remain doubtful that all Spirit-empowered people experience it); (2) tongues constitute a valid form of worship to God (see the chapter on spiritual gifts); (3) the purpose for desiring this gift should be the worship of God rather than spiritual elitism; and (4) tongues used for private worship can strengthen one's prayer life. If some Christians have overemphasized tongues in response to others who have played it down, they have at least called the church back to a biblical appreciation of the gift and, most importantly, called many to a hunger for deeper intimacy with God.

In light of the entire biblical perspective concerning the Spirit, we must focus on the Spirit's provision of an intimate relationship with our risen Lord Jesus and empowerment to make him known and to live out the fruit of God's character. We need the Spirit to transform our hearts to imitate Christ's character and to persevere through testings. Tongues is useful for prayer and can help cultivate our sensitivity to the Holy Spirit; for that reason, we can ask God for the gift, as for others. Though in his wisdom he does not grant every request, God usually delights to bless us with gifts that will draw us closer to him. We should therefore pray expectantly—and then worship however he empowers us.

But if we think ourselves filled with God's Spirit because we speak in tongues, yet neglect his call to evangelize the world and to stand for justice for the oppressed and for the righteousness of God's Word, we deceive ourselves. True, biblical Pentecostals and charismatics must live their whole lives in the power of God's Spirit. If all Christians began speaking in tongues tomorrow, that would not constitute revival. But if all Christians began loving Jesus and one another passionately enough to fulfill the Great Commission, we would experience a revival like the world has never before seen.

10

Why Discern the Spirit?

At age eighteen, after I had been learning to hear God's voice for about one year, I shared my new insight with some friends, one of them a new believer I will call Rhoda (not her real name). A month or two later I left for Bible college, and others discipled her. While I was away, Rhoda grew beyond me in her ability to listen to God's voice, and when I returned from Bible college, I found out that she was having visions. I had never had a vision, and I jealously complained to God that it wasn't fair for him to give visions to her and not to me. I was sure this situation was unfair because I had been a Christian over three years and she had been one less than one year. As you may guess, I was not very spiritually mature, despite my zealous desire for God in some respects.

I believe that Rhoda was indeed walking close to God. I now realize, however, that she was also in some spiritual danger, and had I spent less time being spiritually insecure, I might have proven more helpful to her. When I saw her, she quickly confronted me on why I was becoming a sterile academic. There was a brief period in my spiritual life when I did risk becoming a sterile academic, but this wasn't the time. (Ironically, my sterile period was actually when I began pastoring.) Nevertheless, I probably was too arrogant about the role of information, priding myself on having information that most of my friends didn't have.

On the other hand, Rhoda risked becoming arrogant about her own special ability to hear God in prayer. She explained that the Bible was a helpful record of other people's revelations, but she was getting her own now, so she did not feel badly that she could not spend as much time reading the Bible as she wanted. Less euphemistically, she wasn't reading the Bible much. I began to worry about her a little at that point.

One evening I was scheduled to meet with Rhoda, and before our meeting, I prayed and asked God to speak to me. My motives really left much to be desired: I knew Rhoda would have heard something from God recently, so I figured that I had better hear something from him too, or she would accuse me again of being unspiritual. Because he is gracious, God forgave my motives and spoke to me in prayer, pointing out to me another argument from Scripture I could use to defend the deity of Christ. While we were on the subject, I asked the Lord why he had said that he and the Father were one when in fact the Son is not the Father. He responded that he also prayed that his disciples would be one; that did not make them the same person. That connection had never occurred to me before, and I was quite happy to hear it.

When Rhoda showed up that evening, I eagerly shared with her my new insight about the deity of Christ. She waved her hand dismissively. "God showed me that months ago," she announced. My pride collapsed, again deflated. She insisted on taking me over to the home of the friend who had been discipling her and on the way began sharing with me her new revelation: There wasn't just a Trinity. Eventually, Christians would become God, the *fourth* person of the Trinity.

Although certain that she would chide me for my lack of spiritual insight, I objected, pointing out that the Bible didn't teach that. "Oh, I know," she responded. "The Bible was written a long time ago, whereas this truth was only revealed a few weeks ago."

"But the Bible teaches *against* it," I countered. She retorted that she wasn't saying we are gods; she simply meant we would become divine in the distant future. I pointed to Revelation 22, the final chapter in the Bible, where God's servants serve him before his face forever.

"It's farther in the future than that," she replied. By now we had arrived at the home of her friend, and she and her discipler were ganging up on me, noting that I was holding on to dogma and needed to get their new revelation from the Holy Spirit. Their rebukes of my lack of spirituality made me feel somewhat stubborn, but I kept responding from Scripture. (They said that we would each become saviors of other planets, like Aslan in the Chronicles of Narnia. They had gotten that "revelation" while reading C. S. Lewis.)

Finally, I learned part of the basis for their revelation: The discipler believed that Jesus and the Father were the same person because they were one, so being one with them would make us the same person as God too. Only later did I remember that in prayer earlier that night I had heard the Lord say something quite different on the same subject.

The point here is not that all insights we receive in prayer are wrong. The point is that if they are unscriptural, however, they are certainly wrong. Neither of us could persuade the other that evening; I clung tenaciously to my Bible, and they to their revelations.

Why Must We Discern the Spirit?

My dear friend Rhoda and her discipler both realized their error in time and returned to biblical views about the Trinity. Tragically, however, Rhoda fell away from the faith a year or two later, when she found much resistance in her charismatic church to some of her "prophecies." To this day I mourn when I recall the zeal with which she started her relationship with Christ and my failure to provide better support and correction when she needed it. Yet Rhoda was hardly alone in mistaken "revelations."

In earlier chapters we talked about hearing God's voice and about the Spirit's leading in evangelism and his empowerment for spiritual gifts. Now we must tackle the less pleasant issue of discernment. Discernment is important not only when distinguishing true prophets from false (1 John 4:1–6) or true prophets' accurate from inaccurate prophecies (1 Cor. 14:29). Discernment is also important in hearing God for ourselves.

Mature Christians have witnessed many inaccuracies blamed on the Holy Spirit or, for that matter, on the Bible. Those who have been Christians for several decades undoubtedly remember many unfulfilled claims about the Lord's return. One of the more notorious in my time was a book that calculated the year of Jesus' return: 88 Reasons Why the Rapture Could Be in 1988. The book sold over three million copies—in 1988. The revised edition, providing eighty-nine reasons why Jesus might return in 1989, did not sell as well. (Let it never be said that North American evangelicals are easily deceived—at least not twice in two years by the same author anyway.)[1]

Charismatic Critiques of Charismatics

Revelations, whether based on spiritual insight in prayer or on study of the Bible, can be mistaken and must be tested by Scripture. Given my support of spiritual gifts and my own exercise of some of those gifts, I trust that you will understand that I am not criticizing genuine spiritual gifts here. Instead, I am responding to excesses that have often occurred in circles not grounded in Scripture (what some charismatics playfully call "charismatic granola"—the nuts, fruits, and flakes of the Spirit).

J. Lee Grady, editorial director of *Charisma* magazine, authored a book called *What Happened to the Fire?* which needs to be read by many charismatics.[2] While various readers may differ with some of his examples, Grady, as a charismatic, lovingly but thoroughly documents many examples of charismatic error. He shows that sounder self-criticism is needed if charismatics are to contribute to the larger body of Christ with the gifts God has given them.

My criticisms, like Grady's, are made "in-house." I'm attacking not spiritual gifts but spiritual error propagated in the name of spiritual gifts. Many anticharismatic complaints about the "bad fruit" of charismatic doctrine pertain not to the Spirit or the gifts per se but to the legalism and the opposition to serious Scripture study exhibited by some groups of charismatics. Sometimes these problems are borrowed from noncharismatic popular religion, but whatever the source, since some Christians in error identify themselves as charismatic, sounder charismatics must take special responsibility to lead others away from such practices. This is what I am seeking to emphasize in this section.

Mature charismatics recognize that not everything that passes as the work of the Spirit among Christians today is in fact from the Spirit. A church's label will not tell you in advance whether the Spirit is present. Contrary to their own claims, for instance, some charismatic churches plainly follow a charismatic tradition by rote; by contrast, in some noncharismatic churches (such as the black Baptist church where I was ordained), only the most spiritually insensitive person could fail to sense the overwhelming presence of God's Spirit. Some charismatics who reject the "tradition" of older churches are similarly bound to more recent traditions based on a "revelation" only a few years old, but it is tradition nonetheless.

If we parrot others' teachings without having first checked the context of the passages they quote, we are simply perpetuating tradition, not expounding God's Word faithfully. (One could illustrate how frequently this practice occurs simply by listing the commonly cited texts of many word-of-faith teachers, then examining each in context. Not many texts would remain.) And if we value our church's tradition more than God's Word, it may be our church tradition rather than God we are serving (compare Mark 7:6–13).

Examples of Problematic "Revelations"

Likewise, not every purported revelation comes from the Spirit. One questionable revelation occurred while early Pentecostals were deciding on the nature of the baptism in the Holy Spirit. Under the Baptistic influence of W. H. Durham, many Pentecostals decided that baptism in the Spirit was a second rather than a third work of grace. One of the advocates of three stages, however, then claimed to have had a vision revealing that the devil had instigated the two-stage doctrine to get unsanctified people involved in the Pentecostal movement.

Other "revelations" continued to create problems for early Pentecostal unity. Shortly after much of the Pentecostal movement had settled on the two-stage view, a major segment of the movement split away because one man claimed that one should baptize only in Jesus' name, rendering baptism "in the name of the Father, Son, and Holy Spirit" illegitimate. This revelation led to the view among many that Jesus was the Father and Spirit as well as the Son—the ancient teaching of Sabellianism, which has little support from the Bible.

Many Pentecostals followed the "Jesus only" doctrine, however, lest they dare to question a personal revelation. J. R. Flower, one of the early Assemblies of God leaders, publicly stood against the revelation, declaring it unbiblical. Initially, he was virtually alone in his public declaration, but through his courageous stand, most of the Pentecostals who had accepted the revelation returned to the biblical, trinitarian position. Some, however, have continued to teach the Sabellian ("Jesus only") position to this day.

D. R. McConnell has argued that much of contemporary "faith teaching" stems from an early founder of this movement, who took many ideas from E. W. Kenyon. Although claiming to derive these ideas from direct revelation by the Holy Spirit, this founder's words are sometimes almost identical with Kenyon's earlier words, sometimes for several paragraphs at a time. Kenyon was not Pentecostal; in fact, he opposed tongues. McConnell has shown that Kenyon was significantly influenced by his reading of the New Thought systems that produced Christian Science.[3] An African friend and I cowrote a biblical response to what we believe are some serious errors in the prosperity and "faith" teaching, for use in his home country. Suffice it to say here, I believe that error slipped into many well-meaning charismatic circles, error that has discredited even legitimate charismatics in many wider evangelical and mainline circles.

It is too easy to blame our bad sermons, bad ideas, and so forth on the Holy Spirit. Only when we are humble enough to truly learn the difference between the Spirit's wisdom and our own will we press on to spiritual maturity.[4]

The Bible's Role in Discernment

As important as our own relationship with the Spirit is, we must maintain a sense of proportion. Like many Christians, my friend Rhoda and other Christians mentioned above did not have the Bible in its proper place. God's revelations to all his apostles and prophets in the Bible have already been tested; hence, the Bible serves as a canon, a reliable measuring stick for all claims to revelation today.

Many prophets spoke in Jeremiah's day, but the destruction of Jerusalem revealed that only one of them—Jeremiah—was speaking for God. So guess whose book made it into the Bible? Jeremiah claimed that the earlier true prophets had prophesied judgment and that this left the burden of proof on any prophet who declared that all would go well with God's people (Jer. 28:8–9; compare 23:16–32). History has tested the biblical revelations, and we must use them to evaluate and guide our own sensitivity to the Spirit. Those who learn to recognize God's voice in the Bible will recognize the Spirit when he speaks in their hearts.

Yet hearing God's voice in the Bible is not simply about quoting verses here and there; many people quote verses and use them to argue opposite points against each other. God gave us the Bible not in isolated verses with blank space between them, but one book at a time. This is the way God's Spirit inspired Scripture, and this is therefore the way we can best hear his voice in it. We must learn Scripture in context, passage by passage and book by book, rather than simply depending on our own (or someone else's) revelations. Neglecting the revelation God already gave us in Scripture in favor of a new revelation that violates Scripture is a dangerous practice. It is like one prophet who heeded another prophet's (false) claim of a revelation, neglecting a revelation he already had; he died for disobeying God (1 Kings 13:16–22).

The situation regarding Bible interpretation is more serious than many of us, either charismatic or noncharismatic, realize. Most verses that are randomly quoted in churches are quoted by rote rather than by having first studied them in context. Consequently, many of these verses do not mean what we use them to mean. (For instance, the "thief" in the context of John 10:10 is not merely the devil, nor does "lifting Jesus up" in John 12:32–33 refer primarily to praise—as the interested reader may quickly confirm by checking those passages in context. In Ps. 118:22–24, "This is the day the LORD has made" [NIV] actually refers to a specific, momentous day in history!)

Sincere, zealous brothers and sisters have too often unquestioningly accepted what popular ministers have said, though some of those ministers quote almost every verse they use out of context. Some contend that God can speak through a Scripture verse taken out of context. Granted, God is sovereign and can speak as he pleases—through a proof text, a poem, or Balaam's donkey. But we do not regularly seek out donkeys to tell us how to live. In the same way, we cannot *teach* as authoritative for the rest of Christ's body any interpretation of Scripture that is not genuinely in the text and accessible to all. If we humbly pray for these ministers and they have humble hearts before God, God can lead them to a better understanding. Yet how much better it would have been to correct the error before they began to mislead so many other people!

We who look the other way while God's servants mistreat his Word must share the blame. (If someone misrepresented our intention by quoting us out of context, we might sue!) Let us pray for a fresh revival of the Spirit today—for the awakening of God's church to the truth of his Word.

Unfair Noncharismatic Critiques of Charismatics

I disagree with the conclusion of John MacArthur that miraculous spiritual gifts have ceased, and I am certain that the extreme examples in his book do not represent most charismatics.[5] MacArthur complains that cults and charismatics both affirm new revelation.[6] Yet this comparison should not automatically place them in the same category. First, guilt by association is a form of reasoning that leads to unpleasant results. For example, the

Way International affirmed a pretribulational rapture; so do many Baptists in North America. Are Baptists therefore a cult? Some doomsday cults deny a pretribulational rapture; are most evangelical Presbyterians and Baptist seminary professors who deny pretribulationalism therefore part of a cult? If both those who affirm and those who deny pretribulationalism must be cultic, is it possible to avoid being in a cult? (Lest you think I am therefore advocating mid-tribulationalism—I am not—this was merely an example.)

Second, most cults do accept new revelation, but most cults accept it only as late as the period of their own founding revelation, and they end up denying crucial biblical revelations in the process. This is not what mainstream charismatics do; many are just trying to follow biblical injunctions about being "led by the Spirit" (Rom. 8:14; Gal. 5:18) in their daily lives. In the same way, if some young charismatics' susceptibility to false teaching taints the entire charismatic movement, should tainted charismatics then be thought to taint all their fellow evangelicals? In many parts of the world (such as most of Latin America), most evangelicals are charismatic or Pentecostal.

Further, mainstream charismatics do not accept new doctrinal revelation that they believe is not in the Bible. Finally, MacArthur himself is not above appealing to postbiblical church tradition, so long as it is not charismatic (that is, if it claims to be true wisdom rather than a true "revelation").[7]

Fairer Critiques of Charismatic Excess

Nevertheless, MacArthur's book does provide useful and accurate examples of charismatic excesses, and unfortunately, many long-term charismatics could provide many more examples. In the 1970s I heard of some fringe charismatics who had people cough attitude-demons into jars, which would then be sealed and stored in a basement. Once I was going forward for prayer at a church I was visiting when the minister started casting out a demon from a broken wrist of the woman in front of me. I returned to my seat as quickly as possible! Many of us who affirm and practice spiritual gifts would feel more comfortable among anticharismatics who are at least grounded in Scripture than among such flaky charismatics.

More to the point is MacArthur's critique of some charismatics' Bible interpretation method. Many charismatics (especially in the "faith movement" but also among some noncharismatic pietistic Christians) claim that the Spirit has revealed meanings of Scripture to them when the texts read in context have nothing whatsoever to do with their "revelation." If one is going to get revelations that contradict the inspired meaning of Scripture, why not just get revelations from watching a bird or reading a poem? Why even use the Bible if what God originally inspired it to say is irrelevant?

There is nothing more dangerous than someone acting with the assurance that the Spirit has spoken to him or her when in fact he has not. We dare not preach as if the authority of Scripture is behind us, when in fact Scripture in context does not support what we say. The charismatic early Christians recognized that all claims concerning revelations must be tested (1 Cor. 14:29; 1 Thess. 5:20–22), and they continued in the apostles' teachings (Acts 2:42). It is no wonder that some noncharismatics are afraid that charismatics will go off the deep end. Without careful grounding in Scripture, even well-meaning charismatics, moved by various feelings and predispositions they regard as the Spirit, have sometimes done just that.

The Purpose of Spiritual Gifts (1 Corinthians 12–14)

Spiritual giftedness does not guarantee that we hear from God rightly on every point. The Corinthian church was like parts of the Western church today: socially stratified, individualistic, and divisive. Although Paul commends them for their pursuit of spiritual gifts (1 Cor. 1:5, 7), he reproves them for a deficiency far more serious: They lack love, the principle that should guide which gifts they seek (1 Corinthians 12–14; 1:10).

Spiritual gifts are for building up the body (1 Corinthians 12), and love must coordinate our expression of spiritual gifts (1 Corinthians 13). Thus, prophecy, a gift that builds up others, is more useful publicly than uninterpreted tongues (1 Corinthians 14). Gifts, including prophecy, are no guarantee of spiritual commitment, and one may prophesy falsely or even submit to the Spirit's inspiration without being committed to Christ (Matt. 7:21–23; 1 Sam. 19:20–24).[8] Paul reminds his friends in Corinth that they experienced ecstatic inspiration in Greek religion before their conversion and points out that the message of Christ, rather than inspiration in general, is what is central (1 Cor. 12:1–3). Communicating the content of God's message, rather than how ecstatically one speaks it, is what is central. This principle applies not only to tongues-speakers and prophets but to well-meaning preachers who mistake enthusiasm for anointing while delivering empty religious speeches devoid of sound scriptural teaching.

Paul then reminds his hearers that all the gifts come from the same Spirit (1 Cor. 12:4–11) and that the gifts are interdependent (12:12–26). Paul ranks the leading gifts (apostleship, prophecy, and teaching) and then lists other gifts without explicitly ranking their importance or authority (12:27–30). Paul urges the church to be zealous for the "best" gifts (that is, those that will best build up the church; 12:31), especially prophecy (14:1). Thus, it is appropriate to seek spiritual gifts, but we choose which gifts to seek by determining which gifts will help the body of Christ most. That is, we let love guide our choice (1 Corinthians 13).

Paul covers this point in some detail. Although we sometimes relegate 1 Corinthians 13 to use at weddings, Paul wrote it in the context of a discussion of spiritual gifts. Even if we had all spiritual gifts in their ultimate intensity, we would be nothing without love (13:1–3). The gifts will ultimately pass away, but love is eternal (13:8–13). While noting the priority of love over spiritual gifts, Paul describes the characteristics of love (13:4–8). Many of the characteristics he lists (for instance, not being boastful) are precisely the opposite of characteristics he earlier attributed to his readers in Corinth (see 5:2; 8:1).

Thus, while the Corinthian Christians were strong in Spirit-led gifts, they were weak in Spirit-led character. For this reason, Paul needed to emphasize the importance of the gift of prophecy, which edifies the entire church, over uninterpreted tongues, which edifies only the speaker (1 Corinthians 14). Although Paul focused on what would serve the church as a whole, he was careful not to portray tongues negatively (14:4, 14–19, 39). He exercised this caution even though he could not have known that some later Christians, contrary to 1 Corinthians 14:39, would despise the gift.

Applying Paul's Message Today

The relevance of Paul's words to the Corinthian Christians raises the question of whether Paul would have applied the same argument to all churches in his day. As many Pentecostals and charismatics note, some of his specific restrictions on gifts may have applied to the excessive situation in Corinth rather than to all churches. If, as is likely, most Corinthian house-churches seated only forty members, I suspect that the dynamics of spiritual gifts would apply differently there than in a congregation of two thousand members, where more limits would be necessary, or in a prayer meeting of five members, where fewer would be necessary. Likewise, in churches today in which most spiritual gifts are suspect, prophecy would edify the church no more than tongues would, because even the purest prophecy, approved by other trustworthy prophets, would introduce only division.

Some charismatics insist that the public function of all the gifts, including tongues and prophecy, is so important that we should pursue them (1 Cor. 12:31; 14:1) even if doing so splits a church. Other charismatics, however, (including myself) suggest that this view misses Paul's point. The purpose of the gifts is to make the body of Christ stronger, and if public use of gifts would divide a noncharismatic congregation, charismatic members should honor the unity of the body first and foremost. This is not to say that they should not work through appropriate channels to bring the congregation to greater biblical maturity in the matter of spiritual gifts. But while gifts are important and biblical, they are not the most important issue in the body of Christ. The greatest sign of maturity is love.

When I was part of a congregation that embraced prophecy, the Holy Spirit moved me nearly every week in the service to prophesy. Some weeks the prophecy dealt with issues a number of people were struggling with; some weeks it would call to attention a particular theme, pertaining to the words of a particular biblical text—the text the pastor had felt led to preach on that very week, though neither of us knew how the Lord had been leading the other. After two years there, I returned to a noncharismatic church, going on staff with a Baptist church. The senior pastor told me that I was welcome to exercise whatever gifts the Lord had given me, including tongues and prophecy. At this church I had more opportunities to minister, especially through weekly teaching from the pulpit. Yet the Spirit never once moved me to prophesy in this church. Instead, the Spirit empowered me with the gift of teaching, which was accepted there.

On occasion, with the full support of the senior pastor, I taught about the Spirit's gifts, but this teaching never became a cause of division. Most weeks I did not address spiritual gifts, however, because many other issues needed to be addressed in the congregation—God's demands for sexual holiness, proper treatment of one's spouse, concern for the poor in the neighborhood, and so on. Teachings on abortion, premarital sex, how husbands should treat their wives, and methods for outreach in the community proved far more controversial than tongues or prophecy. The Spirit continued to move in various ways in this congregation, but while some other issues became mildly divisive, spiritual gifts never did.

I never made a secret about my own spiritual experiences, and with the pastor's approval, I ministered privately through prophecy when the Spirit moved me to do so. But some of the friends who ministered to me most deeply there did not share my particular experiences; our unity was rooted in our common fellowship in Christ. Eventually, after I had moved away to a teaching position in another part of the state, some members began to prophesy in the congregation occasionally, and the church has embraced the prophecies without a single complaint. Not every situation works the same way, but 1 Corinthians 12–14 does provide a biblical principle: God gives us the gifts to serve the church, not to divide it.

John MacArthur and other critics of charismatic excess are correct in saying that congregations have often divided over spiritual gifts. I have personally witnessed far more cases, however, in which mainline churches have been rejuvenated and revived by charismatic evangelical ministers or committed members of the congregation. As long as a congregation acknowledges that spiritual gifts may continue today and does not despise those who exercise or fail to exercise particular gifts, spiritual gifts need never be a divisive issue.

The fact that gifts have often been a divisive issue is not an argument against their appropriate use. Often those opposed to the gifts have actually created the division, refusing to live at peace with charismatic members. At other times division has arisen when charismatics have emphasized spiritual gifts or experiences (or some less biblical ideas) while neglecting other aspects of the Spirit's work (such as spiritual fruit or sound understanding of the Bible). The division can come from overzealousness or overreaction on either side. But all believers—from the most fervent Pentecostal to the most committed cessationist—can walk in unity if we dare to love one another as Christ loved us. Unity, after all, comes from the one Spirit among us (1 Cor. 12:13; Eph. 4:3). Many of us believe, however, that one long-term fruit of this unity will not be the diminution of spiritual gifts but their restoration to the entire body of Christ, to whom they rightfully belong (1 Cor. 12:12–26).

Charismatic Separatism

As we have affirmed throughout this book, the gifts are good, but most of us also recognize that they are not everything by themselves. Not only is some of what passes for the Spirit not genuine, but some of what is genuinely of the Spirit may go unrecognized because of our biases and traditions. Although spiritual gifts and fruits rightfully belong to the entire body of Christ, some charismatics of the separatist variety insist that anyone who believes that spiritual gifts are for today must join their kind of church. There is nothing wrong with joining a church that provides for the free exercise of spiritual gifts, but this does not mean that God requires all believers to join charismatic churches.

Many other Christians who affirm and practice spiritual gifts believe God's Spirit has led them into, or led them to remain in, Baptist, Methodist, Anglican, African Methodist Episcopal, Lutheran, Catholic, Presbyterian, Mennonite, or other churches. Many charismatics also serve as biblically faithful voices in circles in which such voices are needed.

Nor are charismatic churches always more Spirit-led than other churches. Charismatic churches can be dominated by ideologies and personalities that conflict with the gospel just as noncharismatic churches can be. Some churches are indeed unfriendly to any word from the Spirit, but this includes some charismatic and Pentecostal churches. Some charismatic churches have distorted the gospel through legalism or cult figures. One charismatic friend told me of a charismatic community to which he belonged years ago that practiced a severe form of "shepherding." When he disagreed with some leaders, he was excommunicated; the leadership became so arrogant and cultic that eventually the church split, the gospel came into great dishonor, and some of the believers left church altogether or took years to recover.

God often has a godly remnant even in congregations that other people call "dead churches" (Rev. 3:4). I have friends who became ministers in such churches, evangelizing not only on the street but during the church services. In many cases, getting long-time church members converted was like pulling teeth, and it would have been easier to start with a much smaller but zealous church and evangelize the community. But God can work either way, and he does call some to bring life to "dead" churches; he never calls any of us only to tasks that are easy.

The way the Bible defines a "dead" church, however, is not what everyone means by the term. Some of the more extremist charismatics have claimed that dead churches are any churches that do not speak in tongues, but this is simply false. Biblically dead churches are those that disobey Christ's call (Rev. 3:1–2) and in which most of the members are not truly Christians (Rev. 3:4–5). The percentage of members who are committed, witnessing, Bible-reading, and Bible-obeying Christians is a far better test of spiritual life in a church than tongues. Nor do tongues necessarily identify even "charismatic" churches: I know many charismatic churches in which tongues plays little or no part in the public church service.

While the operation of charismatic gifts in the church is biblical and desirable, other circumstances being equal, the separatist mentality has serious weaknesses.

First, there are a variety of gifts in Christ's body, some of which are more important for public worship than others. Rare is the church in which all the gifts are in full operation, and that includes most charismatic churches. Teaching is an important gift, yet as we mentioned above and as most sound charismatics recognize, many unsound charismatics exist. Whether or not one is charismatic, if one regularly studies the Bible in context, one will suffer agony while sitting through a sermon in which the minister takes verses out of context.

Although many inadvertently take Scripture out of context and humbly desire God's truth, others arrogantly refuse to admit the need to change, attributing their out-of-context interpretations to the Holy Spirit. One time I heard a minister preach about "let the weak say I am strong" in Joel 3:10, declaring that we need to confess ourselves strong. Of course, God's strength is made perfect in weakness (2 Cor. 12:9–10), but the point of Joel 3:10 in context is something different. God is calling the wicked nations to war against Jerusalem and mocking them: "You are weak, but pretend you are strong against me! I will destroy you" (Joel 3:2–16). We all make mistakes, and I and the minister both made one that day. Mine was that I tried to talk with him about it; I suggested after the service that there was an interesting nugget in the context of that passage. He responded curtly, "I know what the context says. But this is what the Spirit gave me to preach." Unfortunately, what the Spirit gave him was not what the Spirit gave Joel! His mistake, like mine, was pride. He publicly pretended to speak on the authority of the biblical text he was expounding when in fact his point had nothing to do with the point of that text. His point was actually a legitimate biblical one, but if he wanted to claim the authority of Scripture for his message, he should have found a text that fit his message properly (for example, 2 Cor. 12:9–10) or a message that fit his text properly (for example, God's judgment against the proud).

The fact that someone has the gift of tongues, prophecy, or healing does not mean that he or she is a good teacher of Scripture. Though I might well speak in tongues more than most of them—to paraphrase a famous charismatic of the past (1 Cor. 14:18)—I would personally rather work in a noncharismatic (even anticharismatic) church in which the minister expounds the biblical text accurately than in a charismatic church in which the minister blames unsound preaching on the Spirit's guidance. Until those charismatic churches who have poor teaching can supply both spiritual empowerment and sounder teaching, many of them will continue to be only a way station for Christians who need a fresh spiritual experience but who end up taking it elsewhere once they have it. Worse, some churches will nurture believers in a defective spirituality that falls short of the "whole counsel of God," leaving their flock susceptible to future crises in times of persecution, false teaching, or national judgment (Acts 20:26–31).

Second, all the gifts rightly belong to the entire body of Christ. If everyone who privately prays in tongues withdraws into churches that are defined primarily by their public use of particular spiritual gifts, who will remain in noncharismatic churches to introduce others to these gifts in nondivisive ways? Does God call everyone who prays in tongues to worship only in charismatic churches?

Third, all the gifts should build up the body of Christ rather than divide it. Some ministers in the Baptist association in which I was ordained were concerned about charismatic ministers because a number had pulled their churches out of the Baptist association or had deliberately pulled members away from Baptist churches. I think few of our ministers believed that supernatural gifts had ceased; certainly few would have objected to members who personally prayed in tongues or talked about it in a nondivisive way. The fear, however, was division, which does not come from God's Spirit (Rom. 16:17; Jude 19).

Fourth, different churches have different strengths and callings. Ideally, we should be united enough that the strengths of various churches can complement one another. We should be able to learn from and grow in one another's gifts, whether they be teaching, evangelism, or more faith to pray for ailing members in our churches. I went on staff with a Baptist church for the first time partly because I saw the pastor's heart to reach the unreached people of our community in a way few other churches there were doing. The Spirit had given me a passion for evangelism that easily took precedence over attending a church in which people were invited to pray in tongues out loud.

Finally, the common mission that unites us as Christians puts any other particular agenda in second place. Some current issues in evangelicalism undoubtedly are worth dividing over—for instance, whether Jesus is the only way of salvation, an affirmation that I believe is at the heart of the gospel Jesus' first followers preached. I fear that this issue may become a

major point of division in the next decade, as the world's climate of rela-
tivism continues to invade the church. But most issues we debate among
ourselves should not prevent us from working together in our common mission for Christ.

Thus, for instance, I have written elsewhere on issues currently debated
among Christians. But while I may disagree with scholars such as Wayne Grudem on women's ministry and William Heth on divorce, they are two of my
esteemed friends. I may disagree with J. I. Packer on women's ministry but
heartily appreciate his great contributions to the body of Christ. If we broke
fellowship with other believers every time we disagreed on some matter, most
of us would be left with little Christian fellowship! Charismatic tongues, other
spiritual gifts, and beliefs about and experiences in the Spirit may be important, but they do not represent all the issues the Spirit wants us to teach on
or the ultimate basis for unity. Even most charismatic churches do not teach
these subjects all the time. The Spirit can make a difference in how people
look at other issues, but leading people into a deeper relationship with Christ
does not mean just teaching them about tongues. It must include teaching
people how to understand Scripture, how to carry out Scripture's mandates
for evangelism, and how to be sensitive and obedient to God's voice.

Thus, I would urge those who are zealous for spiritual gifts not to abandon noncharismatic churches without good reason; your emphases can
bring renewal to other parts of the body of Christ in areas where they need
it. And in the same way those zealous for particular gifts need other true
Christians' different gifts, even when some of those gifts appear less spectacular at the moment. As Christians, each of us must humble ourselves
before our brothers and sisters in Christ's body (1 Peter 5:5), recognizing
the diversity of gifts God has given (Rom. 12:4–8; 1 Cor. 12:14–26; 1 Peter
4:10). The spiritual discipline of humility, in fact, while one of the least
spectacular signs of all, is a true sign of the Lord's presence in us (2 Cor.
10:1; Gal. 6:1; Eph. 4:2–3).

The ideal, of course, is for all churches to act biblically regarding spiritual gifts—as well as act biblically regarding every other matter. But only
if we pursue the fruit of the Spirit now—including love, peace, kindness,
and longsuffering—can we hope to achieve that goal. If one had to choose
between an emphasis on gifts or on fruit, 1 Corinthians 13 makes clear
where that emphasis should lie. Scripture does not force us to choose, of
course, but it invites us to lay the emphasis where God does.

May the Spirit produce in us his fruits, the image of Christ's character,
so that the world around us may begin to know what God's love for them

looks like. After washing the disciples' feet, as Jesus was getting ready to go to the cross, he commanded them (and us):

> I am giving you a new commandment—that you love one another. You must love one another in the very same way that I have loved you. This is how everyone will know that you are my disciples: if you love one another.

John 13:34–35

Conclusion

I close by returning to the beginning of the book. God gave us the Spirit so we would have God inside us, so we would have an intimate relationship with him. Instead of living life in our strength, we depend on Christ who lives in us (Gal. 2:20). We who yearn to know God more intimately must listen to the voice of the Spirit, who reveals Jesus Christ, the Lord who died to make his body one (Eph. 2:13–15). We must also evaluate the fruit of the Spirit, which reveals God's character in us. We must depend on the Spirit's power for evangelism and for edifying our fellow Christians. God gave us the Spirit so that in all we do in our lives, we can do it depending on him rather than on ourselves. May we seek him in prayer for deeper empowerment and trust that he will not turn us away (Luke 11:11–13).

Conclusion

L ife in the Spirit includes God's power in our lives: empowerment for evangelism, for overcoming testing, and for building up brothers and sisters in Christ by means of select spiritual gifts. But this power flows from an intimate and personal relationship with the Creator of the universe, who has come to live in us by the Holy Spirit. Being led by the Spirit may include some details in our daily lives, but it involves far more knowing, loving, and therefore obeying God.

Although we are complete in Christ, many of us have yet to begin to unlock the treasures of that completeness in our daily experience. In that sense, I can only commend the heart of the state university undergraduate who eagerly announced to me, "I can't get enough of Jesus!" Some writers accurately summarize Paul's teaching on our position in Christ as, "Be who you are." God's Spirit enables us to become in practice what he has already formed us to be in Christ.

We examined knowing the Spirit's voice (chaps. 1–2). We also examined evangelism by the Spirit's power, including God's answers to prayer often confirming our witness (chap. 3). We discussed recognizing and bearing the Spirit's fruit (chap. 4); as we learn God's character in the Bible, especially in Jesus' cross, we learn to recognize what the Spirit's ways sound like when we hear him and look like when we obey him.

Then we turned to some more controversial questions. I argued that the Bible affirms as valid for today all biblical spiritual gifts, and then I examined a number of specific gifts. We discussed the Spirit's role in our conversion, and how this relates to the baptism in the Holy Spirit; we also discussed how the phrase can be applied to the experiences described in Acts and probed the much-debated relationship between baptism in the Spirit and tongues. (I concluded that baptism in the Holy Spirit probably applies to the entire sphere of the Holy Spirit's work; hence, different New Testament writers used the phrase to emphasize different aspects of the Spirit's work in our lives.) Finally, I addressed discernment of the Spirit; affirming that the gifts are for today demands that we be all the more vigilant against counterfeit gifts and against spiritual elitism among those who exercise particular gifts.

Spiritual Gifts and the Life of the Church

One of the more controversial areas of the Spirit's work in today's church has been the practice of gifts, which the Bible says the Spirit supplies to the church; this issue thus invited extended discussion.

In the broadest use of the term *charismatic* (literally, "grace-gifted"), Christ's entire body qualifies, because every member has a gift or gifts to exercise (1 Cor. 12:7–30). To be sure, in most churches many or most members do not exercise their gifts, even in small groups. A few people in the church do all the work, and as a result, most of the work of the kingdom that the church could accomplish never gets done. We need to seek to mobilize all members to do the tasks God has given them, in connection with others (Eph. 4:11–13).

When we examine some of the Bible's teaching on the Spirit's work, we realize that even most Pentecostals and charismatics are less "charismatic" than the Bible invites us to be. Most of us need to experience deeper intimacy with God, fuller power in evangelism, strength in the face of testing, and so on. The Spirit also helps the church through apologetics, teaching, confirming signs such as healing, wise strategies to effectively reach our culture and other cultures, and more.

Thus, it is possible to affirm that all the gifts are for today yet still be a cessationist in practice by neglecting the gifts, or to allow one or two but neglect the others. (To illustrate, some Pentecostal churches practice only tongues and interpretation; some Presbyterian churches practice only teaching; some charismatic churches practice only prophecy; some Baptist churches practice only evangelism; and so forth.) It is even possible to practice some of the gifts yet deny in practice what even cessationists would not deny: that God empowers us for daily prayer, evangelism, and holy living. Our lives of sacrificial love, not simply spiritual experiences, demonstrate how much the Spirit has of our hearts (John 13:34–35; Eph. 5:18–21; 1 John 2:3–6).

In our discussions concerning the fruit of the Spirit and discerning the Spirit, I pointed to the contexts in which the Bible discusses spiritual gifts, especially love (1 Corinthians 13). If we love our brothers and sisters in Christ, we will seek gifts for building up each other. Thus, using the gifts to support pride or separation from fellow Christians is an abuse of the purpose for which God gave us the gifts. The gifts should help the church, not divide it. Conversely, neglecting the gifts means neglecting a resource God gave us to build up each other. In situations in which the operation of particular gifts cause division, the gifts are no more a worthy cause of division than most of our other excuses. Our goal must be to lead the church gently toward a greater biblical openness to the gifts but in a way that honors the unity of the church and also godly leadership.

Some churches may be so closed to spiritual gifts and those who affirm them that dialogue proves impossible. If, as I have argued, the Bible teaches the use of gifts, then churches that oppose the gifts and oppose or disfellowship those who practice them even privately are divisive, even if they call those they oppose divisive. But most churches are more open to nondivisive members and leaders than in times past. And in many churches, spiritual gifts constitute merely one issue among a large number on which churches need to mature spiritually.

Faith makes us all members of Christ's body. Scripture invites us to seek gifts for building up Christ's body (1 Cor. 12:31; 14:1). But those who are mature in the ways of the Spirit are those who have depended on him through hardship and learned to honor Christ's entire body. Those who look down on other Christians because they lack a particular gift or experience, or those who despise a particular gift and look down on Christians who have it, are not demonstrating spiritual maturity. God's goal is our maturity in Christ (Col. 1:28), and that cannot be achieved without us loving and strengthening each other. The deepest lesson to which the gifts point us is to look to the Giver himself—the one who calls us to do his work and supplies us with all that we need for the task.

Conclusion

The Bible summons all Christians to accept the Spirit's empowerment for the various tasks God has assigned us and for evangelizing the world across cultural barriers. Indeed, woe to us in a world like today's if we try to do his work without him!

The one Spirit who makes us one body summons us to serve the one body and to evangelize the world together and worship the Lord together. If we cannot do that, then in practice both our "charismatic" and "non-charismatic" claims to having the Spirit are worthless. We must not only celebrate the Spirit; we must remember why he has come to us. May all of us live like the people of the Spirit that Christ has summoned us to be— the many gifted, fruitful body of Christ.

Afterword
Looking Back on Twenty Years

I f I were writing *Gift and Giver* today, my exegesis of the passages treated in the book—the real heart and majority of the book—would be substantially the same. Of course, I have learned much more since then and discovered more fully how biblical theology of the Spirit fits together, but this would not undermine what the book already says.

My illustrations would, however, change somewhat. The Evangelical Theological Society (ETS) graciously invited me onto their executive committee, and in the year in which I am writing this afterword, I am president of that society. I teach at Asbury, a leading evangelical seminary. I have been program chair for ETS and for the Institute of Biblical Research, and for five years I edited the latter organization's journal.

I still identify myself as a charismatic Baptist, but since my move to Asbury I have worked more closely than before with the Assemblies of God and with Vineyard. I've also gotten to know leaders in some of the younger continuationist movements, such as Rolland and Heidi Baker, Mike Bickle, Randy Clark, Ché Ahn, and their circles, and a yet even newer generation of leaders as exemplified by Daniel Kolenda and the RICE movement. I also engage with academic colleagues in the Society for Pentecostal Studies (SPS) and have cowritten a book with my close friend Michael Brown, a leading charismatic Old Testament scholar.[1]

My life is fully evangelical and fully charismatic. But let me define what I mean by "charismatic," since that term has taken on even wider connotations since the book's first publication. (So has "evangelical," but, not to belabor the point, I refer not to a subculture or to a political label but to those for whom the good news about Christ is central and Scripture is theologically normative.)

Labels

By "charismatic" I do not refer to a particular charismatic theology; there are some fashionable charismatic views, like some fashionable views in other Christian circles, that are not entirely biblical. By "charismatic," I mean a practicing continuationist—that is, someone who believes that the gifts are for today and puts this belief into practice. Charismatics, or renewalists, or global pentecostals (with a small and more inclusive *p*), are thus those who pursue and welcome spiritual gifts.

At the same time, those who wish to obey biblical injunctions to welcome spiritual gifts (1 Cor. 12:31; 14:1, 5, 39–40) must also embrace biblical calls for evaluating them and keeping them on track (1 Cor. 14:29; 1 Thess. 5:19–22). It is rightly said that those who ignore history are doomed to repeat its mistakes. For example, a secular generation devoted to sexual experimentation, ignoring what humanity has learned throughout its history, has left a sad, much-expanded trail of broken families and lives in its wake. In the same way, those who experiment through their own personal experience of the Spirit without paying attention to what the Spirit has already spoken—most definitively, in Scripture—will keep repeating mistakes of baby Christians because they lack millennia of solid foundations.

As R. T. Kendall[2] and others emphasize, we need both Word and Spirit. It is said that early Pentecostal healing minister Smith Wigglesworth lamented the decline of proper foundations in the second generation of the Pentecostal revival. He envisioned instead a coming revival in which Word and Spirit would come together.[3] Bringing together an emphasis on understanding the Bible in context (often associated with evangelicals) and on lives dependent on the Spirit (often associated with charismatics) should be a good thing.

Yet today there are churches with systematic biblical exposition that neglect appropriating vast numbers of biblical passages about the experience of the Spirit. There are also churches experimenting in all kinds of experience with the Spirit that neglect the biblical foundations and safeguards for such experiences. Of course, many churches lie between these extremes and seek both to explain Scripture and to embrace its message about the Spirit. Are we in different parts of Christ's body too proud to learn from each other? And if we disdain and divide from fellow members of Christ's body, do we imagine that we do not cause pain to our own Lord, the one whose body we divide?

Besides Spiritual Gifts

Only a couple chapters in *Gift and Giver* are about spiritual gifts per se; the book is more about the gift of the Spirit and various ways the Spirit works in our lives. That is, the Spirit acts in our life especially in terms of our *relationship* with God (leading us to cry, "Abba, Father," Rom. 8:15), our knowledge of his heart (the Spirit shows us the things of Jesus, John 16:13–15), and our empowerment for ministry (you shall be witnesses, Acts 1:8).

Spiritual gifts tend to remain the key issue of controversy, however, so I will summarize some points in this afterword. But whether or not a reader is a continuationist regarding particular gifts of the Spirit, hopefully all Christians are continuationists regarding the *fruit* of the Spirit. If disagreements over spiritual gifts prevent us from treating fellow believers in Christ lovingly, we are neglecting even more fundamental biblical teaching.

If a fellow believer differs vociferously—even to the point of questioning our salvation—our tendency may be to strike back or walk away. But the way our Lord models for us—even in the face of fatal opposition (Luke 23:34)—is forgiveness. When criticized by fellow believers, we should love them, pray for them, and where possible, lovingly engage them. Admittedly, the extent to which we can do this will also depend on our calling and gifting. The brother whose main ministry is winning people to Christ on the street or the sister whose main ministry is praying for the sick, for example, will not have the same level of engagement as someone whose main ministry is blogging.

If we are continuationists regarding Christ's one body—that is, we believe that *the body of Christ* is still for today—we should not reject as fellow believers those who trust Christ for salvation even when we disagree on many other matters. I work closely with friends who are cessationists regarding certain spiritual gifts that they know I practice. We are friends with much in common for the kingdom.

My concern here is with another brand of cessationists: those who treat all or almost all charismatics as false prophets who do not belong to Christ's body. In the Bible, however, slander is not a spiritual gift, and it certainly is not a fruit of the Spirit. It is a rather deadly sin (Rom. 1:29–32). There are errors in much of the charismatic movement, but humbly serving with one's gift of teaching will bring change more effectively than denunciations will. There are also genuine false prophets, but if everybody who holds some wrong views is a false prophet, we may all be in trouble: "We know in part and prophesy in part" (1 Cor. 13:9). Teaching error in the name of Scripture seems as vulnerable to critique as mistaken affirmations in the name of the Spirit, so long as we claim to be speaking for God. Vocal dismissal of brothers and sisters and their God-given gifts seems to me to fall into that category.

But Also Spiritual Gifts

Nevertheless, God's empowerment of Christ's body for various ministries is expressed in grace-gifts. Nowhere does Scripture state that these gifts will cease any more than it states that Christ's body—which includes arms, legs, eyes, and other parts, with which Paul compares the gifts—will cease. Indeed, the gift of prophecy continues throughout biblical history, predominating especially in times of renewal; its sudden and unannounced cessation is no more biblical than a sudden and unannounced cessation of teaching.

I believe that what Paul says about Christ's body with diverse gifts is for today. Paul nowhere distinguishes "natural" and "supernatural" gifts, describing some as temporary but others as continuing. That distinction reflects primarily the influence of skeptic David Hume on the Western church—not Scripture itself.

Some think that the completed canon makes the gift of prophecy obsolete, but most prophecies deal with matters unrelated to universal revelation. It is more often teaching that expounds universal truths; does the completion of the biblical canon make teaching superfluous? (One of the best expositions of biblical teaching in this regard came from my friend Sam Storms in his ETS presidential address several years ago.)[4]

Some worry that gifts such as prophecy allow for the danger of postbiblical doctrine. But most prophecy was never about introducing new doctrine; it stretched from calling God's people back to Scripture (as often in the books of the prophets) to warning the king when danger awaited (2 Kings 6:8–12) to telling people where their lost donkeys were (1 Sam. 9:20). One can easily have such sorts of prophecy without introducing new doctrine. Certainly praying in tongues (which its detractors sometimes lump with prophecy) has nothing to do with new doctrine. Indeed, the spiritual gift that might most risk introducing postbiblical doctrine is the gift of teaching. Should we reject this gift for today because some have abused it? It is tragic that some popular-level charismatic teachers feel the need to come up with something new so as to market their ministries as special. This fault is not limited to charismatics, however; we seem to require it of doctoral students and monograph writers (sometimes with good results but sometimes with bad ones!).

Cessationism is itself a *postbiblical doctrine* and as such is epistemologically self-defeating. (That is, it is what it complains about.) Obeying biblical injunctions, such as "zealously desire spiritual gifts" (1 Cor. 14:1) and "zealously desire to prophesy, and do not forbid speaking in tongues" (14:39), is far more biblical than to forbid the practice of such gifts on the basis of postbiblical inferences now hallowed as part of our church's tradition.

The claim that continuing prophecies would add to canonical biblical revelation is not consistent, since most prophecies even in biblical times did *not* become part of Scripture. We have little if any record of the prophetic words delivered through prophets in passages such as 1 Samuel 10:5 or 1 Kings 18:4. If the average first-century house congregation each week had just two or three prophecies (cf. 1 Cor. 14:29, 31), even if there were only an average of a hundred house churches during this period, we would be speaking of over 900,000 prophecies. They neither competed with biblical revelation, nor were the vast majority of them included in it. If prophecy could occur while Scripture was being written, without needing to be on the same level as Scripture and hence included in it, why should the situation be different after the canon of Scripture has been completed?

Groundbreaking evangelism in new areas continues to lay new "foundations" (Rom. 15:20), and not surprisingly, genuinely dramatic miracles seem to flourish especially (though by no means exclusively) in such areas, as "signs" confirming the message of Christ's grace (cf. Acts 14:3). Mostly the same range of miracles we see in the Bible—except for events such as the original creation, the exodus, the virgin birth, and Jesus' resurrection, which inaugurated a new creation—continue to be experienced today. (See my two-volume work, *Miracles: The Credibility of the New Testament Accounts*.)[5]

We are one body, so we should value all gifts, from (for example) teaching to evangelism, from encouragement/comfort to worship leading, from financial support to tongues (Rom. 12:6–8; 1 Cor. 12:8–10, 28–30; 14:26). Some churches amputate certain members of the body; some churches pile up the sort of members that other churches have amputated. We can live with some members amputated, but most of us would regard our bodies as in more ideal shape if we have and use all our members.

The New Testament church ideally welcomes the contributions of all members. We cannot accommodate all members' contributions during services in modern megachurches, but megachurch settings with sound biblical teaching also provide special opportunities so long as they are coupled with small groups (Acts 2:46). Small groups, where believers can serve one another with their diverse gifts and in relationships, can more closely approximate the setting of first-century house churches. (Those churches rarely could hold more than forty or fifty people and may have sometimes been closer to ten or fifteen people.)

Pastors (a term used interchangeably in the first century with "elders" and "overseers"; Acts 20:17, 28; Titus 1:5–7; 1 Peter 5:1–2) are necessarily those grounded in Scripture and able to communicate it ("able to teach," 1 Tim. 3:2; 2 Tim. 2:2, 24; Titus 1:9). Those gifted as pastors lead gatherings of believers and therefore help supervise, guard, nurture, and guide other local spiritual gifts to maturity (cf. Eph. 4:11–13). In the New Testament, local churches often had multiple elders balancing one another's gifts, and those who were particularly well trained or gifted, such as Paul's agent Timothy, might pour into multiple congregations and leaders (2 Tim. 2:2). Both prophecy and teaching were valuable in leadership (Acts 13:1).

Charismatic Errors

But there is also a lot of charismatic theology based on (at best) someone's partial insights rather than a solid understanding of Scripture. Today some prophesy on the basis of mathematical or other "clues" in Scripture that do not fit the context of the passages in question. Whether they prove right or wrong in their prophecies (prophecy and teaching are distinct gifts), they should be clear that they are speaking on the authority of their own sense of what the Spirit is saying and not on the authority of any clear message in the biblical passages.

Certainly they should not leave other Bible readers with the impression that this is the normal way to understand Scripture; cleverness often sounds more profound than it is. God can give people insights apart from Scripture: for example, something we hear might trigger our memory to pray for someone else, or a sermon illustration may resonate with something personal in our lives. God sometimes even communicated to prophets with images that recalled a similar Hebrew word (Jer. 1:11–12; Amos 8:2). There is no reason that God cannot do this on a more detailed level with something we read. But the canonical, universal message that we can *teach* on the authority of Scripture itself is what God inspired it to say in its concrete context, language, and setting. It is *in light of* that universal sense that we can teach what it demands of us in our varied concrete settings today.

Some earlier charismatics learned demonology from a book called *Pigs in the Parlor*,[6] which claimed insights that were essentially based on interviews with demons (which, as I understand it, are not reputed to be the most reliable truth tellers). The shepherding movement, attempts to teach people how to speak in tongues through imitation, and self-centered prosperity teaching (as opposed to simply teaching us to trust God's provision for his mission), were other waves of error or excess that blew through popular charismatic circles (cf. Eph. 4:14).[7] Some extreme faith teachers (such as Hobart Freeman) even rejected the use of medicine, claiming it signified a lack of faith.

Many of these errors had some earlier precedents in history. At the same time, believers could have learned from more well-rounded faith teachings earlier in history, modeled by evangelical leaders such as George Mueller or Hudson Taylor (as documented in Paul L. King's excellent *Moving Mountains*).[8] Yes, we need to stand firm in trusting God, but we should not forget that the world is at war in the spiritual sphere.

The kingdom is already/not yet, and much suffering and death will remain in the world until the kingdom's consummation at Christ's return. We should, of course, work for God's kingdom insofar as possible in the present, and faith motivates us to advance in these ways: through extending compassion, healing, support for our communities, and the like. But some excess faith teaching tends toward the view that we must establish God's kingdom on earth fully before Christ's return. They go beyond merely seeking God's empowerment to be an influence for good to, in some cases, expecting political and legal supremacy. Such "dominionism" (an idea originally borrowed from noncharismatic circles) is a form of postmillennialism. Many leading, godly, and effective Christian thinkers of an earlier era were postmillennial. Postmillennialism was popular among devoted Christians during a cultural era of unbridled optimism about progress (and Western empires), especially in the nineteenth century. Yet reality shattered that view in the sufferings of the early twentieth century, and reality is likely to shatter it again.

The idea in some charismatic circles that everything should be kept positive or upbeat can counter some excesses toward pessimism and unbelief, but a gospel that includes the cross as well as the resurrection cannot *only* address what people consider happy. Shepherds need to prepare their flocks for hardship. A summary of Paul's instruction to even new converts is, "We must enter God's kingdom through many afflictions" (Acts 14:22; cf. 1 Thess. 3:3). Paul declares himself innocent of his hearers' blood because he did not withhold from them any of God's purpose (Acts 20:26–27). Facing crises confidently does not entail ignoring hardship.

Some charismatics insist that all prophecies must be positive, risking the danger of prophesying only well-being in the face of impending suffering (Jer. 6:14; 8:11). While it is true that prophecies should reflect God's loving heart, they may warn of suffering (Acts 21:11), exhort (part of the meaning of *paraklēsis* in 1 Cor. 14:3), and reprove (Rev. 2:4–5). Some charismatics reprove cessationists for saying that prophecy has ceased, yet they themselves treat corrective expressions of biblical prophecy as no longer relevant.

Apostolic Movements

I am myself a cessationist regarding some things. We should not anticipate any more virgin births; God became flesh once for all in history. Jesus died once for all, and he rose once for all. Likewise, the canon is closed, since *by definition* the canon is the body of Scripture that the entire church claims to accept as the measuring stick for any other revelation. That does not mean that God has stopped speaking, much less that we should assume that God did not speak through the prophets mentioned in Scripture whose words are not recorded (as noted above). At the very least, all Christians should hear God's Spirit reminding them that they are God's children (Rom. 8:16) and pointing to his love revealed in the cross (Rom. 5:5–9).

Because we regard the canon as closed, some further contend that apostles have ceased. This conclusion, however, need not follow—depending on how we define "apostles." Most of the Twelve did not write Scripture (unless someone considers much later works, such as the Gospel of Thomas or the Acts of Andrew, authentic!), and much of the New Testament was written by those who are not labeled apostles, such as Mark and Luke. The closing of the canon has little to do with whether there are apostles and so does not entail their cessation.

Having said that, I agree that the original first-century apostles have ceased. They have a special place (cf. Matt. 19:28; Luke 22:30; Rev. 21:14). They died and, like all other believers, await the resurrection, but since the first century, the Twelve have "ceased."

But while the Evangelists, especially Luke, restrict the label "apostles" especially to the Twelve, Paul applies the label also to himself and various colleagues in groundbreaking ministry. This is a larger group than the Twelve (Rom. 16:7; 1 Cor. 9:5–6; 15:5–7; Gal. 1:19; 1 Thess. 2:6–7 with 1:1; cf. Acts 14:3). Although not all of them laid foundations for the whole church through history, they could lay foundations for churches or ministries in new regions or spheres (cf. Rom. 15:20; 2 Cor. 10:14–16).

Today many churches speak of "apostolic" missions or "apostolic" church planting. They mean "apostolic" in the wider, Pauline sense of the term. The same is true for many who think of apostles as having special authorization to lead. Many older church traditions speak of apostolic succession, an unbroken chain of appointed leaders going back to the first-century apostles.

Early Methodist leader Francis Asbury attributed to early American Methodism "an apostolic form of Church government" and expected spiritual formation "as in former apostolical days."[9] He sought to return to the New Testament's "true primitive order," "an apostolic order of poverty and itinerancy."[10] Likewise, leaders in the Azusa Street Revival and much of early Pentecostalism considered themselves part of an apostolic faith movement. The idea was not that everyone involved was an apostle but that they were restoring New Testament–style Christianity as in "apostolic" times. In that sense, they were continuing the heritage of other restorationist movements, going back to various earlier awakenings and revivals, the Reformation, some earlier monastic movements celebrating "apostolic poverty," and some ideals even of the Renaissance.

So before we evaluate movements claiming to be apostolic today, it is important to distinguish what various movements and individuals mean by this label. Most churches actually do agree that "apostolic" in some broader sense continues. Scripture does, however, invite us to discern true apostolic ministry from that which is false (Rev. 2:2), and there is no question that, by biblical standards, there are plenty of false apostles today.

Leaders who seek for the sheep to follow them rather than nurturing the sheep for Christ are wolves (Acts 20:29–30). If self-proclaimed apostles are not breaking new ground for the kingdom but are instead boasting in others' labors, they are false apostles, servants of Satan (2 Cor. 10:13–18; 11:13–15). True apostles do not demand or seek honor in this life; characteristically, they suffer to advance the gospel in their spheres (1 Cor. 4:9–13; 2 Cor. 11:23–33). Those who want to be first in the kingdom must be last of all (Mark 10:44; cf. 1 Cor. 12:28 with 4:9).

Today there are people who simply seek to gather other leaders under them, as if having people under them makes them apostles. They value the title "apostle" as a promotion in ministry, often employing a spiritual pyramid scheme that is the inverse of Jesus' model of servanthood. Competing among themselves and with others (2 Cor. 10:12), they try to lure people away from churches with older leadership structures, urging them to catch up with the spiritual times. I have listened to the anguish of Spirit-filled believers in locations as diverse as Cuba, Ethiopia, and India regarding these false apostles and prophets who are dividing the church.[11]

I wish I could be a cessationist regarding false apostles (and false prophets and false pastor-teachers), but they continue today—and we continue to need the gift of discernment today. It takes little discernment to be a cessationist: one can simply discard all prophecies. While I find myself attracted to the simplicity of that approach, Paul explicitly warns against treating prophecies with contempt (1 Thess. 5:20). Yet those of us who believe that God continues to empower his church in a range of ways have a much greater responsibility to exercise discernment, especially with the sorts of prophecies that can do the most harm when they are mistaken. (Believers have the same responsibility to evaluate teaching on the basis of Scripture.)

Gifts, ministries, and experiences different from ours are not necessarily wrong. But behavior unbecoming of the kingdom, such as self-aggrandizement, is wrong. Prophecies that distract from instead of exalt Jesus are wrong; prophecies that irresponsibly weaken the faith and health of God's people are wrong.

Learning and Growing

Since writing *Gift and Giver*, I have learned more from other continuationist scholars writing about the Spirit, including Robert Menzies, Max Turner, Youngmo Cho, James D. G. Dunn, Randall Harrison, Ken Hemphill, Zeb Bradford Long, Julie and Wonsuk Ma, Jon Ruthven, Anthony Thiselton, my many colleagues in SPS, and a further array of friends and colleagues too vast to mention. Some whom I cited in the original version of *Gift and Giver* have also produced improved, revised editions of their work, such as Jack Deere's marvelous classic, *Surprised by the Power of the Spirit*.

I have also had further experience with God's Spirit, including some pleasant experiences with miracles and unpleasant encounters with demons. Talking about these personal experiences is uncomfortable in academic settings because Western readers who have not experienced such encounters can easily doubt my sanity. Happily, passion for truth usually motivates me more than what colleagues think of me in this life. Were I updating *Gift and Giver* or writing it from scratch today, many illustrations would differ. Nevertheless, I need not rehearse such experiences. Scattered references to some of them appear in some books published after *Gift and Giver*, and biblical teaching is sufficient regardless of the subsequent accounts we might use to illustrate it.

One major change in my life since writing *Gift and Giver* has been more learning from the global church, especially from my wife, Médine, whom I married a year after *Gift and Giver*'s publication. She hails from the Evangelical Church of Congo, the mainstream Protestant denomination in her Central African nation. Although she did not speak in tongues, she has prophetic dreams and has a sister who was raised after three hours of being, so far as anyone could tell, dead. Even if I did not pray in tongues, I might call myself charismatic the way James Dunn rightly calls himself charismatic: I have a *charisma* of teaching. Even so, some African noncharismatic experience has taught me beyond my own Western charismatic experience. Admittedly, I have been prophesying less frequently when awake in recent years than in some earlier ones, but I have been growing in prophetic dreams, relishing the heart of Jesus and other experiences beyond where I was before.

The heart of what I have been learning from Médine appears in our story together, *Impossible Love* (2016).[12] Although prophetic guidance moves some of the story, it highlights our brokenness, especially Médine's experiences as a war refugee for eighteen months after her Ph.D. The New Testament recounts not only empowerment but also suffering, and we must learn about both. Indeed, Jesus' power is expressed especially in weakness, just as the cross is the womb of the resurrection.

Research for my book, *Miracles: The Credibility of the New Testament Accounts* opened my eyes further, through testimonies of and sometimes medical documentation for miracles around the world that far exceeded my own experiences. These stretched my faith, inviting me to trust God further. Baker will be publishing a shorter, more readable account of some of my more recently documented discoveries in this area (probably in 2021), and of course, other readily readable resources on the subject exist (particularly recently).[13]

My 4,500-page *Acts: An Exegetical Commentary*[14] required such intense attention over the span of a decade—it took me about fourteen months just to index all the references in the four volumes—that I am able to function as a normal person afterward only by God's grace and my family's gracious patience. So many years of sixty-hour weeks of research and writing, not including teaching and other academic responsibilities, left me socially underdeveloped and mentally burned out. Recovering sanity took a couple years! (After I regained my sanity, Cambridge published a one-volume version in 2020.)

Living closely in the text of Acts for so long, however, exposed me more intensely to God's wonderful works, including how he loves to surprise us as he moves the gospel message forward. The most important insight I gleaned was seeing how often various community experiences of the Spirit—something like what we call "revival"—followed occasions of prayer (see esp. Luke 11:13; Acts 1:14; 4:31; 8:15–17). And although the insight was not new, it changed me. It was a great honor to deliver a plenary lecture at ETS on the Spirit in Acts in 2018.

When I worked on *The Mind of the Spirit* (2016),[15] I grew in understanding about how the Lord empowers our minds. Some charismatic circles emphasize only the affective dimension of spiritual experience, but Scripture emphasizes God's work in the cognitive sphere as well. Some other churches seem to restrict God's work to the cognitive dimension, as if God did not engage the rest of our person. For Paul, however, the Spirit who testifies to our spirits (Rom. 8:16) also gives us a new way of thinking (8:5–7). Likewise, spiritual gifts include not only prayer with our spirit (in tongues) but also prayer with our understanding (with interpretation; 1 Cor. 14:13–15). That is, the Spirit works with both the affective and cognitive dimensions of our persons. Some of us may be gifted more in one way or the other, but we are whole people and can welcome God to renew even those aspects of our personality that we have closed off to him.

Many errors have circulated publicly in particular kinds of charismatic circles, where they are often blamed on the Holy Spirit. Cessationists are absolutely correct to challenge such excesses and the popular desire for novel "revelations" rather than sound teaching. Too often those who seek what is novel do not grasp even fundamental details already offered in the biblical text. Unfortunately, in a pattern characteristic of the increasingly polarized culture in the United States, extremes tend to react against each other. Indeed, both cessationism and imbalanced charismatic teaching have been growing in much of the world. These extremes polarize God's church instead of inviting church-wide appreciation for both the Spirit-inspired Scriptures and the experience of the Spirit to which Scripture testifies.

It was partly this concern that motivated me to accept the invitation to write *Spirit Hermeneutics* (2016)[16] in an attempt to further bring together Word and Spirit, exegesis and depending on God. We read Scripture in light of the inspired text itself, in its context, and also in light of (and feeding into) our relationship with the God who inspired the text. That is, mechanical exegesis as a purely academic exercise can generate some useful *raw materials* for devotion, but as Christians we go beyond collecting raw materials. One of the contexts in which we read Scripture is the reality of the God we are learning to know.

Moreover, I find myself sympathizing with my elders who report that the older they get, the less they know. Life has a way of maturing our epistemic humility, and life with God brings trust in God's faithfulness beyond what we can explain. God's Word is so vast that there is always more for us to learn. (Perhaps this is the point of Ps. 119:96.) I may have many more stories to tell now than I did in 2001, but as a Bible teacher I am also tempted to displace those stories with more observations about stories in Scripture, especially stories that reveal the character of our wonderful Lord, Jesus Christ.

Nevertheless, for a nontechnical summary of what I would say exegetically about the Spirit in the New Testament, *Gift and Giver* still remains the best place to start.

Appendix
What Can Bible Stories Teach Us?

A lthough few of our conclusions have rested on narrative alone, some readers may feel uncomfortable with the way we have used narratives from Acts and elsewhere as models for today, even when those narratives portrayed the perfect activity of God rather than the fallible behavior of his followers. Because others have already written so much on Paul's treatment of the Spirit,[1] in this book I often emphasized the narrative portions of the New Testament—that is, the New Testament stories. Stories can be true stories (like biblical history or biography) or fictitious stories (like parables), and we read history and parables somewhat differently. But both kinds of stories share some common narrative devices, such as a plot and characterization, and in some respects we approach them in the same way. When we read any kind of biblical story, we look for its moral (1 Cor. 10:11).

This approach becomes especially clear when we compare the differences between the Gospels or the overlapping material in Kings and Chronicles. Because Jesus did and taught so much, no one Gospel writer could have told us everything about him (as John 21:25 explicitly points out). Rather, each Gospel writer emphasized particular points about Jesus, the way we do today when we read or preach from a text in the Bible. This means that when we read Bible stories, we not only learn the historical facts about what happened, but we listen to the inspired writer's perspective on what happened—that is, the lessons to be drawn from the story. When the writer "preaches" to us from the stories he tells us, he often gives us clues for recognizing the lessons. For example, a Gospel writer often selected a number of stories with the same basic theme or themes that repeatedly emphasized particular lessons.

Different Approaches Today

Many evangelical restoration movements (for example, German Pietists, Moravians, Wesley's first followers) looked to Acts for appropriate patterns for church life. Similarly, Baptists base their case for believers' baptism by immersion on historical precedent in the New Testament, arguing from what baptism meant in first-century Palestine. (Admittedly, even the most rigorous Baptists do not practice baptism exactly the way first-century Jews did. Formal Jewish baptism rituals were performed nude, and those being baptized probably immersed themselves face forward. Undoubtedly, John's public baptisms in the Jordan were done a little differently.) Many churches even base practices on precedents in church history after the completion of the Bible. In other words, we have a great deal of historical precedent for finding historical precedents in Bible stories!

Despite such historical precedent, many conservative North American Christians today seem nervous about getting theology from narrative (Bible stories). Although few would dismiss the doctrinal value of narrative altogether, many suggest that one should find in narrative only what is plainly taught in "clearer," more "didactic" portions of Scripture.

Although some of these scholars are among the ablest exegetes regarding other portions of Scripture, I must protest that their approach to Bible stories violates the most basic rules for biblical interpretation and in practice jeopardizes the doctrine of biblical inspiration. Did Paul not say that *all* Scripture was inspired and therefore useful for "doctrine," or teaching (2 Tim. 3:16)? I freely admit that I myself do not understand some portions of Scripture—for example, how to provide reproof from the genealogies in Chronicles. But other obscure parts began to make sense to me after I understood the cultural context they addressed (for instance, the design of the tabernacle in Exodus).

To be sure, specific examples of how God worked in narrative often provide only principles rather than promises: For instance, the fact that Jesus healed a leper shows God's power and Christ's compassion but need not guarantee the healing of all lepers under all circumstances. Some texts are more useful for addressing situations today than others, but all biblical texts, including narratives, have some purpose.

What Was the Point?

One of the most basic principles of Bible interpretation is to ask what the writer wanted to convey to his contemporary audience. This principle applies to narratives such as the Gospels as much as to epistles such as Romans. If one could simply write a "neutral" Gospel that addressed all situations universally, it would undoubtedly have been included in the Bible. Instead, the Bible offers us four Gospels, each one selecting different elements of Jesus' life and teachings to preach Jesus to the needs of various readers in relevant ways. The Gospels' selectivity also provides us with a model for how to preach Jesus in relevant ways to our hearers. The way God chose to give us the Bible is more important than the way we *wish* he would have given it to us.

Further, we must learn to read each book first of all as a self-contained unit, because that was how God originally inspired these books. Books such as Mark or Ephesians were written independently by inspired authors addressing specific situations. The first readers of Mark could not refer to Ephesians or John to figure out an obscure point in Mark; they had to read and reread Mark as a whole until they grasped the meaning of each passage. When we read a book of the Bible, we need to read each passage in light of the total message and argument of the book as well as read the book in light of the passages that constitute it.

This is not to say that we cannot *compare* the results from our study of Ephesians with the results from our study of Mark and show how they fit together. But we miss the complete character of Mark when we resort to Ephesians before we have finished our examination of Mark. This approach is not a bias adopted from secular scholarship; I learned it as a young Christian when I was reading the Bible forty chapters a day and noticed that this was how the Bible demanded we approach it.

An example from Mark may suffice. The opposition Jesus faces for healing a paralytic provides a lesson for the hostility we can expect from the world for doing God's will. The opposition to Jesus that builds in early chapters of Mark and climaxes in the cross parallels the suffering believers themselves are told to expect (8:31–38; 10:33–45; 13:9–13; 14:21–51). Mark summons Christians to endure and provides negative examples of this principle (for example, 14:27–52) as well as positive ones to reinforce his point. Such examples also show Christians' inability to fulfill this call in their own strength. That Jesus is popular in Mark 2:2, however, is not a general model for Christian ministry; the rest of Mark itself shows that eventually crowds denounced Jesus (15:13–14). From these narratives we might learn to use any popularity for good at

226

the moment but not to count on it enduring. Reading the part in light of the whole thus allows us to learn theology from narrative by discerning whether patterns and examples are intended as positive or negative.

Cultures and Consistency

Most cultures in the world teach lessons through stories. Westerners are often the ones who are unable to follow the point of narratives in the Bible. But not even all Western Christians find Bible stories inaccessible. Black churches in the United States have for generations specialized in narrative preaching. In most churches, children grow up loving Bible stories, until they become adults and are taught that they must now think abstractly rather than learn from concrete illustrations.

The fact that our traditional method of extracting doctrine from Scripture does not work well on narrative does not mean that Bible stories do not send clear messages. Instead, it suggests that the way we apply our traditional method of interpretation is inadequate because we are ignoring too much of God's Word.

When Jesus' followers were writing the New Testament, everyone understood that narrative conveyed moral principles. Ancient biographers and historians expected readers to draw lessons from their examples, whether positive or negative. Students regularly recited such stories in elementary school exercises, and in more advanced levels of education they learned how to apply these examples to drive home moral points.

Using only nonnarrative portions of the Bible to interpret narrative is not only disrespectful to the narrative portions but also suggests a misguided approach to nonnarrative parts of the Bible. Everyone acknowledges, for instance, that Paul's letters are "occasional" documents—that is, they address specific occasions or situations. Thus, had the Lord's Supper not been a matter of controversy in Corinth, we would know little about it except from Matthew, Mark, and Luke. If we then were to interpret the narrative portions of Scripture only by other portions, we might assume that we do not need to observe the Lord's Supper today. Of course, Jesus teaches his disciples about the Lord's Supper within the narrative. But since the teaching is within the narrative, we can always protest that he addressed this teaching only to a select group of disciples. A few hundred years ago Protestants explained away the Great Commission in just such a manner. Today, many similarly explain away teachings found in the Gospels and Acts about the usefulness of signs and wonders for evangelism.

Not only is the traditional "doctrinal" approach inadequate for interpreting the Gospels, but it is inappropriate for interpreting the Epistles as well. The "narrative" way of interpreting Bible stories, in fact, shows us how to read the Epistles properly. Paul never wrote just to say hello; he wrote to address specific needs of churches. While the principles Paul employs are eternal and apply to a variety of situations, Paul expresses those principles concretely to grapple with specific situations. Before we can understand his principles, we often must first understand the situations with which he is grappling. Paul's concrete words that deal with real situations are case studies that show us how to address analogous situations today. Paul's letters presuppose a sort of background story—he is responding to events and situations that arose among his original audience. In other words, we must read even Paul's letters as examples. This is how Paul read the Old Testament—drawing theology (especially moral teaching) from its examples (1 Cor. 10:11).

Saying that narratives have teaching value does not solve the problem of determining what they teach, of course, as evangelical scholars such as J. Ramsey Michaels, D. A. Carson, and Gordon Fee have rightly pointed out when addressing the tongues issue. But students of the Bible must examine the narratives in the Bible as thoroughly as any other part of the Bible, for the teaching God chose to provide there is no less important than what he offered elsewhere in Scripture. The fact that many of the examples in Acts show patterns of God's action suggests that these models remain valid for understanding how God has chosen to work (in contrast to examples more bound to the cultures of their day).

I suspect that many scholars—including myself in earlier years—feel uncomfortable finding theology in narrative largely because of their academic training. In the theological academy, one can feel content addressing important issues such as Christology while ignoring equally necessary personal issues such as domestic abuse and how to witness at work. But pastors, door-to-door witnessers, and other ministers cannot ignore issues that exceed the bounds of traditional doctrinal categories. We should not forget that those general doctrinal categories were established by medieval theologians who were not always involved with the daily issues with which most of their contemporaries struggled. The issues they addressed were important, but they were hardly exhaustive. I believe that the more we are forced to grapple with the same kinds of situations the writers of Scripture had to face, the more sensitively we will interpret the texts they wrote. When that happens, we will need to reappropriate all of Scripture—including its stories—for the life and faith of the church.

Notes

Chapter 1

1. For more detailed suggestions on hearing God's voice, see Jack Deere, *Surprised by the Voice of God* (Grand Rapids: Zondervan, 1996), not available to cite when I wrote *3 Crucial Questions about the Holy Spirit* (Grand Rapids: Baker, 1996).

2. Dallas Willard, *In Search of Guidance: Developing a Conversational Relationship with God* (New York: Harper Collins, 1993), 26.

3. See my more detailed comments in Craig Keener, *Revelation*, NIV Application Commentary (Grand Rapids: Zondervan, 2000), 196–97; cf. ibid., 179–81.

Chapter 2

1. For documentation on comments about friendship here, see my article on "Friendship" in *Dictionary of NT Backgrounds*, ed. Craig Evans and Stanley Porter (Downers Grove, Ill.: InterVarsity, 2000), 380–88; or my forthcoming commentary on John.

Chapter 3

1. Craig Keener, "Spirit at Work," *Discipleship Journal* (January/February 1996): 43; see full article 43–47.

2. Full documentation for the New Testament exegetical portions of this chapter appears in *The Spirit in the Gospels and Acts: Divine Purity and Power* (Peabody, Mass.: Hendrickson, 1996), 190–213 (on Acts 2) and 49–90 (on Mark 1:8–11). That book's title is something of a misnomer (I do not usually get to name my books); I simply noted two basic themes about the Holy Spirit and provided sample studies in some Gospels and Acts passages that might reflect or develop these themes.

3. On the connection between Luke's portrayals of Jesus and the Spirit-baptized community of Acts, see Roger Stronstad, *The Charismatic Theology of Saint Luke* (Peabody, Mass.: Hendrickson, 1984), 34–48, and 51 (following Talbert); R. L.

230   Notes

Brawley, *Luke-Acts and the Jews*, Society of Biblical Literature Monograph Series
33 (Atlanta: Scholars Press, 1987), 24–25; R. F. Zehnle, *Peter's Pentecost Discourse*,
Society of Biblical Literature Monograph Series 15 (Nashville: Abingdon, 1971),
128. On Luke's emphasis on the prophetic empowerment dimension of the Spirit,
see especially R. P. Menzies, *The Development of Early Christian Pneumatology with
Special Reference to Luke-Acts*, Journal for the Study of the New Testament Sup-
plement 54 (Sheffield, England: Sheffield Academic Press, 1991).
    4. Baptism "in Jesus' name" in Acts always occurs only with the passive voice—
receiving baptism in Jesus' name. That is, contrary to the antitrinitarian interpretation, baptism "in Jesus' name" concerns one's own profession of faith in Christ, not
a formula someone else pronounces over one during baptism (see Acts 2:21; 22:16).
    5. On the parallels among figures in Luke-Acts, see especially M. D. Goulder,
Type and History in Acts (London: SPCK, 1964); Charles H. Talbert, *Literary Patterns, Theological Themes, and the Genre of Luke-Acts*, Society of Biblical Literature Monograph Series 20 (Missoula, Mont.: Scholars Press, 1974); and Robert
C. Tannehill, *The Narrative Unity of Luke-Acts: A Literary Interpretation*, vol. 1,
The Gospel according to Luke (Philadelphia: Fortress, 1986); vol. 2, *The Acts of the
Apostles* (Minneapolis: Fortress, 1990).
    6. See Anil Stephen, "The Church on the Top of the World," *Christianity Today*
(3 April 2000): 56–59, esp. 56, 58.
    7. See the discussion in my *Revelation*, 289–303. See also G. K. Beale, *The Book
of Revelation*, NIGTC (Grand Rapids: Eerdmans, 1999), 572–85.
    8. In many parts of the world, the church, less shaped by Western rationalism,
already views Christian apologetics especially in terms of power encounter; see,
for example, the African perspectives summarized in William A. Dyrness, ed.,
Emerging Voices in Global Christian Theology (Grand Rapids: Zondervan, 1994),
11–12. In the Bible see Exod. 7:8–13; 12:12; 1 Kings 18:20–40.
    9. In more detail, see my *Spirit in the Gospels and Acts*, 49–90. Matthew adds
that those who revile the Spirit's testimony to Jesus (12:24, 31–32) thereby reject
Jesus' Messianic identity (see Matt. 12:18, 28). Other writers also emphasize how
the Spirit empowered Jesus both to perform signs (e.g., Acts 10:38) and to suffer
(Heb. 9:14). The Spirit is also central in the act of resurrection (Rom. 8:11; 1 Peter
3:18; cf. Rev. 11:11).
    10. "The Need of the Hour," *Discipleship Journal* 7 (January 1982): 24–26; see
also *Discipleship Journal* 61 (January 1991): 31–33.

Chapter 4
    1. That the particular forms of dancing are often culturally expressed may be
illustrated by some traditional African American churches, in which specific forms
of dance (like the "shout," with roots in emotionally forceful African worship)
become a vehicle for expressing exuberance about God's presence, or by many
Messianic Jewish congregations, in which the horah and other dances are incor-
porated into the often charismatic worship.
    2. See most fully, recently, and persuasively, Deirdre J. Good, *Jesus the Meek
King* (Harrisburg, Pa.: Trinity Press International, 1999), who shows that ancients
meant "meekness" as a self-disciplined moral strength, not a weakness.

3. In keeping with traditional Jewish usage, "in the Spirit" probably suggests the Spirit's inspiration, although this could include worship in one's own language (1 Chron. 25:1–7) as well as in tongues.

4. I expressed my views elsewhere (*Paul, Women, and Wives* [Peabody, Mass.: Hendrickson, 1992], 139–224), which resemble those of charismatic scholars such as Gordon Fee, Peter Davids, Ben Witherington, or Rebecca Merrill Groothuis. Other charismatic scholars, however, including my friend Wayne Grudem, have argued the opposite position; one's views or practice of spiritual gifts do not necessarily determine one's views in these matters.

Chapter 5

1. For a reasonable and balanced modern cessationist position that does not restrict God's activity as many cessationist positions have, see Daniel B. Wallace, "Who's Afraid of the Holy Spirit?" *Christianity Today* (12 September 1994): 35–38. For more arguments in favor of cessationism, see Richard B. Gaffin Jr., *Perspectives on Pentecost* (Phillipsburg, N.J.: Presbyterian and Reformed, 1979); John F. MacArthur Jr., *Charismatic Chaos* (Grand Rapids: Zondervan, 1992). The cessationist position is difficult for me to identify with, but I have deeply committed Christian friends who hold it (including two authors in this note), and my disagreements imply no lack of respect for them.

2. Willard, *In Search of Guidance*, 110–11.

3. For a balanced view of charismatic gifts in history, see D. A. Carson, *Showing the Spirit: A Theological Exposition of 1 Corinthians 12–14* (Grand Rapids: Baker, 1987), 165–68. See further James D. G. Dunn, *Jesus and the Spirit: A Study of the Religious and Charismatic Experience of Jesus and the First Christians as Reflected in the New Testament* (London: SCM, 1975), 192; from a charismatic historian's perspective, Eddie L. Hyatt, *2000 Years of Charismatic Christianity* (Chicota, Tex.: Hyatt International Ministries, 1996).

4. See Gary Shogren, "Christian Prophecy and Canon in the Second Century: A Response to B. B. Warfield," *Journal of the Evangelical Theological Society* 40 (4 December 1997): 609–26; Ronald A. N. Kydd, *Charismatic Gifts in the Early Church* (Peabody, Mass: Hendrickson, 1984); the sources in Siegfried Schatzmann, *A Pauline Theology of Charismata* (Peabody, Mass.: Hendrickson, 1987), 82 n. 40; and John Wimber with Kevin Springer, *Power Evangelism* (San Francisco: Harper & Row, 1986), appendix A, 157–74.

5. Stanley M. Burgess, "Evidence of the Spirit: The Ancient and Eastern Churches," 3–19, and "Evidence of the Spirit: The Medieval and Modern Western Churches," 20–40 (esp. 20–26), in *Initial Evidence: Historical and Biblical Perspectives on the Pentecostal Doctrine of Spirit Baptism*, ed. Gary B. McGee (Peabody, Mass.: Hendrickson, 1991).

6. Anti-supernaturalism was part of Thomas Paine's Deism (see Mark Noll, *History of Christianity in the United States and Canada* [Grand Rapids: Eerdmans, 1992], 166); see critiques of secular anti-supernaturalism, e.g., in William A. Dembski, *Intelligent Design: The Bridge between Science and Technology* (Downers Grove, Ill.: InterVarsity, 1999), 49–69; essays in R. Douglas Geivett and Gary R. Habermas, eds., *In Defense of Miracles: A Comprehensive Case for God's Action in*

History (Downers Grove, Ill.: InterVarsity, 1997) (the essayists would not all agree with my anticessationism).

7. For those who doubt that Pentecostals are mainstream evangelicals, the Assemblies of God, a Pentecostal denomination, is at the time of writing the largest denomination in the National Association of Evangelicals in the United States.

8. See Jack Deere, *Surprised by the Power of the Spirit* (Grand Rapids: Zondervan, 1993), 219–27, for a broader list of arguments. Himself a former cessationist professor, he also supplies responses to many particular objections to which we cannot devote space here.

9. Likewise, one who would argue that the "other" tongues merely represent the disciples' own languages (Greek and Aramaic) likewise unreasonably stretches the sense of the text to support one's own thesis. Aramaic and Greek were hardly "other" tongues—both Greek-speaking and some Aramaic-speaking foreign Jews (who are Luke's primary focus in the text) and all the more so local Jews were conversant with these languages. No ancient texts suggest that local languages in Palestine could have been viewed as "other" tongues; this suggestion also makes inexplicable the nature of the tongues in Acts 10 and 19. Explaining away the supernatural empowerment to speak in languages the disciples had not learned requires ignoring both details of the text and features of the culture, no matter how well one may argue some individual points that contribute to this thesis.

10. Although the Bible is certainly not against medicine or doctors (Col. 4:14; 1 Tim. 5:23), John MacArthur's presentation of Acts 28:9 is tendentious: He thinks this verse represents Luke healing as a physician because the Greek word is different from the term in 28:8 (MacArthur, *Charismatic Chaos*, 219). The difference is undoubtedly due to literary variation, a typical part of Luke's style, however; far from being nonmiraculous, Luke frequently uses the term for Jesus' healings!

11. Schatzmann, *Pauline Theology of Charismata*, 101 (see also Dunn, *Jesus and the Spirit*, 263, 297). Note the definition of *charismatic* from *charisma* in Schatzmann, 1–7. Such Pauline *charismata* rightly belong to Christ's entire body. Schatzmann, 18, also rightly observes that Paul sometimes applies the term *charisma* to the gift of eternal life (see Rom. 16:23), making *all* Christians charismatic in the sense of having received God's gracious gift.

12. For traditional dispensational cessationist arguments on tongues, see a number of articles in *Bibliotheca Sacra*, e.g., C. L. Rogers, "The Gift of Tongues in the Post Apostolic Church (A.D. 100–400)," *Bibliotheca Sacra* 122 (1965): 134–43; Z. C. Hodges, "The Purpose of Tongues," *Bibliotheca Sacra* 120 (1963): 226–33; S. L. Johnson, "The Gift of Tongues and the Book of Acts," *Bibliotheca Sacra* 120 (1963): 309–11; and on 1 Corinthians 12, S. D. Toussaint, "First Corinthians Thirteen and the Tongues Question," *Bibliotheca Sacra* 120 (1963): 311–16. Cessationism is not, however, a mandatory element of modern dispensationalism (see Robert L. Saucy, *The Case for Progressive Dispensationalism* [Grand Rapids: Zondervan, 1993], 186). We address one of the traditional Reformed approaches below in more detail, via Gaffin; the interested reader will also find more material in Benjamin B. Warfield, *Counterfeit Miracles* (1918; reprint, Carlisle, Pa.: Banner of Truth, 1972) and some articles in *Westminster Theological Journal*.

13. See especially Paul Elbert, "Face to Face: Then or Now?" (paper presented to the seventh annual meeting of the Society for Pentecostal Studies, Springfield,

Mo., December 1–3, 1977). Elbert takes into account hundreds of Koine Greek examples to show that this passage refers to the second coming. See also G. D. Fee, *The First Epistle to the Corinthians*, New International Commentary on the New Testament (Grand Rapids: Eerdmans, 1987); and *Gospel and Spirit: Issues in New Testament Hermeneutics* (Peabody, Mass.: Hendrickson, 1991), 7–8; also G. D. Fee and Douglas Stuart, *How to Read the Bible for All Its Worth* (Grand Rapids: Zondervan, 1982), 60.

14. Gaffin, *Perspectives on Pentecost*, 109. See further Harold Ellis Dollar, "A Cross-Cultural Theology of Healing" (D.Miss. diss., Fuller Theological Seminary School of World Mission, 1981), 48; Wayne A. Grudem, *The Gift of Prophecy in 1 Corinthians* (Lanham, Md.: University Press of America, 1982), 210–19. For the related view that tongues, prophecy, and knowledge passed away in the church's infancy (faith, hope, and love existing for the present and only love for the future), see R. L. Thomas, "'Tongues . . . Will Cease,'" *Journal of the Evangelical Theological Society* 17 (1974): 81–89. But the passing of the imperfect and the arriving of maturity corresponds in 1 Corinthians 13:12 to seeing Christ face to face, and Paul's "now abides" refers to the time of Christ's return, since "greatest" in 13:13 is not temporal. D. A. Carson has shown that the Greek middle form of "cease" (1 Cor. 13:8) does not here mean "cease of themselves" and that New Testament usage does not support such a distinction (*Exegetical Fallacies*, 2d ed. [Grand Rapids: Baker, 1996], 76–77; see also *Showing the Spirit*, 66–67).

I document additionally here because it will be some time before my academic work on Paul, in contrast to my work on the Gospels, is in print. Later Jewish teachers understood Jeremiah 31:31–34 as promising the fullness of knowledge in the age to come (W. D. Davies, *Paul and Rabbinic Judaism*, 4th ed. [Philadelphia: Fortress, 1980], 224; compare the Babylonian Talmud, Shabbat 63b, in Davies, *Torah in the Messianic Age and/or the Age to Come*, Journal of Biblical Literature Monograph Series 7 [Philadelphia: Society of Biblical Literature, 1952], 82). The idea that one can have perfect knowledge in this age Irenaeus attributes to Gnosticism (*Against Heresies*, 2.28).

15. Deere, *Surprised by the Power*, 134–43.

16. See Gaffin, *Perspectives on Pentecost*. Apart from the cessationist arguments, most of the exegesis in the book is useful.

17. Fee, *Gospel and Spirit*, 77.

Chapter 6

1. For perhaps the most thorough scholarly study of healing in biblical theology to date, see Michael L. Brown, *Israel's Divine Healer*, Studies in Old Testament Biblical Theology (Grand Rapids: Zondervan, 1995).

2. Carson, *Showing the Spirit*, 40.

3. On this point I differ from my friend Wayne Grudem, although I am in sympathy with his basic direction on prophecy and greatly appreciate his important work on the subject; see my *Paul, Women, and Wives* (Peabody, Mass.: Hendrickson, 1992), 245. Grudem's primary concern seems to be to keep canonical revelation on a higher level than any current prophecies, which must be tested by what has already been proven and now constitutes Scripture. I fully concur with this concern

and with the absolute priority of canonical revelation; see below under the gift of "discernment of spirits."

4. Acts 19:6 exhibits a special construction, distinguishing "speaking in tongues" from "prophesying"; the Greek wording of Acts 10:46 technically allows tongues and praise to be identified.

5. See the various responses, pro and con, to William Graham McDonald's "Biblical Glossolalia—Thesis 7," *Paraclete* (spring 1994) and *Paraclete* (winter 1995), including articles by David Bundrick and Benny Aker. Bundrick cites others within the Assemblies of God who hold that the primary function of public tongues is prayer (Anthony Palma and Gordon Fee) and notes that it does not violate the denomination's doctrinal parameters (Bundrick himself finds some implicit scriptural support for the position).

6. Paul's view of self-edification in 1 Corinthians 14:4 cannot be negative, since he encourages private uninterpreted tongues in 14:5 (Carson, *Showing the Spirit*, 102 n. 89).

7. Carson, *Showing the Spirit*, 84–86.

8. Sometimes biblical writers use "first, second, third" merely to summarize chronologically without ranking (Gen. 32:19; Matt. 22:25–26). But in 1 Corinthians 12:28 Paul enumerates specific items where chronology is irrelevant and numbering was unnecessary. In contrast to many scholars, I believe that the listing of at least the first three offices, with apostles at the top, does suggest rank.

9. Compare Michael Green, *I Believe in the Holy Spirit*, 2d rev. ed. (Grand Rapids: Eerdmans, 1989), 252–53; Carson, *Showing the Spirit*, 41–42. For the use of the imperative in 1 Corinthians 12:31 and 14:1, 39, see also Carson, *Showing the Spirit*, 57–58.

Chapter 7

1. I have provided fuller documentation for John's treatment of the Spirit and purification in *The Spirit in the Gospels and Acts*, 135–89; for proselyte baptism, ibid., 63–64; or *A Commentary on the Gospel of Matthew* (Grand Rapids: Eerdmans, 1999), 120–22.

Chapter 8

1. For Wesleyan, Anglican, and Catholic views of the second experience, see W. J. Hollenweger, *The Pentecostals* (Peabody, Mass.: Hendrickson, 1988), 21, 26 n. 2; see at greater length H. I. Lederle, *Treasures Old and New: Interpretations of "Spirit-Baptism" in the Charismatic Renewal Movement* (Peabody, Mass.: Hendrickson, 1988), who provides a full survey of views; Vinson Synan, *The Holiness-Pentecostal Movement in the United States* (Grand Rapids: Eerdmans, 1971), 18–21; and for the most thorough treatment of the terminology's Wesleyan and Holiness roots, see Donald W. Dayton, *Theological Roots of Pentecostalism* (Metuchen, N.J.: Scarecrow; reprint: Peabody, Mass.: Hendrickson, 1994). Because the usual sacramental uses of the phrase (in Catholic and Anglo-Catholic circles) differ from the experiences we are discussing here, but do not rule out these experiences, we do not treat them as part of this particular debate.

2. For Finney, see e.g., John L. Gresham Jr., *Charles G. Finney's Doctrine of the Baptism of the Holy Spirit* (Peabody, Mass.: Hendrickson, 1987); for Torrey and Gor-

don, see Gary B. McGee, "Early Pentecostal Hermeneutics: Tongues as Evidence in the Book of Acts," 96–118, in *Initial Evidence* (Peabody, Mass.: Hendrickson, 1991), 101; on Puritan and Reformed Sealers, see Lederle, *Treasures*, 5; Dayton, *Theological Roots*, 37. See also Frederick Dale Bruner, *A Theology of the Holy Spirit: The Pentecostal Experience and the New Testament Witness* (Grand Rapids: Eerdmans, 1970), 76, 323–41, who disagrees with subsequence but documents the subsequence positions of Wesley, Finney, Torrey, Andrew Murray, A. J. Gordon, and F. B. Meyer.

3. For a much more detailed treatment of early Jewish understandings of the Spirit (and points below such as the antiquity of Jewish proselyte baptism), see the extensive first chapter and relevant points in subsequent chapters of my *Spirit in the Gospels and Acts* (Peabody, Mass.: Hendrickson, 1997). See also the excellent works by R. P. Menzies, *The Development of Early Christian Pneumatology with Special Reference to Luke-Acts* (Sheffield, England: Sheffield Academic Press, 1991), emphasizing the prophetic aspect of the Spirit, and Max Turner, *The Holy Spirit and Spiritual Gifts* (Peabody, Mass.: Hendrickson, 1996), helpfully emphasizing a broader range of activities of the Spirit than either my or Menzies's works.

4. Although I struggled to these views on my own, others have articulated similar positions. See, for example, David Watson's views (as summarized in Lederle, *Treasures*, 151): All Christians have the Spirit, but not all are filled with the Spirit—the phrase "baptism in the Spirit" including either one—and the power and reality matter more than the terminology anyway.

5. See Gordon D. Fee, *God's Empowering Presence: The Holy Spirit in the Letters of Paul* (Peabody, Mass.: Hendrickson, 1994) and his lexical arguments on this passage. His case is not likely the result of mere presuppositions; Fee rightly disavows most proposed "second work" readings of Paul. He believes that both Paul and Luke show "that the gift of the Spirit was not some sort of adjunct to the Christian experience, nor was it some kind of second and more significant part of Christian experience. It was rather the chief element of the Christian life from beginning to end" (*Gospel and Spirit: Issues in New Testament Hermeneutics* [Peabody, Mass.: Hendrickson, 1991], 98).

6. For an argument that these "disciples" were already Christians, based in part on the grammar of Paul's question, see Stanley M. Horton, *What the Bible Says about the Holy Spirit* (Springfield, Mo.: Gospel Publishing House, 1976), 159–62. Although Horton's book offers many good points throughout, many exceptions to the grammatical rule he cites make an argument from grammar tenuous here either in support of or against his position.

7. Bruner, *Theology of Holy Spirit*, 177–78, carefully surveys Pentecostal writers (although many Pentecostals today would differ from many of the older positions summarized) and provides a serious analysis of New Testament texts from a charitable noncharismatic perspective. He argues that the delay in Samaria was abnormal and that the Spirit here completes the experience of Christian baptism. If the text implies that the experience was abnormally delayed, we still must ask whether the sort of event depicted here is possible without an experiential dimension; if not, then conversion should normally include a dramatic experience of the Spirit, one that is sometimes delayed (probably more often today than then). This would fit the view of some charismatics who view Spirit baptism as a completion

of salvation (in contrast to my own view above, that it represents a different kind of empowerment of the Spirit).

8. James D. G. Dunn, *Baptism in the Holy Spirit: A Re-examination of the New Testament Teaching on the Gift of the Spirit in Relation to Pentecostalism Today* (Philadelphia: Westminster; London: SCM, 1970), addresses Acts 8 on pages 55–72. Acts 8 is certainly not a *normative* pattern—God may have allowed the delay to heal the Jewish-Samaritan schism (so Michael Green, *I Believe in the Holy Spirit*, 2d rev. ed. [Grand Rapids: Eerdmans, 1989], 167–68; D. A. Carson, *Showing the Spirit: A Theological Exposition of 1 Corinthians 12–14* [Grand Rapids: Baker, 1987], 144–45). But it does illustrate that God could allow delay; and if he allowed it then, he could also allow it (for different reasons and under other circumstances) today.

9. Dunn, *Baptism in the Holy Spirit*, 55.

10. Clark Pinnock, foreword to Roger Stronstad, *The Charismatic Theology of Saint Luke* (Peabody, Mass.: Hendrickson, 1984), vii.

11. Dunn, *Baptism in the Holy Spirit*, 55–72.

12. On many of these points, see Howard M. Ervin, *Conversion-Initiation and the Baptism in the Holy Spirit* (Peabody, Mass.: Hendrickson, 1984), 28–32. Although I would more often agree with Dunn against Ervin, I believe that Ervin has the exegetical upper hand in Acts 8.

13. Fee, *Gospel and the Spirit*, 96–99, 117–19.

14. Carson, *Showing the Spirit*, 160. Some of us have lost count!

Chapter 9

1. Carson, *Showing the Spirit*, 50 (compare also 186).

2. One reason I enjoy being a Baptist is that we are supposed to have no "creed" but Scripture alone; my commitment is to what I find in Scripture (whatever denominations that evidence might support on some issues), and on that count I happily continue praying in tongues. Perhaps the other side of being a Baptist who prays in tongues might be described by my fellow Baptist Tony Campolo, who has a book, *How to Be Pentecostal without Speaking in Tongues* (Dallas: Word, 1994).

3. James D. G. Dunn, *Jesus and the Spirit: A Study of the Religious and Charismatic Experience of Jesus and the First Christians as Reflected in the New Testament* (London: SCM, 1975), 189–91.

4. In "Evidence and Movement," in *Initial Evidence: Historical and Biblical Perspectives on the Pentecostal Doctrine of Spirit Baptism*, ed. Gary B. McGee (Peabody, Mass.: Hendrickson, 1991), 136, Henry Lederle claims that only 35 percent of all Pentecostals have prayed in tongues.

5. McGee, "Hermeneutics," 108–10. For dissent among early Pentecostals, see McGee, "Hermeneutics," 107, and H. I. Lederle, "Initial Evidence and the Charismatic Movement: An Ecumenical Appraisal," in *Initial Evidence*, 131–32. Lederle, *Treasures*, 29–31, also summarizes early Pentecostal theologians who held other views, noting that doctrinal freedom on major issues secondary to the gospel characterized early Pentecostalism (see esp. 29; see also Hollenweger, *Pentecostals*, 32, 331–36). For a well-crafted exegetical defense of the classical Pentecostal position, see Donald A. Johns, "Some New Directions in the Hermeneutics of Classical Pentecostalism's Doctrine of Initial Evidence," in *Initial Evidence*, 145–67. His-

torically the nineteenth-century Catholic Apostolic Church, whose last apostle died the year the modern Pentecostal movement was born (1901), viewed tongues as a prominent sign of Spirit baptism (see David W. Dorries, "Edward Irving and the 'Standing Sign' of Spirit Baptism," in *Initial Evidence*, 41–56; compare Gordon Strachan, *The Pentecostal Theology of Edward Irving* [Peabody, Mass.: Hendrickson, 1973]; Larry Christenson, *A Message to the Charismatic Movement* [Minneapolis: Bethany Fellowship, 1972]).

6. See Cecil M. Robeck Jr., "William J. Seymour and 'the Bible Evidence,'" in *Initial Evidence*, 81–89; Synan, *Holiness-Pentecostal Movement*, 180. Some of Parham's original ideas concerning tongues, such as that it was xenoglossa or that only tongues-speakers would experience a pretribulational rapture (see James R. Goff Jr., "Initial Tongues in the Theology of Charles Fox Parham," in *Initial Evidence*, 64–65, 67), were quickly rejected by other Pentecostals, as was his advocacy of British Israelitism. For the usual breaking down of racial barriers in early Pentecostal circles, conflicting with broader societal prejudice, see Synan, *Holiness-Pentecostal Movement*, 80, 109–11, 165–69, 172, 178–79, 182–83, 221; Synan, "Seymour, William Joseph," in *Dictionary of Pentecostal and Charismatic Movements*, ed. Stanley M. Burgess, Gary B. McGee, and Patrick H. Alexander (Grand Rapids: Zondervan, 1988), 778–81; Leonard Lovett, "Black Holiness-Pentecostalism," in *Dictionary of Pentecostal and Charismatic Movements*, 76–84, esp. 83; Burgess, McGee, and Alexander, "The Pentecostal and Charismatic Movements," *Dictionary of Pentecostal and Charismatic Movements*, 3.

7. Stanley M. Burgess, "Evidence of the Spirit: The Medieval and Modern Western Churches," in *Initial Evidence*, 33–34; McGee, "Hermeneutics," 107–8.

Chapter 10

1. For a more complete listing of such false predictions of the end, see my *Revelation*, NIV Application Commentary (Grand Rapids: Zondervan, 2000), 61–65. Other examples could be multiplied, e.g., George Bell predicted the end of the age for February 28, 1763, and though Wesley had excluded him, it brought reproach against the early Methodists; see *Christian History* 2, no. 1 (1983): 11.

2. J. Lee Grady, *What Happened to the Fire? Rekindling the Blaze of Charismatic Renewal* (Grand Rapids: Chosen, 1994).

3. See D. R. McConnell, *A Different Gospel: A Historical and Biblical Analysis of the Modern Faith Movement* (Peabody, Mass.: Hendrickson, 1988), 137–40.

4. Examples of "self-promoting" revelations could likewise be multiplied. In 1965, Homer Tomlinson, son of a former overseer of a Pentecostal denomination, announced that he was king of the world. Like other "end time prophets" before him such as John Alexander Dowie or William Branham, however, his revelation failed to commend itself to most of his subjects. He died in 1969 (Vinson Synan, *The Holiness-Pentecostal Movement in the United States* [Grand Rapids: Eerdmans, 1971], 196–97; for Dowie and Branham, see David Edwin Harrell Jr., *All Things Are Possible: The Healing and Charismatic Revivals in Modern America* [Bloomington, Ind.: Indiana University, 1975], 13–14, 27–41, 159–65).

5. John F. MacArthur Jr., *Charismatic Chaos* (Grand Rapids: Zondervan, 1992), throughout.

238   Notes

6. Ibid., 80–81.
7. Ibid., 75, for example.
8. The latter example is the more remarkable considering Saul's inspiration from an "evil spirit" in 1 Samuel 18:10. Although the nature of this spirit is debated and some of my knowledgeable colleagues in Old Testament doubt that 1 Samuel 18:10 refers to a demon, I am inclined to think that it probably does (especially in light of some work by my former student Emmanuel Itapson).

Afterword

1. Michael L. Brown and Craig S. Keener, *Not Afraid of the Antichrist: Why We Don't Believe in a Pretribulation Rapture* (Bloomington, Minn.: Chosen, 2019).
2. R. T. Kendall, *Word & Spirit: Truth, Power, and the Next Great Move of God* (Lake Mary, Fla.: Charisma House, 2019).
3. George Stormont, *Wigglesworth: A Man Who Walked with God* (Tulsa: Harrison House, 1989), 114.
4. Now published as Sam Storms, "Revelatory Gifts of the Spirit and the Sufficiency of Scripture: Are They Compatible?," in *Scripture and the People of God: Essays in Honor of Wayne Grudem*, ed. John DelHousaye, John J. Hughes, and Jeff T. Purswell (Wheaton: Crossway, 2018), 79–97.
5. Craig S. Keener, *Miracles: The Credibility of the New Testament Accounts*, 2 vols. (Grand Rapids: Baker Academic, 2011).
6. Frank and Ida Mae Hammond, *Pigs in the Parlor: A Practical Guide to Deliverance* (Kirkwood, Mo.: Impact Christian Books, 1973).
7. Kenneth E. Hagin himself eventually challenged some excesses (*The Midas Touch: A Balanced Approach to Biblical Prosperity* [Tulsa: Faith Library Publications, 2000]). For recent readable critiques from charismatic scholars of popular errors, see Michael L. Brown, *Playing with Holy Fire: A Wake-Up Call to the Pentecostal-Charismatic Church* (Lake Mary, Fla.: Charisma House, 2018); Eddie L. Hyatt, *Angels of Light: False Prophets and Deceiving Spirits at Work Today in the Church and the World* (Grapevine, Tex.: Hyatt, 2018); Paul L. King, *Is It of God? A Biblical Guidebook for Spiritual Discernment* (Newberry, Fla.: Bridge Logos, 2019).
8. Paul L. King, *Moving Mountains: Lessons in Bold Faith from Great Evangelical Leaders* (Bloomington, Minn.: Chosen, 2004).
9. From Francis Asbury's valedictory address of 1813, "The Patriarch Broods over His Family's Future," reproduced in *Christian History* 114 (2015): 39.
10. Kenneth Cracknell and Susan J. White, *An Introduction to World Methodism* (Cambridge: Cambridge University Press, 2005), 48.
11. Cf. more fully my comments in "Recognizing False Apostles," *The Christian Post*, April 23, 2019, https://www.christianpost.com/voices/recognizing-false -apostles.html; "Leading New Testament Scholar Reveals How to Recognize False Apostles," *Charisma Leader*, April 30, 2019, https://ministrytodaymag .com/leadership/calling/25997-leading-new-testament-scholar-reveals-how-to -recognize-false-apostles.
12. Craig Keener and Médine Moussounga Keener, *Impossible Love: The True Story of an African Civil War, Miracles, and Love against All Odds* (Grand Rapids: Chosen, 2016).

13. See esp. Lee Strobel, *The Case for Miracles* (Grand Rapids: Zondervan, 2018). A sample of just a few other recent works includes James L. Garlow and Keith Wall, *Real Life, Real Miracles: True Stories That Will Help You Believe* (Minneapolis: Bethany House, 2012); Harold J. Sala, *What You Need to Know about Healing: A Physical and Spiritual Guide* (Nashville: Broadman & Holman, 2013); Daniel Fazzina, *Divine Intervention: 50 True Stories of God's Miracles Today* (Lake Mary, Fla.: Charisma House, 2014); Dean Merrill, *Miracle Invasion: Amazing True Stories of the Holy Spirit's Gifts at Work Today* (Savage, Minn.: BroadStreet, 2018).

14. Craig S. Keener, *Acts: An Exegetical Commentary*, 4 vols. (Grand Rapids: Baker Academic, 2012–15).

15. Craig S. Keener, *The Mind of the Spirit: Paul's Approach to Transformed Thinking* (Grand Rapids: Baker Academic, 2016).

16. Craig S. Keener, *Spirit Hermeneutics: Reading Scripture in Light of Pentecost* (Grand Rapids: Eerdmans, 2016). Cf. more concisely, "Pentecostal Biblical Interpretation / Spirit Hermeneutics," in *Scripture and Its Interpretation: A Global, Ecumenical Introduction to the Bible*, ed. Michael J. Gorman (Grand Rapids: Baker Academic, 2017), 270–83.

Appendix

1. Fee's *God's Empowering Presence* is the most extensive in this regard. Carson's *Showing the Spirit* is also excellent and is probably the best work devoted specifically to spiritual gifts.